Ireland: The Politics of Independence

D1760347

Also by Mike Cronin

SPORT AND NATIONALISM IN IRELAND: Gaelic Games, Soccer and Irish Identity since 1884

THE BLUESHIRTS AND IRISH POLITICS

THE FAILURE OF BRITISH FASCISM: The Far Right and the Fight for Political Recognition (*editor*)

Also by John M. Regan

THE IRISH COUNTER-REVOLUTION 1921–36: Treatyite Politics and Settlement in Independent Ireland

Ireland: The Politics of Independence, 1922–49

Edited by

Mike Cronin
Senior Research Fellow
De Montfort University
Leicester

and

John M. Regan
Research Fellow
Wolfson College
Oxford

First published in Great Britain 2000 by
MACMILLAN PRESS LTD
Houndmills, Basingstoke, Hampshire RG21 6XS and London
Companies and representatives throughout the world

A catalogue record for this book is available from the British Library.

ISBN 0–333–72050–4 hardcover
ISBN 0–333–72051–2 paperback

First published in the United States of America 2000 by
ST. MARTIN'S PRESS, INC.,
Scholarly and Reference Division,
175 Fifth Avenue, New York, N.Y. 10010

ISBN 0–312–22787–6

Library of Congress Cataloging-in-Publication Data
Ireland : the politics of independence, 1922–49 / edited by Mike
Cronin and John M. Regan.
p.   cm.
Includes bibliographical references and index.
ISBN 0–312–22787–6 (cloth)
1. Ireland—Politics and government—1922–1949.   I. Cronin, Mike.
II. Regan, John (John M.)
DA963.I735   1999
641.5082'2—dc21   99–40610
                                                        CIP

This book is printed on paper suitable for recycling and made from fully managed and sustained
forest sources.

10   9   8   7   6   5   4   3   2   1
09   08   07   06   05   04   03   02   01   00

Printed and bound in Great Britain by
Antony Rowe Ltd, Chippenham, Wiltshire

Contents

Abbreviations

BL   British Library
CAI   Cork Archive Institute
NAI   National Archive of Ireland, Dublin
NLI   National Library of Ireland, Dublin
PRO   Public Record Office, Kew
TCDL   Trinity College Dublin Library
UCDA   University College Dublin Archives

Notes on the Contributors

Mike Cronin is Senior Research Fellow in History at De Montfort University, Leicester. He is the author of *The Blueshirts and Irish Politics* (Four Courts Press, 1997), *Sport and Nationalism in Ireland: Gaelic Games, Soccer and Identity* (Four Courts Press, 1999) and editor of *The Failure of British Fascism. The Far Right and the Fight for Political Recognition* (Macmillan, 1996).

Pauric Dempsey is a doctoral student in the School of Modern History, Queen's University, Belfast, and researcher with the *Dictionary of Irish Biography* based at the Royal Irish Academy in Dublin.

Richard Dunphy is Senior Lecturer in Political Science and Social Policy at the University of Dundee. He is the author of *The Making of Fianna Fail Power in Ireland* (Oxford University Press, 1995) and has published widely in edited volumes and academic journals on Irish and European political culture.

Richard English is Reader in Politics at Queen's University, Belfast. He is the author of *Radicals and the Republic: Socialist Republicanism in the Irish Free State 1925–37* (Oxford University Press, 1995) and of *Ernie O'Malley: IRA Intellectual* (Oxford University Press, 1998).

Donal Lowry is Senior Lecturer in History at Oxford Brookes University. He has published widely on aspects of the connections between Ireland and the British Empire. He is the editor of *The South African War* (Manchester University Press, 1999).

Finín O' Driscoll studied history at University College Cork and is a doctoral student at Wolfson College, Cambridge.

Senia Paseta is a Fellow of St Hughes College, Oxford. She was formally the Irish Government Senior Scholar at Hertford College, Oxford, and a Junior Research Fellow at Merton College, Oxford. She has written *Before the Revolution: Nationalism, Social Change and Ireland's Catholic Élite 1879–1992* (Cork University Press, 1999).

John M. Regan is a Research Fellow at Wolfson College, Oxford. He was formally the Irish Government Senior Scholar at Hertford College, Oxford, and a holder of a British Academy post-doctoral fellow at

Wolfson College. He has written *The Irish Counter-Revolution 1921–36: Treatyite Politics and Settlement in Independent Ireland* (Gill & Macmillan and St. Martin's Press, 1999).

Susannah Riordan completed her doctoral thesis at the University of Cambridge and is a Faculty of Arts Fellow and lecturer in the Department of History at University College Dublin.

1
Introduction: Ireland and the Politics of Independence 1922–49, New Perspectives and Re-considerations

John M. Regan and Mike Cronin

Whether what occurred in Ireland between 1912–23 was a revolution or not remains a matter of debate.[1] The fact that there is still a degree of discomfiture over applying the word 'revolution' to this period and the war of independence is indicative of a historiography which has yet to resolve some of the most fundamental questions of twentieth century Irish history. That what happened in Ireland, in the decade before the two Irish polities north and south were formed, was a revolution is accepted here. Though as a revolution it was peculiarly narrow in its focus and decidedly limited in its results. Revolutionary change swept the entire island of Ireland after 1912. Its initial force came from within Ulster Unionism as it reacted and armed in response to the prospect of home rule in the period before the First World War. Ulster Unionism introduced the gun to twentieth century Irish politics and it also initiated the militarisation of Irish society with the formation of the Ulster Volunteer Force and in response the nationalist Irish Volunteers. By 1921, militant Ulster Unionism had been reconciled in a six-county political administration in the north-east of the Ireland, known somewhat ambiguously as Northern Ireland. The main force for revolutionary change after 1914 came from the south, and with the advent of sustained revolutionary violence in late 1919 more particularly the extreme south-west of the island, leading to the creation in 1922 of a self-governing dominion within the Commonwealth: the Irish Free State. It is the southern 26-county polity in its many constitutional forms – Southern Ireland, Free State, Eire-Ireland, and Republic – which interests us here and throughout the rest of this volume.

There is little evidence of a social component within the Irish revolution and less again in its settlement. Such potential as there was for social upheaval had to a great extent been defused by the transfer of land back to native ownership under a series of reforming land acts at the end of the nineteenth, and the beginning of the new century. The conservativeness of the Irish revolution was underpinned by a rural peasant proprietorship, nationalist in outlook but classically liberal in its economic interest. The Irish administration built by the British emerged from the period divided into two new constituencies but for the most part unscathed and unchanged. The immediate post-revolutionary settlement in the 26 counties jarred with the rhetorical aspirations of many of the revolutionaries who had put the revolution through. No new Gaelic Jerusalem was built. Nor did a republic hermetically sealed against perfidious Albion come into being. The personnel controlling political power in Southern Ireland did, however, change in the decade after 1912, and were a product of revolutionary and also counter-revolutionary violence. The Irish parliamentary party elite, the pre-war nationalist establishment, were moved aside and Sinn Féiners, with their multi-coloured ideologies, took control of the new state. In this aspect alone the changes which occurred in Irish society and political organisation deserve the term revolution, but only just.

Part of the tendency to retreat from using the definition of revolution in the Irish context has been to concentrate on the results of armed struggle, rather than the processes which produced armed struggle. The problem with such an approach is that it interprets the process of revolution and state formation as being continuous and uninterrupted. In fact revolution and state formation were intersected by a significant counter-revolution. The decision of revolutionaries, led by Michael Collins, to accept a settlement with Britain on the terms dictated in the Anglo–Irish treaty of 1921 demanded a countering of revolutionary forces which ultimately led to a civil war in Southern Ireland. The new state, its institutions, and the political culture of its elite were created out of reaction to revolution rather than as a product of it. Examining the edifice of the Free State, and its preservation of the old order through the administration of government and social conservativeness, tells us a great deal more about counter-revolution in Ireland than the revolution it attempted to snuff out. If Irish society appeared to have turned full circle by 1923 only to resemble what existed before 1914, then it was through the agency of a counter-revolution rather than the absence of a revolution in the first place.

Even dispelling the idea that the sum of a revolution is manifest in the end product, the Irish revolution remains a conservative affair. Led for the most part by a Catholic nationalist bourgeois elite with few exceptions – James Connolly being the most notable – it represented a substantially undefined broad nationalist front which even on the issue of its republicanism was incapable of fully reconciling internal differences. The most radical aspect of the revolution was its violence perpetrated by the militarist republicans of the IRA. Such violence as there was turned out to be short-lived, sporadic, and of low intensity. At the point of consolidation, the signing of the treaty in December 1921, the revolution was politically immature and, more pointedly, its violence had not reached its full potential. Neither side had resorted to all-out war. For the British that meant full-scale mobilisation rather than a paramilitary police action. For the IRA it meant unrestricted terrorism with perhaps greater use of reprisals carried out in both Ireland and Britain. In the revolutionary war in Ireland the Marquess of Queensberry was abandoned, but the gloves were left on. Revolutionary violence radicalised those who supported it and perpetrated it. It also suppressed internal debate within a diverse movement, establishing instead the ascendancy of republican and militarist values. A war of longer duration and greater intensity might well have produced more virulent strains of republicanism among a radicalised population and further established the dominance of the republican ideal within the Sinn Féin movement. As it was, the conclusion of the conflict in July 1921, after just 18 months of sniping, assassination and counter-assassination, ensured that the radicalising effects of revolutionary violence had less of an impact on the revolutionary elites and the general population than would otherwise have been the case. The low intensity of the Irish revolutionary war contributed to the survival of moderation and a civil component within the revolutionary movement in the form of Cabinet Government, Dáil, and its Departments. The survival of moderates through a short violent campaign ensured that the revolutionary movement, or its less radicalised parts, could reach a compromise with the British. It was the conservative consolidationist wing of Sinn Féin which was to triumph over the more radical militarist republicans and succeeded in eventually building a state as an institutional bulwark against revolution and revolutionaries.

The Irish revolution remains an ill-defined, under-researched and contentious historical being. With the exception of a few pioneering and innovative regional studies and even fewer national studies, the precise nature of what happened to Irish society and its political elites in the decade before independence remains for the most part speculative: though there is much promising work in prospect. The history of the revolution, or struggle as some still prefer, was viewed, and often when taught in schools south of the border, as a linear progression towards independence – from Ulster crisis in 1912, to the formation of the volunteers in 1913, the 1916 rising, a war of independence, the signing of the Anglo–Irish treaty, leading to collapse into civil war and ultimately vindication with the advent of Fianna Fáil in power under de Valera. It was a historiography defined by the idea of republican pre-destination in which all Irish history was part of a process supposedly leading to the republic in which de Valera, briefly interrupted by the treaty sell-out, enjoyed a second coming in 1932. The 1916 Proclamation, with its declaration of a republic and appropriation of previous uprisings for the republican cause, still gives popular expression to this idea in what is the most commonly reproduced and displayed primary source document in contemporary Ireland. It seems that few public houses, and many private houses, are not complete without their own framed affirmation and illustration of republican pre-destiny and martyrdom. Leaving aside the inconsistencies with what has been called the 'Fianna Fáil school of historical revisionism',[2] it is clear that such a self-serving 'story' had little room for the complexities and diversities of the revolutionary period. Republican teleology had no use for Irish parliamentarians, Redmondite politics, Irish Volunteers in France, Flanders and Galipolli or the first ten years of independence. As a result, such personalities, ideas and common experiences were expurgated from a well cultivated historical past. Even the professional historical community did not venture far outside the parameters established by this republican Whiggism until recently. Institutional prohibitions, and the restricted access to archive material, also meant that the revolution as a historical subject worthy of research was surrendered to any who would take up the business of history writing, and by default or by intent were happy to perpetuate notions of republican predestination to the exclusion of other important forces for change.

Accepting the relative immaturity of the revolutions' historiography, to undertake a study or a series of specialised studies of the politics of independence after the revolution may appear to be putting the cart before the horse. All of the essays in this volume are concerned with the multifarious tensions and relationships between revolution and post-revolutionary settlement. Whatever the precise nature of the revolution which created the circumstances by which a sovereign Irish state could incrementally come into being between 1922 and 1949, it was the processes of consolidation and settlement, involving the interpretation of the revolution and significantly its negation, which gave that process its lasting institutional and cultural importance. In as far as the revolution is explored in this volume it is done through the retrospection of its protagonists, and those who its train by-passed. In this sense what matters in this volume is not what happened to Irish society during the revolution, but what the various groupings represented in these essays believed the revolution had been about, in terms of its goals and their achievements, after the event. Treatyites, Fianna Fáilers, socialist republicans, Catholic intellectuals and social thinkers, as well as the old nationalist and southern unionist elites, justified their experience of revolution in the context of their own place in the new order. The difference between aspiration and reality demanded for all the invention or rejection of historical pasts which became part of their political and sometimes ideological furniture. The founders of 'Fianna Fáil: the republican party' championed their teleological republican history by refusing to recognise the inconsistency of not declaring the much vaunted republic while in power. Southern Unionists could become new nationalists. The old parliamentary nationalists could reinvent themselves as new Sinn Féiners within Cumann na nGaedheal. What happened to Irish society during the revolutionary years in historical terms may for the moment remain *terra incognita*, but its products – social, cultural, political and institutional – can still be studied profitably. The horse may be of uncertain pedigree, but that does not prevent us from dismantling the cart.

The historiography of independent Ireland, or at least its politics, is in a better state of health than its revolutionary precursor. Ronan Fanning's *Independent Ireland*,[3] a model synthesis of text book and primary research, offers a broad introduction to the process of state formation and the politics of independence. J.J. Lee's *Ireland: Politics and Society 1912–85*[4] provides the most exhilarating distillation of writing and primary research on the revolution and its settlement treated within the context of Lee's performance thesis. Dermot Keogh's *Twentieth Century Ireland*,[5] offers a detailed and the most comprehensive account of independence south of the border. David Fitzpatrick's *The Two Irelands*[6] deals with both revolution and settlement in an innovative and all-embracing dual approach to both unionism and nationalism, and the polities they created after 1920. One of the factors all of these studies share is the degree to which their authors have hewn their material from the archival coal-face rather than synthesising an existing historiography. To this extent writing on independence has been the preserve of a few pioneers probing deep into primary sources without the assistance of an extensive secondary literature either at monograph or article length. Nowhere is this lacuna more

evident than in the provision of sophisticated biographical interpretations of the key players of revolution and settlement in Ireland. Of
necessity, the shape of the resulting historiography has been defined
by the possible and the accessible. Consequently the political, institutional and constitutional history of the new state is decidedly more
advanced than either cultural or intellectual historiography. While any
book dealing with the politics of independence will intersect with
these central themes, the works produced here will at least make a contribution to the diversification of the historiography of independence
and post-revolutionary settlement in independent Ireland.

In commissioning the essays the contributors were asked to introduce their specialism for a general/undergraduate reader and to present
new research, or a reconsideration of their field, with regard to their
own work. The only parameters established by the editors were that the
work should address the political experience of independence. Such a
broad remit might well have produced a collection of essays which
failed to interconnect. That in itself would not have been a problem
but in the essays represented in this volume several themes, ideas and
even personalities recur. The retrospective relationship with the revolution has already been mentioned. John M. Regan, Richard Dunphy and
Richard English consider party-political organisation and mobilisation
in their respective studies of the treatyite parties, Fianna Fáil and the
socialist republican political culture. Both Susannah Riordan and Finín
O'Driscoll consider the influence, or lack of it, of lay Catholic intellectuals in the age of Catholic Action. The continuity of policy both
economic and foreign in the pro- and anti-treaty regimes are treated by
Mike Cronin and Donal Lowry. And the reconciliation of the old elites –
nationalist and unionist – within the new settlement are approached by
Senia Paseta and Pauric Dempsey. The volume therefore concerns itself
with both the centre-ground of Irish politics and the outfield. While
offering challenging interpretations of some familiar ground it also
makes room for marginal men and women and their interests. If any
preliminary conclusion can be drawn from the explorations in this collection it is that those who found themselves outside of what emerged
as the consensus of nationalist politics in the first two decades were to
remain very much in the cold. This nationalist consensus which both
the main parties of government supported (Cumann na nGaedheal
later Fine Gael and Fianna Fáil), despite their differences over the
treaty, meant that the central issues of church–state relations, the legitimacy of the state and majority rule, the rights of the individual, the
right to private property, party–state relations, and the nature of
Ireland's relationship with the commonwealth were all settled, where

they were in doubt at all, by the mid-1930s at the latest. Some of the essays in this volume are concerned with those who did not fit squarely inside the new consensus and found themselves losers in the politics of independence. The old nationalist and unionist elites, Catholic social thinkers, the republican socialists and even the treatyites after 1932 found themselves locked out of a new nationalist consensus which became increasingly synonymous with the one great winner in the politics of independence: Fianna Fáil. History, as has often been pointed out, is written by the winners for the winners. In politics, as in aviation, success and failure are critical absolutes, both equally deserving of study, and this volume considers both the flyers and those who found themselves for many reasons grounded or ditched after the revolution.

Explorations of the post-revolutionary settlement in the first three decades of independence remain crucial to our understanding of the shape of Irish society to the present. The new state's institutions, its two largest political parties which exclusively dominated government in our period, were forged with remarkable rigidity in the immediate post-1922 period. Indeed the settlement which evolved during the first two decades, a confessional Catholic democracy equipped with a dominant set of cultural values, dominated after 1932 by one party, and for that matter one leader, was set to remain in place for the next fifty years. For many reasons, post-revolutionary settlement in Independent Ireland championed a narrowly focused mono-culture which remained remarkably impervious to sources of pluralism. In this sense the Irish society which has developed over the past decade and continues to evolve with such élan – north as well as south – is still involved within an ongoing debate about the nature of the post-revolutionary settlement. Even in the age of the European integration, the Celtic tiger and the peace dividend, political culture, institutions and indeed the constitutional arrangements which bind Irish public and private life remain substantially defined by the events and culture of the 1920s and 1930s. There remains an ever-live debate over the meaning of independence. In a speech in 1997 the leader of Fine Gael, John Bruton, claimed that buoyant economic performance of the Irish economy in recent years came as a direct legacy of the founders of the state and his political party. Taking this as yet another attempt at the appropriation of the historical past, John Waters the *Irish Times* journalist and cultural commentator responded:

> He [John Bruton] did not mean to refer to those who had fought for independence, or those whose passionate thoughts and deeds had

inspired their generation to expel the conqueror for good. He meant, quite precisely, those who had founded the State. He meant the generation that, in the wake of the War of Independence and the bloody Civil War of 1922–23, had appropriated the country, nation, society, on behalf of the Irish middle classes... The 'Irish Free State', created at that moment of compromise and disillusion, was itself a compromise, snatched from the idealists who had sought a free and united republic.[7]

Whether the new state was 'snatched' or saved from idealists remains like much else from the period a matter of contention. The confusion of the settlement is something which Tom Garvin has addressed in a series of provocative and innovative essays, *1922: The Birth of Irish Democracy*. Garvin, however, after dismissing the democratic credentials of the idealists of 1922–23, makes an equally impassioned counter-argument in relation to the ongoing peace process and its historical origins:

Democracy in Ireland was the child of strange parents... Its crucial moment came in 1922–23, when force was used to prevent it being forcibly disestablished by insurrectionist 'republicans' who mouthed democratic slogans but whose violent actions belied their words. Since the Free State victory of 1923, no alternative regime has been taken seriously in Ireland. No all-Ireland polity, were one to emerge in the future, could ever be established without the clear consent of the Northern majority. It was the democratic founders of independent Ireland who first said this openly and did so at the founding moment of the state. Now seventy years later, the descendants of their opponents, the leaders of Fianna Fáil, have finally, after years of prevarication, openly agreed with William Cosgrave, someone whose name they have sometimes virtually forgotten or which they remember only as that of a traitor.[8]

Garvin is of course correct in identifying a continuous dialogue about the nature of the Irish state and relations on the island spanning from 1920 to the Downing Street declaration of 15 December 1993, to which he alludes. No matter what position one takes on the debates of the 1920s or the present, the point remains that constitutionally, legally, culturally and intellectually modern Irish society is still attempting to redefine itself against its own revolutionary settlement.

   Unlike nearly all other western European societies in the period between the First World War and the present, no great war or strife impinged upon a twenty-six county consensual nationalism to shake it from its complacency or to challenge its assumptions. Nor did any foreign occupation with its attendant miseries challenge assumptions established in the post-revolutionary settlement. There was of course trauma in post-revolutionary Irish society, symbolised by economic under-performance resulting in chronic poverty and immigration. Partition, although decidedly more traumatic north of the border than south, also cast a long shadow over the post-independence settlement. The outbreak of violence in Northern Ireland did bring military occupation, violence and war, some of which spread southwards across the border, but southern politics and historical assumptions remained remarkably impervious to the northern situation. No general election was fought on the issues emanating from the north, and political support for those parties championing them in the Republic remained minuscule. Economic stagnation and partition served to add to the immutable nature of the revolutionary settlement in the southern state by exporting potential problems outside of the settlement. Emigration bled off potential forces for change, while partition removed from the independent Irish state the problem of dealing with a significant minority culture, and the demands of inventing a genuinely pluralist nationalism. After 1923, southern Irish society, by European standards, enjoyed a remarkably docile and stable political experience which was capable of surviving the internal collapse of the post-revolutionary settlement in Northern Ireland.

The most significant forces for change, which are only now beginning to distance contemporary Irish society from the revolutionary settlement, have been of the non-traumatic kind – at least to date. One of the most remarkable transformations has been the quiet secularisation of Irish society over the past three decades. By 1995 such a process could claim, but only just, to have overthrown by referendum the prohibition on divorce: itself part of what might be termed the post-revolutionary moral settlement. Increases in wealth and subsequent mobility since the 1960s and economic and educational interaction with Britain, North America and the rest of Europe have created a new breed of bipolar Irish pluralisms. Emigrants can now, if they choose, live an amphibious existence darting back and forth between Ireland, Britain, the Continent and North America. The banter of passengers on the Friday evening flights from Heathrow to Cork or Dublin bears its own testimony to the fact that both cities are now part of the Celtic commuter belt of London and the City. Conversely, places like Kinsale and Templebar have been cultivated as chic and not so chic weekend resorts of the British travelling public. The western littoral from Clonikilty to Mallen Head now enjoys dispersed colonies of Europeans in search of their own hidden Irelands. The cultural barriers erected after the revolution through censorship, and a static emigrant culture exasperated by poverty, have substantially disintegrated with access to economic travel between Ireland and the outside world.

Of equal significance has been the revolution in media technology since the mid-1980s which has introduced a degree of pluralism – even if it is largely defined within an Anglo-American culture – which was inaccessible until the advent of video, satellite, cable, and a liberalisation of the censorship laws, officially and otherwise. The first cyber-cafes opened in Dublin in 1992, giving access to an uncensored medium to Irish 'surfers' for the first time. With the advent of the World Wide Web an Irish businessman, school child and now any public library user is a global communications operative. Such observations, of what is now commonplace, may seem of little import but they represent the very sudden end of what might be termed the official post-revolutionary moral and cultural settlements. These innovations do however seem remarkable when set against the 1970s, when a diligent customs officer might deprive a reader of a copy of Edna O'Brien's *The Country Girls*, or during the 1980s of a copy of Alex Comfort's *Joy of Sex*. As recently as August 1996 the American soft-porn magazine *Playboy* went on sale for the first time on Irish newsagents' top shelves inside a protective wrapper without frightening Irish horses: revolutionary or otherwise. These events, so recent and now suddenly so surreal, represent both the cultural inertia of the official post-revolutionary moral and cultural settlements and their almost instant irrelevance within the last half-decade. Any absolute definition of cultural experience between the revolution and the present is of course redundant. It was varied and inordinately complex as between rural and urban, middle class and working class, those who had access to foreign media and foreign travel and those who did not. But at a popular and official level the post-revolutionary settlement in these spheres has only just collapsed. We are only now beginning to trample over its rubble. Advances in technology have provided cultural as well as intellectual choices which the post-revolutionary establishment struggled against, and ones that they had been largely successful, until the very recent past, in denying to the Irish public. What is happening to Irish society as it travels so far so fast is impossible to say, but the concept of the post-revolutionary settlement as an area of study and reflection at least gives us a reference point from which a much-needed discussion can develop.

The mono-culture resulting from the longevity of the political, moral and cultural settlement in independent Ireland tended towards producing a mono-history narrowly defined by an ongoing partisan debate over the events of 1921–22, and the nature of the new state's relationship with Britain and Northern Ireland. The leadership of 1916 and 1921 lingered on into the late 1950s, in de Valera's case into 1970s, and posthumously in Michael Collins' case into the consciousness of the 1990s. Much of the debate about the meaning of independence, even seventy years on, appears somewhat circular and still fought – for those still prepared to engage – in atavistic and for that matter the *chiaroscuro* terms of treaty and anti-treaty; right or wrong; them and us. The more one examines twentieth-century Irish political culture south of the border and the issues which divided the revolutionary Sinn Féin movement in 1922, the more apparent it becomes that the divisions within 26-county nationalism are characterised by the slightest subtleties.

The essays in this volume do not address directly what are commonly held to be the seismic, or landmark events in the history of independence: the treaty negotiations; the civil war; the collapse of the boundary commission; the transfer of power in 1932; the new constitution five years later; nor that exercise in linguistic autarky, the 'Emergency', otherwise the Second World War. There is of course no question that these events, the dot-to-dot of most narrative histories of independence, remain of crucial importance. By broadening the debate which surrounds the experience of independence and by re-examining the central players and including peripheral groups something more can be added, not only to our knowledge of what the settlement means, but to better inform a debate which appears locked in a monochrome dialogue still obsessed with personality, defined by party, motivated by the need to apportion blame or, conversely, to take credit for supposed triumphs. If books can have ambitions, then the ambition of this volume is to explore at one and the same time the diversity and commonality of the political experience of independence which lurks behind all too often deceptive and unhelpful flags of convenience: treatyite; socialist republican; Fianna Fáiler; parliamentary nationalist; southern unionist; and the Catholic intelligentsia.

Notes

1   For a consideration of the debate see Ronan Fanning, 'Michael Collins – An Overview', in Gabriel Doherty and Dermot Keogh (eds), *Michael Collins and the Making of the Irish State* (Dublin, 1998), pp. 202–10.

2 T. Garvin, *1922. The Birth of Irish Democracy* (Dublin, 1996), p. 30.
3 R. Fanning, *Independent Ireland* (Dublin, 1983).
4 J.J. Lee, *Ireland 1912–85, Politics and Society* (Cambridge, 1989).
5 D. Keogh, *Twentieth Century Ireland* (Dublin, 1994).
6 D. Fitzpatrick, *The Two Irelands, 1912–1939* (Oxford, 1998).
7 J. Waters, *An Intelligent Person's Guide to Modern Ireland* (London, 1997), p. 27.
8 T. Garvin, *1922*, pp. 206–7.

2

Ireland's Last Home Rule Generation: The Decline of Constitutional Nationalism in Ireland, 1916–30

Senia Paseta

We all took it for granted that if Home Rule was achieved, we would be among the politicians of the new Ireland. A Home Rule Parliament in College Green in those days would, no doubt, have been dominated by the Irish Party, which would have earned the credit for its establishment. We, in the College, had many connections with the Irish Party... We all confidently expected that in a short time we would be exercising our oratory, not in the dingy precincts of the old Physics Theatre in 86 [Earlsfort Terrace], but in the 'Old House in College Green'. It was because of this hope that we took our debates so seriously. We had heard that future prime ministers were picked out because of their performances at the Oxford Union, and we believed that, when the chair at the 'L. & H.' was taken by distinguished visitors, such as John Dillon, some future Irish Prime Minster might attract influential attention if his oratory aroused sufficient admiration. Debating took such a large part of our energies that I remember Arthur Cox saying to me that there were only three positions for which we were being fitted by our education – prime minister, leader of the opposition and Speaker of the House of Commons.[1]

The final years of the Irish Parliamentary Party are shrouded in tragedy and misfortune. Although recent scholars have underlined both the Party's very real achievements and the political acumen of John Redmond,[2] the years 1900–18 have frequently been represented as a time of political preparation and consolidation for Irish republicans and years of decline for adherents of constitutional Home Rule. A republican-dominated historical perspective has obscured the majority view in late nineteenth and early twentieth century Ireland, and an influential generation of young constitutionally-minded Irish men and women who became 'lost' through the radicalising of Irish politics has been afforded little more than a marginal role in the subsequent construction of the history of Ireland in the twentieth century.

The presentation of the victory of revolutionary politics as inevitable has undermined the importance of a number of salient issues which influenced the evolution of modern Ireland. Ireland at the turn of the twentieth century seemed ripe for change, both political and social. The environment for the development of a new Catholic intelligentsia was ideal: the rise of cultural nationalism, the growth of social and political movements such as feminism, the inroads into the professions made by Irish Catholics and, importantly, an unprecedented level of prosperity in the evolving Catholic middle classes fuelled the desire for change.

This emerging elite was by no means homogenous; it was divided by both social and economic background and its political vision for its country. Some, schooled in the 'greats' of Irish nationalism – Tone, O'Connell, Davis and Parnell – were convinced that they would one day claim a place in this long line, and saw Home Rule as a central aspect of twentieth century Ireland. Others, however, believed the maintenance of the Union was desirable and indeed necessary if Catholics were to climb to the top of professional and social ladders. Advocates of republicanism were rare and contributed little to the dynamic political culture which was increasingly dominated by a coterie of University College Dublin students and graduates.

Student life was revived after a long period of apathy by the resurrection of the University College Literary and Historical Society in 1897. The list of 'L&H' auditors included Thomas Kettle, Arthur Clery, Hugh Kennedy and Francis Sheehy Skeffington and the Society discussed such topics as Ireland under Home Rule, the University Question and women's suffrage. The establishment in 1901 of *St Stephen's*, a University College magazine, signalled the drive by educated young nationalists to stamp their influence on Irish political life. Enthused by the reunification of the Irish Parliamentary Party and convinced of the inevitability of Home Rule, student politicians affirmed their allegiance to constitutional Home Rule time and time again:

> The political opinions of the University College students are those to be found throughout Nationalist Ireland. As one might expect, the College has a larger proportion of extreme nationalists than is to be found in other parts of the country. But with the exception of a

considerable minority who profess themselves believers in separation, the bulk of the students hold the orthodox Home Rule view.[3]

Advocacy of Home Rule did not, however, signify unquestioning
approval of the Parliamentary Party. A desire for new ideas and new
blood led to the foundation of the Young Ireland Branch (YIB) of the
United Irish League, the national organisation of the Irish Parliamentary
party, in 1905. Established and led by Thomas Kettle, the YIB constituted a separate Dublin branch of the United Irish League and its first
committee included Kettle as chairman, Eugene Sheehy, William
Fallon, Richard Hazelton and Hanna and Francis Sheehy Skeffington.
The YIBs revolted 'against the party machine',[4] braving Redmond's criticism by denouncing the Council Bill of 1907 which proposed to give
control of 48 government departments to a national council elected on
the existing local government franchise. The organisation regularly
offered similarly controversial and progressive opinions on issues
including women's suffrage and industrial and economic development
which ignored or challenged official Parliamentary Party policy.

Their enthusiasm invigorated student culture and reflected the
increasing involvement of young nationalists in activities on the cut-
ting edge of Irish cultural and political life. Arthur Clery, a student and
future Professor of Law at University College, Dublin, described the
years from 1897 as 'undescribably brilliant and interesting',[5] while the
writer, Mary Colum, emphasised the importance of youth to the new
national movements:

> Almost everything in the Dublin of that period was run by the
> young, eagerness, brains, imagination, are what I remember of every-
> body. There was something else that was in all of them: a desire for
> self-sacrifice, a devotion to causes; everyone was working for a cause,
> for practically everything was a cause.[6]

The Gaelic League also sought student support and articles written in
Irish began to appear in *St Stephen's*. The influence of D.P. Moran, the
Irish-Irelander and editor of the *Leader*, was also apparent as graduates
including Arthur Clery, the barrister William Dawson and future Chief
Justice of Ireland, Hugh Kennedy, began to contribute to the *Leader*.
While the mission to 'de-anglicise' Ireland and to expose 'West
Britonism' certainly won the approval of some young nationalists, the
influence of the YIB remained strong and the political fortunes of lead-
ing YIBs, Thomas Kettle and Richard Hazelton, were monitored closely

by leaders of the Irish Parliamentary Party. Kettle's outspokenness and his willingness to question political orthodoxy appealed to the young men and women who advocated Home Rule, but questioned the effectiveness of the Parliamentary Party:

> But the idea which found expression these meetings, and which were soon to reach a wider public through the medium of Kettle' weekly, the *Nationist*, and the Young Ireland branch of the UIL, of which he was chairman and many from the society were members, showed that a new and more keenly critical outlook on national affairs had awakened among the younger generation of educated Irishmen. So far as University College was concerned, the spirit of revolution was not yet above the horizon. But a definite and lasting discontent with ineffective political methods had manifested itself...[7]

The Irish Party supported the parliamentary ambitions of Kettle and fellow YIB, Richard Hazelton, but continued to overlook other talented young politicians such as Cruise O'Brien and Francis Sheehy Skeffington.[8] Kettle was elected Member of Parliament for East Clare in 1906, but he continued to pursue extra-parliamentary activities, often in the company of fellow YIBs. He had founded the *Nationist*, a 'weekly review of Irish thought and affairs' in 1905 and edited it with the assistance of Francis Sheehy Skeffington. Although both men had played prominent roles in the production of *St Stephen's*, the *Nationist* allowed them the freedom to pursue in detail a number of cultural and political issues without the inclusion of college gossip and what Sheehy Skeffington described as Gaelic League 'propaganda'.[9]

Kettle espoused the Parliamentary Party's political agenda through the pages of the *Nationist*. He explained that his support for the Party was based on 'realism in politics' and argued that the Party possessed the experience, machinery and results which would secure Home Rule for Ireland.[10] His strident advocacy of the constitutional agenda reflected his growing impatience with what he identified as the tendency to dismiss politics as 'counting for nothing at all'.[11] Scathing of much gaelicist rhetoric and concerned about the fragmentation in the national movement, he appealed to Irish-Irelanders to join with constitutionalists in the Home Rule campaign:

> We have appealed to the men of the younger movements to throw themselves into the political movement. We have shown Gaelic Leaguers that Home Rule stands for mastery of our educational

systems, and industrialists that Home Rule stands for mastery of our purse. Will they not, then, join with us to obtain Home Rule?[12]

Although Kettle insisted that many young constitutionalists had supported the Gaelic League,[13] both he and Skeffington expressed increasing disapproval of the League's prescriptive tendencies and its flirtation with separatism. In contrast to the Gaelic League and commentators such as D.P. Moran, Kettle continued to emphasise the importance of established political activity as represented by the Irish Party and to defend the political institutions which he maintained were central to democratic government. 'The State', for example, was

> the name by which we call the great human conspiracy against hunger and cold, against loneliness and ignorance, the State is the foster-mother and warden of the arts, of love, of comradeship, of all that makes life a brave and beautiful adventure.[14]

Sheehy Skeffington tackled the Gaelic League through publications which included the journals *Dana*, the *National Democrat* and the *Irish Citizen*. With his friend and fellow socialist, Frederick Ryan, he challenged the notion that 'the mere desire to speak another language' correlated 'with the active desire for political freedom'.[15] Moving rapidly to the left, he became an outspoken critic of the conservatism which permeated Irish social and political life.

> There are, it is to be feared, too many in the Nationalist ranks today who regard the attainment of Irish autonomy as an end in itself, or, if a means to any end, to the establishment of a conservative [order], supporting and supported ecclesiastical and capitalist hierarchies. Logically, however, Irish autonomy will not be an end, but a beginning.[16]

Kettle similarly urged his readers not to view Home Rule as a panacea or as an easy answer to Ireland's many problems:

> Assuredly, we must not seem to suggest that in an autonomous Ireland public life will be all nougat, velvet, and soft music. There will be conflicts, and vehement conflicts, for that is the way of the twentieth century ...[17]

In 1907 Kettle and Sheehy Skeffington joined forces with Ryan and the writer, Maurice Joy, in order to found a 'National Democratic

Committee' which was to 'link forces with the British Labour Party and Davitt's last battle with clericalism'.[18] The organisation failed to progress beyond the planning stage, but it indicated a willingness to move beyond the concerns of the Parliamentary Party and into open conflict with the Catholic hierarchy, one of the Party's most important backers. But, while Sheehy Skeffington veered further to the left and became increasingly involved with feminism and pacifism, Kettle's impatience with competing nationalist organisations such as Sinn Féin seemed to steer him closer to Parliamentary Party orthodoxy and away from the radicalism he had once flirted with.

The two men's political priorities diverged sharply over the issue of women's suffrage. Sheehy Skeffington resigned from the YIB and the Parliamentary Party in 1911 because of its anti-feminism, in particular its refusal to support women's suffrage.[19] He had earlier resigned his position as registrar to University College because of its refusal to admit women to its classes. Like Sheehy Skeffington, Kettle was an intimate of many prominent feminist campaigners including his sister-in-law, Hanna Sheehy Skeffington. He had advocated women's suffrage, but abandoned the cause in the interests of the Party and the safe passage of the third Home Rule Bill.[20] Sheehy Skeffington wrote bitterly of this defection:

> It was a pretty tale, full of friendships, of election pledges and platform appeals from those who 'have always been our best friends', but who were always fatally debarred from action at 'critical junctures', and who in the sacred cause of party were regretfully obliged to shelve our cause when there was a likelihood of its winning.[21]

Sheehy Skeffington maintained his antipathy, criticising John Redmond and vowing to disregard the Party's refusal to allow women to enjoy the same political rights and privileges as men.[22] Hanna Sheehy Skeffington protested against the menial role women played in the YIB, claiming that the obstacles placed in the way of women who were used to working alongside men in other nationalist organisations, but were prevented from participating in the Irish Party and associated organisations such as the YIBs ensured that they often turned instead to the Gaelic League or Sinn Féin.[23]

Kettle and the Sheehy Skeffingtons further diverged over Ireland's involvement in the British war effort. Kettle argued that the war represented a test of Ireland's commitment to freedom and democracy.[24] In common with many nationalists, he believed the European War '[held] out to Ireland fair and high promise of the future',[25] and argued:

> Yet the separate existence of the Irish Brigades is a thing to dwell on, for they are the living symbol of the truth that this war is Ireland's war, and that Ireland for the first time in the passage of long centuries sends out her sons fully accredited to fight for the sake of Ireland and for Ireland's cause.[26]

In the first issue of the *Nationist*, Kettle had urged his readers to 'learn to accept Ireland as a great complex fact; an organism with all the complications of modern society'.[27] Implicit in his view of Ireland in the twentieth century was its place within modern Europe. He further argued that Irish students should play a prominent role in the political life of their country just as their counterparts had in other parts of Europe.[28] The Great War threatened Kettle's vision of a liberal and democratised Europe: 'we have lived to see Europe – that Europe which carried the fortunes and hopes of all mankind – degraded to a foul something which no image can so much as shadow forth'.[29]

University College Dublin students responded to Redmond's call to arms; in common with Kettle, many viewed the War as a test of 'the sincerity of [their] professions of faith'.[30] Kettle himself decided to enlist after travelling to Belgium to obtain guns for the Volunteers. 'Belgium', he claimed, 'is in agony'.[31] 'It is impossible not to be with Belgium in the struggle. It is impossible any longer to be passive.[32] He condemned the '"physical force" school of Irish nationalist thinking' as 'naïve and Prussian',[33] and reiterated his conviction that Ireland's struggle for political autonomy paralleled the allied campaign against German aggression in Europe:

> If we take our stand against Prussia we have got to take our stand with England. No Man could condemn more strongly than myself the weary centuries of English blackguardism in Ireland. But the poisoners of Owen Roe O'Neill are dead, and the hangers of Emmet are dead. Even in our own time, and in the last ten years of it, a new world has come into existence. The England of 1914 is on the side of the Ten Commandments, and it does not reside in the spiritual tradition of Ireland to desert the 'Ten Commandments' in order to gratify a hatred of which the mainsprings have disappeared.[34]

Kettle referred rather frivolously to the Easter Rising as the 'Sinn Féin nightmare' which 'upset [him] a little'. 'But if', he explained, 'you tickle the ear of a short tempered elephant with a pop gun, and he walks out on you that is a natural concatenation of events'.[35] His friend and former political ally, Francis Sheehy Skeffington, was executed by a British army firing squad at Portobello Barracks after attempting to prevent looting during Easter week 1916.[36] Kettle was himself killed at Givenchy in September 1916. The deaths of Thomas Kettle and Francis Sheehy Skeffington injured the development of liberalism, Europeanism and intellectual life in Ireland. They had at one time represented the most modern and dynamic wing of the Parliamentary Party and had pursued numerous political and social ideals in the face of growing opposition. More importantly, they represented youth, a tantalising glimpse of a possible future Irish government, and, most importantly, the potential for Irish nationalism to develop along peaceful and constitutional lines. Many of their former allies remained politically active, but were often forced to adjust to unprecedented new circumstances. The cause of Irish nationalism remained paramount for most and energies were poured into new movements such as Sinn Féin. But old agendas and beliefs did not disappear and continued to exercise an influence over political behaviour post-1916.

While continuing to consider themselves loyal nationalists, some former Party supporters denounced the radical shift in Irish politics and the implications of republican status with as much bitterness as their Unionist counterparts. Former Gaelic League member and staunch Home Ruler, John Horgan, declared, for example:

> Thus the proclamation of a non-existent Irish Republic, combined with the pretence that Irish was the real language of Ireland, led, not only to the Civil War, but to the permanent division and present anomalous position of our country, for Mr de Valera's political 'strategies and spoils' are the natural offspring of the union between the men of 1916 and the Gaelic League. We cannot hope to recover the integrity, physical or spiritual, of the nation until we have frankly recognised this fact.[37]

Like Kettle and Skeffington before him, Stephen Gwynn, a former leading member of the Irish Party, likewise despaired of Ireland's political situation and slide into provincialism and fanaticism:

> What is a Gaelic Ireland? I do not know ... But we do need in Ireland to get a civilised State, and we can only do that by adopting some of

the patterns which are established in Europe, to which we belong. It is a great deal more important to be civilized than to be Gaelic ... Gaelic Ireland exists in about as much reality as Mr de Valera's presidency of an Irish Republic to-day [May 1923]. They seem to me meagre phantoms for which to kill or burn – but so long as people continue to offer them this costly homage it will remain the duty of our Government, and all of us, to insist by all necessary means that such savage rites shall cease.[38]

Claiming that Sinn Féin was becoming increasingly 'bolshevist',[39] Gwynn hoped to attract like-minded Irish men and women to a new political party whose aims owed much to Redmond and his party. Launched in 1919, the Irish Centre Party rejected partition and advocated Irish self-government within the Empire. The new party outlined a social policy which emphasised reform in areas including health and housing. It also insisted upon the protection of minority rights, promising that a state-funded education system would be 'controlled on lines which allow free development alike for the Catholic and Protestant ideals of teaching'.[40]

The Irish Centre Party merged with the Dominion League in 1919, assuming the role of pressure group and ostensibly leaving party politics behind. Gwynn and Sir Thomas Esmonde represented the old Irish Party in the new organisation, but Gwynn acknowledged new political circumstances by insisting that the new organisation claimed more from the British government than the old Party ever had. A central demand was the right of a self-governing Ireland to control its own taxation.[41] The organisation continued to claim support from the very constituencies the Parliamentary Party had once appealed to

> Sinn Féin in asking for an Irish Republic is simply putting up a bargaining demand; but, at all events, [Plunkett] knows that outside the ranks of declared Sinn Féiners, and declared advocates for maintaining government as it is at present by armed force, there is the 'middle public', including vast numbers of businessmen, perfectly prepared to accept the status of a self-governing dominion, subject to the necessary strategic limitations.[42]

Former YIB and brother-in-law of Thomas Kettle, Eugene Sheehy, offered his legal expertise to the new Irish government by serving as Judge Advocate-General in the Free State Army during the Civil War. But former affiliations coloured the participation in the new political order of former Home Rulers. As Conor Cruise O'Brien has astutely noted:

> The new government needed such allies, but its relations with them were necessarily a little constrained. Eugene, after all, had been in the British Army at John Redmond's call throughout the World War, including 1916. The new government was made up of Sinn Féiners, all of whom had denounced the wearing of the British uniform as treason to Ireland. Eugene could hardly forget this. The new government could hardly forget it either. Allies like Eugene were needed, in the struggle against the extreme Republicans, but they were compromising allies.[43]

Some could not find a place in the new Ireland and many who stayed continued to mourn earlier times whose distance was measured in momentous political change rather than years. The Catholic doctor, Patrick Heffernan, yearned for 'the hey-day of the middle-classes before the modern revolution came',[44] while George O'Brien found solace in the company of landed Catholics who had little sympathy for self-government and the language movement.[45] His only personal association with Gaelic revivalism was with like-minded people in the 'Ruskin-Morris traditions of arts and crafts, of the intelligentsia redeeming the vulgarity of trade'.[46]

But O'Brien, in common with many other political moderates also found solace in the Irish Dominion League (IDL) and associated organisations. Launched by Horace Plunkett in 1919, the IDL advocated 'self-government of Ireland within the Empire'.[47] The organisation boasted prominent members including Viscount Gormanston and the Earl of Fingall, and leading political figures including Mary Kettle (widow of Thomas), feminist and historian Mary Hayden, Stephen Gwynn and Eugene Sheehy. Although in no way officially aligned to the Parliamentary Party, the IDL produced manifestos which were reminiscent of earlier Parliamentary Party rhetoric. In his outline of the League's aims, prominent member Colonel Pope-Hennessy, for example, declared:

> Even if it were politically obtainable, which we are sure it is not, we see no advantage for Ireland in the status of a Republic, but many grave disadvantages which, as a Dominion, she would not have to fear.[48]

Plunkett's pragmatism fuelled his drive for dominion status; he believed that Unionism was no longer viable and that the only hope of avoiding both Anglo-Irish and extreme Nationalist–Unionist conflict was to persuade the British government to grant greater political concessions to Ireland. He was the first to admit that the prevailing political climate rendered this a difficult task, acknowledging in 1918 the existence of 'a hatred of Britain more virulent just now, it must be admitted, than in living memory, aggravated as it is by contempt for British statesmanship and utter distrust of British promises'.[49]

Plunkett and the IDL maintained, however, that 'moderate opinion' had been under-estimated and under-represented. Stephen Gwynn claimed that

> All the information which I gather supports my own reading of the situation – that the persons actually in charge of Irish nationalist policy do not represent the mind of the country to-day. Ireland wants a settlement. The vast majority of those who voted for Republicans at the last election did not understand what they were doing. They though they were putting up a bargaining demand... They did not foresee war, [and] did not want war.[50]

The IDL aimed explicitly at winning the support of middle-class Ireland; Lord Monteagle, for example, advocated the lobbying of 'the business community and the learned professions', 'judges and magistrates' and the 'clerical and medical professions'.[51] The organisation offered a forum for liberal conservatives (some of whom were former Unionists), political moderates and former supporters of the Irish Party, and served as a kind of refuge for the politically-minded men and women who could not identify with the intransigence of hard-line Unionists and the single-mindedness of republicans:

> its object, briefly described, was to afford the means for Irish people of all shades of political conviction and antecedents to combine in advocacy of Dominion Status for Ireland as the only possible arrangement by which the antagonism between Ireland and Great Britain and between North-East Ulster and Ireland could be amicably adjusted.[52]

Although scathing of extreme republicans, the IDL was clearly influenced by the radicalisation of Irish politics. The organisation considered that Redmondite Home Rule or simple repeal of the Union would no longer appease Irish demands for self-government.[53] 'I believe', explained Plunkett, 'in a much wider measure of self-government than might formerly have sufficed, but not in an Irish Republic'.[54] Dominion status, insisted the IDL, would grant Ireland full powers of taxation and customs and excise; the military would remain under central control, but the power to impose compulsory military service would rest with the new Dublin parliament.[55]

Although the IDL self-consciously presented itself as a moderate alternative to both Unionism *and* extreme nationalism, it clearly identified Sinn Féin as its most formidable rival in the competition for public opinion.[56] The organisation thus urged middle Ireland to reject republicanism and Sinn Féin. Significantly, it also urged moderate Sinn Féiners to accept dominion status. George F.H. Berkeley, a leading member of the London IDL branch, claimed that Sinn Féin could have been persuaded to accept Dominion Home Rule in 1920, had the British government cooperated. Although Lloyd George had assured Plunkett and Henry Harrison (secretary to the IDL) that 'he would negotiate matters on [their] lines' if they managed to organise a strong centre party, leading IDL members (including Berkeley) came to doubt his sincerity.[57] Their misgivings deepened in line with their condemnation of government policy during the 'War of Independence'. Claiming that the government and the press had enforced a 'conspiracy of secrecy', Berkeley denounced Lloyd George, arguing that the 'champion of freedom for the people was now the promoter of a secret campaign of repression and outrage'.[58]

Lord Monteagle – who was 'almost worked off his feet' during his attempt to introduce a Dominion Bill into the Lords in 1920[59] – maintained contact with a 'leading Sinn Féin acquaintance who [was] in close touch with Griffith'.[60] After conferring with his 'acquaintance', he formed the opinion that Sinn Féin would accept Dominion status 'under protest'. Berkeley also testified to Griffith's willingness to be persuaded, claiming that he had accepted a scheme of Dominion Home Rule offered by Lloyd George in 1921, but subsequently rejected the offer.[61] Monteagle believed that the almost certain exclusion of Ulster or parts of Ulster from the legislation was the major stumbling block to Sinn Féin's acceptance of Dominion status. He understood that Ulster Sinn Féiners would swear loyalty to the Dublin parliament and attempt to send members to it. Ulster would thus eventually be brought into the Dominion scheme without the introduction of any further legislation.[62] In retrospect this strategy appears naïve in the extreme, but Ulster remained the largest stumbling block to the success of any settlement.

Although distinct in some ways, the various solutions to the partition issue offered by prominent IDL members commonly insisted that Ulster must not be forced into any scheme and that minority rights (of unionists) would be protected under a Dominion settlement. The country 'must face frankly and meet fairly the Ulster difficulty'.[63] Arguing that partition was unacceptable, the Irish Centre Party advocated the establishment of a national parliament *and* provincial assemblies.[64] Monteagle suggested that if the majority of the representatives of counties Antrim, Armagh, Fermanagh, Down, Londonderry and Tyrone refused to accept a new constitution, they should be permitted to present a memorial to the Imperial Conference. If the new Irish constitution were rejected at a subsequent plebiscite, the counties would be 'excluded from its operation'.[65] Henry Harrison broadly agreed with Monteagle, and suggested that the northern counties might exercise their options as a unit or as two units. He added: 'I believe that Ireland would accept this method of "calling Ulster's bluff"'.[66]

The IDL organised and financed the Irish Peace Conference of 1920, but the country plunged further into crisis while the League continued to call for a peaceful settlement. Civil war loomed and the importance of finding a settlement gained momentum. Berkeley explained: 'we were all in deadly earnest about it [the Dominion Bill], because we felt it was the last chance of arranging a compromise; in fact the only remaining alternative to civil war'.[67] Plunkett and the IDL continued to condemn 'government repression', but their commitment to Dominion status was increasingly undermined by divisions within the organisation over partition. Monteagle and a section of the organisation came out for partition in the interests of peace; Plunkett, who continued to oppose partition, consequently wound the organisation up.[68] The organisation 'dissolved itself' in 1921, claiming that its aims had been achieved. A note attached to its final report seemed to vindicate its campaign: 'As this Report is going through the Press the world has been rejoiced by the publication of the "Treaty between Great Britain and Ireland"'.[69] Berkeley expressed similar enthusiasm upon the announcement of the Treaty:

> I well remember our feelings, but they are hard to describe. I think the first general sentiment was that we could hardly trust it: it was too good to be true. Will it last? What ought we to do clinch it, to make it permanent?[70]

Such endorsement of the Treaty led almost inevitably to support for Cumann na nGaedheal. Henry Harrison applauded the efforts of the treatyites, arguing that 'under the Free State Government, Ireland has crawled painfully and determinedly out of the frying pan, and now the Anti-Treaty republicans want to throw her altogether into the fire'.[71] Stephen Gwynn praised Cumann na nGaedheal's political programme of April 1924, claiming that

> the eight headings under which the programme is further itemised would all command the assent of any among the old Nationalists and there is no mention of the Republic. As a student of history, I should be prepared to contend that the demand for a republic is not in accord with the national tradition, but that is an abstract discussion.[72]

Despite the Treaty and the continuing electoral success of Cumann na nGaedheal, some former constitutional nationalists could not adapt to Ireland's changed political circumstances. Founded by Captain William Redmond in 1926, the National League Party managed to win eight seats in the June 1927 election. Advocating a policy of cooperation with Britain and Northern Ireland, the new party marketed itself as the heir to the old Parliamentary Party.[73] Its support waned and its remnants merged with Cumann na nGaedheal between 1931–32. Despite this decline in the political fortunes of former constitutionalists, a sentimental attachment to the values of an earlier generation remained. Organisations with strong links to the Parliamentary Party such as the Ancient Order of Hibernians promoted the 'bringing together in social intercourse many of the Nationalists who have retained their loyalty to all that the old constitutional movement and the Irish Party typified'.[74] But, by the early 1930s, the voice of pre-Independence constitutional Ireland had all but disappeared from the public stage.

Memories of participation in and support for the Great War stood at the heart of the shared political history which continued to bind some former Home Rulers. Many members of the IDL, the Irish Centre Party and the National League Party had served in the war or had supported the British war effort; most had lost friends and relations during the War. Horace Plunkett, for example, claimed that 'at the beginning of the war a large number of Irish nationalists, ... acted as I felt'.[75] He argued in 1918 that 'by every tradition this is Ireland's war, and every friend of Ireland so regards it',[76] but by that time war weariness and the threat of conscription had intensified the increasingly hostile attitude towards the War and the Irish men and women who had participated in it. Sinn Féin had, moreover, achieved a measure of political and

moral superiority. The veteran parliamentarian William O'Brien captured the national mood in 1918 when he credited Sinn Féin with
saving Ireland from 'the three plagues of Partition, Conscription and
Corruption'.[77]

But a small number of persistent commentators continued to extol
the virtues of the war dead and to condemn Sinn Féin and associated
organisations for encouraging the erosion of their memory:

> The action of Irish soldiers was thwarted and frustrated by the
> action of a very few separatists, with a very small expense to them-
> selves in bloodshed. But the tribute to the work of the Gaelic League
> is that Ireland accepted them and rejected us.[78]

Such men and women as Lawrence Kettle, Eugene Sheehy, Mary Kettle
and Stephen Gwynn found some solace and an outlet for their grievances in organisations such as the IDL which upheld many of the ideas
which their friends and relations had died for. Henry Harrison was perhaps the most dogged of all, founding *Irish Truth* through which he
campaigned for the remuneration and recognition of Irish men who
had served in the British army during the war. Claiming that Irish soldiers had experienced greater difficulty settling into civilian life than
former soldiers from any other part of the Empire, he continued to
insist that they had not compromised their nationality by serving in
the British army:

> They have had none too easy a time since disbandenment. But the
> vast bulk of them served because they were told that it was for
> Ireland's interest and honour than they should, and he [Harrison] is
> proud of the magnificent record of their gallantry. And they are none
> the less good Irishmen for having served on the side of the Allies.[79]

Although the memory of Ireland's role in the Great War dead faded
in tandem with the remaining members of Ireland's last Home Rule
generation, the attempt to commemorate Ireland's war dead periodically aroused controversy. The establishment in 1916 of the T.M. Kettle
Memorial Committee signalled the commencement of a long battle
between Kettle's like-minded contemporaries and government officials.
By 1917 the committee – which was at various times comprised of people including W.G. Fallon, Joseph Devlin, Oliver St John Gogarty and
William Dawson – had collected over £500 and a site in St Stephen's
Green had been chosen for the placement of a portrait-bust. It was

decided to postpone the unveiling of the bust until after the War, but in 1923 the committee decided that the bust could not be erected 'so long as present circumstances last in Ireland'.[80] The bust was due to be unveiled in 1927, but the ceremony was held up when the Commissioners of the Office of Public Works objected to the committee's request that the following lines (which Kettle had composed shortly before his death) be inscribed on the memorial:

> Died not for flag, nor King, nor Emperor,
> But for a dream born in a herdsman's shed
> And for the secret scripture of the poor.[81]

Eager to avoid controversy, the Commissioners of the Office of Public Works insisted that

> the unveiling of the Memorial is to be in the nature of a ceremonial to which only the original subscribers and some friends will be invited, that no prior announcement of the date of the ceremony will be made in the public press and that any address delivered will be of a non-political character.[82]

The Commissioners also objected to the inscription of the words 'killed in France', but agreed to allow the committee to inscribe on the pedestal the three allegedly controversial words and the sonnet 'at a later date say within the next six months'.[83] The Kettle family, however, insisted that the inscription be added.[84] The commissioners withdrew their objection in 1928, but the bust languished in the National Gallery until the inscription was added and the bust was unveiled (without an official ceremony) in 1937. The bust was stolen in 1960 and was later retrieved from a pond in St Stephen's Green.

Kettle prophesied in 1916: 'what we have said and done is to be remembered and is to rise up in judgement against us in the new Ireland that is coming'. Kettle and like-minded nationalists were judged harshly by their more extreme counterparts and virtually ignored until recently by historians. The political (mis)fortunes of John Redmond, John Dillon and Joseph Devlin have rightly been highlighted by historians working on the final years of constitutional Home Rule. John and Willie Redmond have in particular come to be viewed as martyrs to the Home Rule cause just as Patrick Pearse has come to represent the sacrificial aspect of republicanism. But the dramatic careers and deaths of some of the best-known advocates of Home Rule have come to over-shadow the little-known but important activities of a younger generation of Home Rulers, a generation poised to inherit and lead a self-governing Ireland. The demise of constitutional nationalism dealt a death blow not only to the Irish Party but to the men and women who had been prepared to lead Ireland in the new century.

Notes

1 George O'Brien cited in J. Meenan, *George O'Brien: A Biographical Memoir* (Dublin, 1980), p. 33.
2 See, for example, P. Bew, *John Redmond* (Dundalk, 1996) and P. Bew, *Ideology and the Irish Question* (Oxford, 1994), *passim*.
3 *National Student*, November 1914, p. 2.
4 F. Sheehy Skeffington, 'Frederick Ryan', *Irish Review*, no. 27, May, 1913, p. 118.
5 A. Clery, *Dublin Essays* (Dublin, 1919), p. 55.
6 M. Colum, *Life and the Dream* (Dublin, 1966), p. 131.
7 T.F. Bacon 'Fathers of the Society of Jesus', in *The Centenary History of the University College, Dublin, Literary and Historical Society, 1855–1955* (Tralee, 1957), p. 71.
8 F.S.L. Lyons, 'Decline and Fall of the Nationalist Party', in O.D. Edwards and F. Pyle (eds), *1916: The Easter Rising* (London, 1968), pp. 57–8.
9 *St Stephen's*, December 1901, p. 75.
10 *Nationist*, 21 September 1905, p. 5; and Kettle, 'A Note on Sinn Féin', p. 52.
11 *Nationist*, 2 November 1905, p. 101.
12 *Ibid.*, 16 November 1905, p. 133.
13 T.M. Kettle, 'A Note on Sinn Féin', *North American Review*, clxxxvi, January, 1908, p. 48.
14 T.M. Kettle, *The Philosophy of Politics* (Dublin, 1906), p. 16.
15 F. Ryan, 'Is the Gaelic League a Progressive Front?', *Dana*, no. 7, November 1904, p. 217.
16 *National Democrat*, no. 1, February 1907, p. 8.
17 Draft notes, n.d., T.M. Kettle Papers, LA34/289(i), UCDA.
18 F. Sheehy Skeffington, 'Frederick Ryan', p. 117.
19 T. Lawlor to F. Sheehy Skeffington, 4 October 1911 and 21 October 1911. Sheehy Skeffington Papers, MS 21, 622(v), NLI.
20 See J.B. Lyons, *The Enigma of Tom Kettle: Irish Patriot, Essayist, Poet and British Soldier, 1880–1916* (Dublin, 1983), pp. 208–13.
21 F. Sheehy Skeffington, 'The Women's Movement – Ireland', *The Pioneer*, 1, February 1911, p. 227.
22 F. Sheehy Skeffington to J. Redmond, 11 November 1909, Sheehy Skeffington Papers, 21, 634(x), NLI.
23 H. Sheehy Skeffington, 'Women and the National Movement', 1909, Sheehy Skeffington Papers, MS 22, 266, NLI.
24 T.M. Kettle, *An Open Letter to the Man on the Land in Ireland* (Athlone, 1915).
25 S. Gwynn and T.M. Kettle, *Battle Songs for the Irish* (Dublin and London, 1915), p. vi.

26   *Ibid.*, p. v.
27   *Nationist*, 21 September 1905, p. 4.
28   *Ibid.*, 2 November 1905, p. 101.
29   T.M. Kettle, 'Why Ireland Fought', draft, Kettle Papers, UCDA, LA34/390.
30   *National Student*, no. 1, November 1914, p. 1.
31   *Daily News*, 26 August 1914, T.M. Kettle Papers, UCDA, LA34/365.
32   *Daily News*, Kettle Papers, UCDA, LA34/664(I).
33   T.M. Kettle, draft of an article about the threat posed to Ireland by the German military domination of Europe, Kettle Papers, UCDA, LA34/394.
34   *Ibid.*
35   T.M. Kettle to M. McLaughlin, 7 August 1916, Kettle Papers, UCDA, LA34/397.
36   L. Levenson, *With Wooden Sword: A Portrait of Francis Sheehy-Skeffington, Militant Pacifist* (Dublin, 1983), pp. 222–33.
37   J.J. Horgan, *Parnell to Pearse: Some Recollections and Reflections* (Dublin, 1948), p. 288.
38   S. Gwynn, *Observer*, 13 May 1923, Gwynn Newspaper Cuttings, NLI.
39   *Ibid.*, 16 February 1919.
40   *The Irish Centre Party*, c. 1919.
41   S. Gwynn, *Observer*, 29 June 1919, Gwynn Newspaper Cuttings, NLI.
42   *Ibid.*, 15 June, 1919.
43   C.C. O'Brien, *States of Ireland* (Frogmore, 1974), p. 102.
44   P. Heffernan, *An Irish Doctor's Memories* (Dublin, 1958), p. 43.
45   George O'Brien cited in J. Meenan, p. 99.
46   *Ibid.*, p. 96.
47   R. Pope-Hennessy, *The Irish Dominion League: A Method of Approach to Settlement* (London, 1920), p. 28.
48   *Ibid.*
49   H. Plunkett, *Home Rule and Conscription* (Dublin and London, 1918), p. 14.
50   S. Gwynn, *Observer*, 12 December 1920, Gwynn Newspaper Cuttings, NLI.
51   Monteagle to Jellet, 26 June 1920, Monteagle Papers, NLI, MS 13, 417.
52   *The Irish Dominion League Official Report, Setting Forth a Summary of Results Achieved Together with the Proceedings on Dissolution* (Dublin, 1921), p. 7.
53   H. Harrison, *The Irish Case Considered* (Dublin, 1920), p. 14.
54   H. Plunkett, *Dominion Self-Government* (Dublin, 1919), p. 4.
55   *IDL Official Report*, p. 13: These ideas were not of course new. Erskine Childers had outlined a similar form of Home Rule in his *The Framework of Home Rule* (Dublin and London, 1911).
56   Berkeley even identified support for Sinn Féin in the 'extraordinarily broad-minded' atmosphere of the Kildare Street Club; G.F.H. Berkeley, 'My Experience with the "Peace With Ireland Movement, 1920–21"', George F. H. Berkeley Papers, NLI, MS 10, 924.
57   *Ibid.*
58   *Ibid.*
59   *Ibid.*
60   J.S. Douglas to Monteagle, 26 June 1920, Monteagle Papers, NLI, MS 13, 417.
61   Berkeley, 'My Experience'.
62   *Ibid.*
63   *Irish Statesman*, vol. 1, no. 1, June 1919, p. 2.

64 Irish Centre Party.
65 Monteagle Papers, NLI, MS 13, 417.
66 H. Harrison, 1 June 1920, Monteagle Papers, NLI, MS 13, 417.
67 G.F.H. Berkeley, 'My Experience'.
68 T. West, *Horace Plunkett: Co-operation and Politics, An Irish Biography* (Gerrards Cross, 1986), p. 194.
69 Note attached to IDL, *Official Report*.
70 G.F.H. Berkeley, 'My Experience'.
71 *Irish Truth*, vol. 1, November 1924, p. 267.
72 S. Gwynn, *Observer*, 29 April 1924, Gwynn Newspaper Cuttings, NLI.
73 See election leaflets in the W.G. Fallon Papers, NLI, MS 22, 581.
74 J. Nugent to W.G. Fallon, 5 October, 1934, Fallon Papers, NLI, MS 22, 581.
75 H. Plunkett, *Dominion Self-Government*, p. 3.
76 H. Plunkett, *Home Rule and Conscription*, p. 15.
77 W. O'Brien, *The Downfall of Parliamentarianism: A Retrospect for the Accounting Day* (Dublin and London, 1918), p. 52.
78 S. Gwynn, *Irish Books and Irish People* (Dublin, 1919), p. 3.
79 *Irish Truth*, vol. 1, August 1924, p. 5.
80 W.G. Fallon to Secretary of the Office of Public Works, 6 February 1923, W.G. Fallon Papers, NLI, MS 22, 598.
81 Secretary of the Office of Public Works to Fallon, 4 March 1927, Fallon Papers, NLI, MS 22, 598.
82 *Ibid.*
83 *Ibid.*
84 L.J. Kettle to W.G. Fallon, 11 March 1927, Fallon Papers, NLI, MS 22, 598.

3
The Politics of Utopia: Party Organisation, Executive Autonomy and the New Administration[1]

John M. Regan

The construction of a new state with enduring democratic institutions, an army subservient to the civil power, an unarmed police force, and a meritocratic civil service free from political interference are seen quite rightly as the great achievement of the treatyite regime between 1922–32. The success in bringing about a viable Irish democracy is all the greater given the historical context of the new state's birth. For the previous decade Ireland had experienced revolution, accompanied by the militarisation of Irish society. During the course of 1922 a new elite, led until their deaths in August by Michael Collins and Arthur Griffith, was propelled from being the administrators of revolutionary Sinn Féin's proto-state to ministers responsible for a well-equipped functioning modern state with a full range of departments. The two regimes were of course very different. The revolutionary Sinn Féin proto-state was of necessity clandestine and other than the Departments of Local Government and Finance its ministries were amateurish or even fictional affairs. Ministers consequently treated their portfolios as part-time or sinecures. It was also a one-party regime supported, manned and protected by revolutionaries with goals which most assumed to be the same. The executive, legislature, administration, army and ancillary departments were elements of a party which had spawned a rebel counter-state to undermine the British civil administration in Ireland.

Within this arrangement personnel moved freely within an administrative market defined by talent, energy and patronage. Michael Collins, to take a famous example, could be a Dáil Deputy, a vice-president of the Sinn Féin party, Director of Intelligence in the army, head of the IRB, and Minister of Finance between 1918–21. Likewise James A. Burke, was a Dáil Deputy, Sinn Féin envoy to the United States, and civil servant in the Department of Local Government.[2] The separation of powers civil from military, and legislative from administrative mattered for little or nothing in a revolutionary political culture defined by expediency. The new situation the treatyite government took over from the British during the course of 1922 demanded a different approach. In the first instance the Free State inherited from the British the old civil service almost in its entirety, fully trained, professional, theoretically apolitical and by 1922, predominantly Irish-born.[3] In the circumstances of 1922, this was an enormous boon to the nascent Free State guaranteeing administrative personnel removed from the complex ideological strains and loyalties of a Sinn Féin movement at war with itself for supremacy in Southern Ireland. However, the process of taking over British institutions and their personnel also meant abandoning the Sinn Féin proto-state. The treatyite government's willing acceptance of the British administration rather than the expansion, if indeed such were possible, of the Sinn Féin administration meant that the revolutionaries who had come down on the side of the treaty were for the most part immediately locked out of the new administration. In the crisis of 1922, this transition did not emerge as a significant issue. Civil war and a rapidly expanding Free State army provided, in the short term at least, both distraction and an alternative source of state sponsored patronage.

This chapter examines the manner in which the treatyite elite dealt with its supporters' revolutionary aspirations – ideological and material – in the process of establishing what was to be an enduring post-revolutionary settlement. In particular this study focuses on the tensions which emerged between the treatyite government, its party and organisation, and the civil administration as the treatyites attempted to move from an all embracing one party regime to a modern parliamentary democracy in which the powers and functions of government, party and army were separated. The transition was complicated by a number of factors; chief among which being the attempt by the treatyite party organisation to create a dynamic party machine, fuelled by state sponsored patronage and a populist political agenda. In the process the treatyite elite in government found itself in a power struggle with its party over the independence of state institutions: military and civil. That this dispute was settled in favour of the new state's institutions was crucial to the democratic development of the Irish State, although such an outcome was by no means certain.

One distinguishing factor of post-independence politics in Ireland has been the organisational inequality of the two largest political parties. The treatyite parties, Cumann na nGaedheal (1922–33) and later Fine Gael (1933–), have apparently laboured under an organisational deficit, while their main opposition, Fianna Fáil, was able to create and, more importantly, sustain a large-scale and effective party-political machine. Within a year of its foundation in 1926 Fianna Fáil had established 1307 cumainn or local branches. Although there was a lapse in 1929 when numbers fell to 703, the organisation, after being fine-tuned by Sean Lemass, could mobilise 1404 cumainn in the decisive 1932 and 1933 general elections.[4] In contrast, the treatyite parties failed repeatedly during the crucial period 1926–33 to organise an extra-parliamentary parties which could match the Fianna Fáil machine. Moreover, the organisational disparity which begun in the 1920s was to remain a characteristic of Irish politics in Ireland into the 1960s and 1970s.[5] A number of theories have been put forward in order to explain the contrasting performance of the extra-parliamentary political organisations of the two largest parties in the state. Tom Garvin has argued that its origins lay in the anti-treatyites' abstentionist policy:

> Cumann na nGaedheal suffered from a serious lack of organisation and strength at local level, in part because the leadership, which had never witnessed competitive party politics of a normal kind, and was insensitive to the need for regular branch organisation in the late 1920s. Cumann na nGaedheal's dominance in the Dáil was somewhat artificial, as it depended on the self-imposed boycott of the Free State Dáil by the [anti-treatyite Sinn Féin] republicans and early Fianna Fáil.[6]

Also addressing the issue of organisational inequality Ronan Fanning has argued succinctly that it was borne of the treatyite elite's complacent political culture and its failure to realise the full potential of a party organisation:

> Cumann na nGaedheal were … at a disadvantage electorally because its leaders were already in government before they founded the party; *having* power they did not, unlike de Valera, conceive of their party as an instrument for *winning* power.[7] (Emphasis in original)

Jeffrey Prager while omitting to address in any detail the issue of party organisation in his study of state formation and democracy in the first decade of independence, has put forward what might be properly described as the *Masada* theory.[8] Prager argues the treatyite governments made an absolute priority of selflessly creating strong state institutions at the expense of any party political considerations eventually resulting in electoral suicide when Fianna Fáil swept to power in 1932. Of treatyite political culture Prager has written '... the decision by Cumann na nGaedheal leaders to sacrifice their own popularity for democratic order probably knows few parallels in other nations.'[9]

A lone attempt to examine the nature of treatyite intra-party politics has been made by Maryann Valiulis in a study of the conflict between the Cumann na nGaedheal party organisation and its governmental elite over the fidelity of the civil service and the ideology of the Cumann na nGaedheal party during the course of 1924–26.[10] Valiulis has correctly identified that in the course of the ministerial elite's defence of the new civil service it suppressed its own party organisation and directed the Cumann na nGaedheal party as a whole towards a more moderate and conservative brand of nationalism. Valiulis argues that the negation of revolutionary nationalism within Cumann na nGaedheal was the central reason for the party organisations' decline along with the parliamentary party after the mid-1920s:

> It was a Pyrrich victory ... Henceforth Cumann na nGaedheal [party organisation] would enjoy the same reputation as the government and would, therefore, be castigated as anti-nationalist, elitist, conservative faction in Irish politics. This reputation would lead the party to defeat in 1932 and keep it in the political wilderness of opposition until 1944 [sic]. Had it listened to its dissident wing, the party's electoral history might have been different. The traditional nationalist section of the party, schooled in the writing of Arthur Griffith and the ideas of Irish-Ireland and weaned on the lofty aspirations of the revolutionary struggle engendered, understood more clearly than the government the people's hopes for the first indigenous Irish government. The promise of independence was a concept that the Cosgrave government never seemed to understand.[11]

Though the reasons for this organisational asymmetry remain less than clear, all commentators are agreed that it placed the treatyite parties at a material disadvantage in early electoral contests and facilitated Fianna Fáil's spectacular advancement after 1926.[12]

Such an organisational deficit was also obvious to the treatyites early on. In the late summer of 1924 the Standing Committee of the

Cumann na nGaedheal extra-parliamentary party received a preliminary report on policy and organisation which it had commissioned:

> Recent events, both without and within the organisation, make nec-
> essary a clearer and more detailed statement of policy, which would
> have the double effect of preventing further secessions and of show-
> ing the country some immediate benefits from the Treaty. The
> maintenance of the Treaty position will for years depend on it being
> upheld by a united and well-organised popular movement; but such
> a movement will be impossible, and rightly so, unless those who
> stand for the Treaty can show that it provides solid advantages for
> the people, while showing no tendency towards weakening the
> National Tradition.
>
> It is clear that neither the Party nor the Organisation as a whole
> are homogenous in regard to policy except upon the question of the
> Treaty... It should be an immediate task to find and formulate such
> elements of policy as will serve to give a common basis to those
> who support the Treaty.[13]

The report reflected the remarkably inchoate and despondent nature of
treatyite politics two and half years after the Anglo–Irish treaty's acceptance by Dáil Éireann. The treatyite party which metamorphosed during 1922–23 into Cumann na nGaedheal was defined by external
factors rather than an internal ideological agenda: the anti-treaty military threat to the state during the Civil War, and the ongoing crisis of
stability which followed its cessation in May 1923. This afforded the
Executive Council, as the Cabinet was styled, considerable latitude
with regard to the implementation of its policies and the maintenance
of the autonomy it had preserved from the Cumann na nGaedheal
party and organisation during the course of the Civil War. The unaccountable cabinet culture of the revolutionary Dáils continued in the
new Free State regime.[14] During the protracted crisis of 1922, Griffith,
Collins and their successors in the provisional and national governments did not consult the treatyite deputies regarding any major decisions during the summer of 1922. At a meeting of Cumann na
nGaedheal deputies, on the second day of the third Dáil 10 September
1922, Deputy Liam de Róiste recorded in his journal:

> ... Dick Mulcahy [Commander-in-Chief and Minister of Defence] in
> speaking of Party Whips' duties, inadvertently spoke of 'Shepherding
> the sheep'. [Walter] Cole [T.D.] laughingly commented on this – 'We

are the sheep I suppose.' and self remarked 'Take care! there may be some rams in the flock!'[15]

There was more truth than humour in Mulcahy's remark, and the same was ultimately true of Cole's interjection. During the protracted crisis of 1919–23 revolutionary government had enjoyed the luxury of compliant and subservient parliamentary parties, and for that matter party organisations. Such a relationship was all the more crucial in the context of the Civil War, but it was underpinned among the treatyite elite by a profound distrust of organisational politics after the experience of Sinn Féin bifurcation's during 1922. The Extraordinary Árd Fhéis called in February 1922 to decide on revolutionary Sinn Féin's attitude towards the treaty and reconvened three months later in May had been packed by the anti-treatyites. Using intimidation and even physical violence, the cumainn had been radicalised between December 1921 and February 1922 by the IRA which materially effected the anti-treaty majority within the 3000 delegates at the February meeting of the Extraordinary Árd Fhéis.[16]

During the drafting of the new treatyite party constitution in September–December 1922, Ernest Blythe, Minister of Local Government in Cosgrave's National Government formed in September, intervened on behalf of the ministerial elite. Blythe ensured the adoption of his proposal that only constituency executives of the organisation would return delegates to the annual conventions of the new party: and then only in numbers equal to the number of seats in the constituency and not as was the practice before to nominate one delegate per cumann.[17] This new arrangement broke with the Sinn Féin tradition, and of the United Irish League before it, of sending delegates from each cumainn or branch. It also significantly devalued the political importance of the cumann as the local unit of the organisation while at the same time making the annual convention a smaller and more manageable affair from the elite's point of view with a maximum of 153 delegates, equivalent to the numbers of deputies in the Dáil, eligible to attend. Blythe's early intervention was decisive in both ensuring that the party organisation could not exert the same influence in the new regime as it had in the old one, and in also defining the relationship of the elite to the party.

In the period between the signing of the treaty and the outbreak of the Civil War, the treatyite governments' ministers evolved into a separate political entity away from the rest of the political party within the emergent regime. Nowhere was this isolation, enormous responsibility and attendant paranoia better expressed than in Kevin O'Higgins' description of his fellow ministers as '... simply eight young men in the City Hall standing amidst the ruins of one administration, with the foundations of another not yet laid, and with wild men screaming through the keyholes.'[18] Dedicating themselves to the work of constructing a new state, the treatyite elite withdrew with senior civil servants to centres of administration in City Hall, Dublin Castle and government buildings in Merrion Street which with the onset of war took on the appearance of ministerial bunkers. The dominant rationale of this closeted elite was the centralisation of power in a democratically elected parliament and ultimately in that institution's executive. In achieving this the treatyite governments (the provisional and Dáil governments existed in parallel from January 1922 but acted in effect as one institution after May 1922) went to war against the anti-treaty IRA after the 'pact' general election in June 1922 had given it a somewhat qualified electoral mandate.[19] The treatyite governments, however, also faced significant threats to their stability from inside the new regime.

Uncertain loyalties, the anti-treaty policy of infiltrating pro-treaty institutions and dissatisfaction with conditions led to several mutinies in the army and police force between 1922–24.[20] The treatyite parliamentary party and extra-parliamentary organisation possessed much of the diversity of ideology and mixed temperament of the revolutionary party from which it had evolved.[21] Its composition of stepping-stone republicans, Griffithite monarchists, free traders and protectionists, not to mention ideological agnostics and the disillusioned meant that there was considerable potential for schism. Internal dissent within the agencies of the new state leading to mutiny or revolt had the potential to do as much damage to the new regime as those who lined up in arms against it: O'Higgins' screamers were to be found on both sides of the door. The ministerial elite were determined in such circumstances that they would, in the interests of governmental stability during the crisis of 1922–23, resist policy initiatives coming from supporters of the regime still espousing revolutionary and in some quarters republican rhetoric. This could prove to be divisive and destabilising to the fragile coalition Collins and Griffith had cobbled together during the treaty debates. Towards the end of 1923, with the Civil War over and a majority electoral mandate secured by Cumann na nGaedheal at the August 1923 general election, executive autonomy began to be challenged by elements within the parliamentary party and the Cumann na nGaedheal organisation's Standing Committee who demanded   advancement on what they interpreted as the revolutionary agenda.[22]

The Standing Committee, in effect the Dublin-based residents of the National Executive elected at the first Cumann na nGaedheal Convention in April 1923, met weekly and attempted to oversee the day-to-day running of the party's organisation. Under the stewardship of Seamus Hughes, its mercurial General Secretary, it hoped to steer the government towards a more populist agenda in a bid to reverse the fortunes of what appeared to all informed commentators as a moribund party organisation following a weak performance in the 1923 general election.[23] The electorate returned 63 Cumann na nGaedheal deputies with 39 per cent of the poll, against an outstanding electoral result for the abstentionist anti-treaty Sinn Féin party which secured 27.5 per cent and 44 seats within 12 weeks of their military defeat.

In a bid to improve on Cumann na nGaedheal's flagging performance, the Standing Committee through late 1923 and early 1924 called for a more aggressive national policy from the government. Hughes in particular wanted to create a dynamic party organisation which he saw as being the civilian arm of the government and committed to voluntary work on behalf of the state. To this end the Standing Committee submitted proposals for the establishment of a boy scout movement and drafted a catechismal code for civic responsibilities.[24] In July 1922, Seamus Hughes, on behalf of the Standing Committee, had sponsored a proposal to use the party organisation as a police auxiliary or what looked in the abstract like an Irish *fascisti* which Collins had the foresight to veto: albeit after some initial hesitation.[25] Members of the party organisation also hoped that a more populist and aggressive national policy would placate discordant supporters of the treaty. The Executive Council's refusal in March 1924, temporarily led by O'Higgins in Cosgrave's absence, to reinstate mutinous army officers provided a cause around which dissident sentiment in the Cumann na nGaedheal parliamentary party could rally. The officers had delivered an ultimatum to the government on 6 March demanding promotions and a more progressive and republican interpretation of the treaty. After the intervention of the Minister of Industry and Commerce, Joseph McGrath, the mutinous officers retracted their statements and publicly accepted the unqualified authority of the civil government. Though they were led to believe they would be reinstated in the army, the government, still under O'Higgins' direction, refused to restore their commissions. McGrath resigned and initially intended to retire from public life following what he saw as the Executive Council's reneging on assurances personally given to him. He was, however, prevailed upon to remain within the Dáil and consequently he resigned only his Cumann na nGaedheal party whip on 25 March, declaring his intent to set up his own party 'as an independent republican'. His departure from the party was soon followed by eight other Cumann na nGaedheal deputies ostensibly sympathetic to the mutinous officers but who also objected to the authoritarian and isolationist attitude of the elite.[26] The self-styled National Group led by McGrath articulated, throughout its short existence, grievances and prejudices which resonated below the public facade of Cumann na nGaedheal – the ministry's insularity and arrogance in matters of policy; the belief that the government had turned its back on the revolutionary aspirations, notably Griffith's protectionism and Collins progressive stepping-stone interpretation of the treaty; and the recurring accusation that the ministers relied on civil servants whose loyalties, if not pro-British, were controlled by – that old Griffithite chestnut – the Freemasons. Sean Milroy, a non-republican member of the National Group, articulated these sentiments publicly after his resignation from the Dáil in late 1924:

> Government in the Saorstat is in imminent danger of becoming government by a clique inspired and directed by the extant rump of officialdom of the old regime or government by a few young men who suffer from the delusion that they are gifted with political infallibility… The Government seems determined to muddle along ignoring public feeling, estranging public confidence, contemning national interests and pandering to the old Ascendancy Gang… we avow our opposition to government from Molesworth Street[27] as heartily and emphatically as our opposition to government from Whitehall.[28]

The Cumann na nGaedheal organisation and parliamentary party under the pressure of the March 1924 army crisis and the secession of the National Group deputies once again recoiled and regrouped behind their Government as they had done during 1922–23. At the local level, however, the March mutiny scarcely impacted on the party organisation at all. By 1924 the dominant political agenda of the revolution – republicanism, gaelicism, and the aspiration for national unity – had taken second place to more mundane material concerns. Of 27 resolutions sent by constituency committees to the 1924 annual conference, 25 were concerned with drainage; the provision of cheap railway transport; the provision by a government agency of business credit loans to entrepreneurs; the encouragement of Irish insurance companies; the extension of urban district boundaries; and the division of the county Galway constituency and the administration of the party.[29] One resolution was also submitted from the north-east Mayo executive calling for members of the clergy of all denominations who were supporters of the Cumann na nGaedheal to be made ex-officio members of cumainn but this was in due course turned down. The army mutiny and National Group secession, both of which had their roots in the interpretation of the treaty's ongoing relationship with revolutionary aspirations resulted in just two Dublin cumainn breaking away from Cumann na nGaedheal in March and April 1924. The politics of the revolution appeared to have evaporated from within the party at large.

The passive reaction of the Cumann na nGaedheal organisation to the division of the parliamentary party revealed either the existence of a profound loyalty to the government or the existence of a different political agenda in local cumainn which appears to have been largely unaffected by issues of the revolution's political settlement. By mid-January 1924, Cumann na nGaedheal had 274 cumainn in the Free State most of which had come into existence during the 1923 general election campaign and two in Northern Ireland. As the General Secretary's report to the General Executive Council recorded outside Dublin, the 'main stimulus' for joining was the 1923 Land Act introduced by the Minster of Agriculture, Patrick Hogan, which continued the land distribution begun by the British at the end of the nineteenth century as well as introducing measures to expedite the collection of debts which had accumulated during the troubled period of 1919–23.[30] The agrarianism which had been a contingent and, in its more radical mode, a troublesome part of revolutionary Sinn Féin's support in some western counties continued to be a motivating factor for joining Cumann na nGaedheal.[31] At the formation of the Clonguish cumann in county Longford a press release was issued:

> ... all members wishful to join are earnestly requested to attend as by the programme unlimited are the benefits to be obtained by a strong organisation of Cumann na nGaedheal, one of which, the repopulation of the untenanted lands, should attract the attention of the men of Clonguish as they have in their midst that long fought-for agitation known as the Douglas Ranches yet unpopulated [sic].[32]

The cumann was cast as the intermediary between the Land Commission and a land hungry local tenantry. P.J. Ryan, Cumann na nGaedheal organiser for Leinster, informed a Longford meeting that as ranches were being broken up

> ...it was for the people to put themselves under the guidance of an organisation which was in a position to help them. There was also the matter of obtaining payments in connection with subscribers to the old Dáil Eireann loan; and the organisation were interesting themselves in seeing that subscribers who belonged to the organisation would be paid. A great deal was also being done in the matter of obtaining Old Age Pensions, and furthermore the organisation was helping to see that people to whom accounts were due either by the old IRA or the National Army were paid.[33]

Ryan's attempt to entice new members into the Cumann na nGaedheal organisation with the promise of preferment and privilege was not the work of an isolated party worker but part of a policy initiated by Seamus Hughes.[34] Cumann na nGaedheal in Government jettisoned much of revolutionary Sinn Féin's policy and its attendant rhetorical republicanism after the August 1923 general election. In the process it had failed to replace them with either an alternative ideological agenda or a forward-looking policy which could enlist enthusiastic support for the party beyond the promise of land distribution through the laboriously slow agency of the Land Commission. Hughes' expansion scheme demanded that the consolidation of the progress he had made on the further promise of patronage would depend on the party organisation's ability to deliver preferment and patronage. Hughes was not only writing cheques the party organisation could not pay but was doing so in a currency the government ministers were determined not to recognise.

Hughes' initiative met with some early success, and the organisation grew during early 1924 from 247 branches at the beginning of January, to 328 by the end of February. Organisational strength in real terms as opposed to the number of branches is, however, difficult to determine with any degree of accuracy. Branches varied in size from ten to over a hundred members, and they surfaced and submerged with remarkable frequency: most notably influenced by general and by-election campaigns.

If the number of first preference votes given to Cumann na nGaedheal candidates in the 1923 general election is divided by the number of branches in each constituency, it is possible to arrive at a cumann:voter ratio indicating, roughly, the level of organisational support among Cumann na nGaedheal supporters in the 1923 general election. During the general election campaign Kildare, Wicklow, South Mayo, Laois/Offaly, Cavan, Galway, and Sligo/Leitrim, all have a ratio of less than 1100 first preference votes per cumann in each constituency. Cumann na nGaedheal's best electoral performances in the 1923 general election tended to be in cities, with 48.4 per cent in North Dublin, 52 per cent in South Dublin and 43.3 per cent in Cork Borough, but these constituencies were amongst the worst organised coming nineteenth, twenty-first and twenty-second in the order of cumainn to votes ratios. Cumann na nGaedheal's popularity at the polls did not translate into a similar distribution of organisational strength. Louth which returned two Cumann na nGaedheal deputies to the three seats in the constituency with 46.4 per cent of the vote could muster only one branch. Limerick returned three deputies with 41.5 per cent of the vote whilst having just ten branches. Kildare, where Cumann na nGaedheal achieved just 27 per cent of the first preference votes in 1923, had the highest branch:voter ratio in the country with one branch for every 210 first preferences. Branch numbers and a structured party organisation evidently did not translate into votes on polling day for Cumann na nGaedheal in 1923.

The overwhelming wish within Cumann na nGaedheal's Standing Committee after March 1924 was to come to an understanding with the National Group and reunite the treatyite party. Ultimately the loss of nine pre-treaty Sinn Féiners from the Cumann na nGaedheal party further weakened the aggressive nationalist, Irish-Ireland, protectionist and republican lobbies within the parliamentary party. For those who shared these aspirations within the party and organisation, rapprochement leading to reunification with the dissidents would, it was hoped, also act to counterbalance the government's autonomy and its reluctance, as they defined it, to pursue the policies of Griffith and Collins. With a view to affecting reunion the National Group was invited to a meeting with the Cumann na nGaedheal organisation's governing body the Árd Comhairle or General Executive Council on 13 May, but after an ill-tempered disagreement over the agenda the National Group's representative, Sean Milroy, walked out. The meeting proceeded without him and a motion demanding that deputies and the organisation be given advanced warning by ministers of 'unpopular measures' was discussed.[35] During the course of the debate objections arose to, what was claimed to be, the disproportionate influence of senior civil servants. The elite's response was typically one of proposed accommodation followed by inaction. Cosgrave, taking his customary conciliatory line, agreed that

> ... it would be well if the actual work done by the Government were known in detail by the members of the Organisation. Disagreements in a political party representative of all sections were inevitable and they ought to be faced and thrashed out. A Government, like a family, will have its differences but the Government was not the slave of the Civil Servants. He had never known a case where Civil Servants dominated policy.[36]

Kevin O'Higgins, Vice-President and Minister of Home Affairs, argued 'nothing could be more disastrous than the virtual isolation of the Government. A responsible Government meant one that had to answer to the people'. The distinction between people and party, synonymous in the rhetoric of revolutionary Sinn Féin, was not lost on O'Higgins. Frustrated by platitudes the party organisation's Standing Committee decided at the end of May to take matters into their own hands and appointed a sub-committee to 'draw up a national and economic policy for adoption by the Organisation' consisting of: Senator Jenny Wise Power, an Irish-Irelander and treatyite-republican; George Nesbitt, one of Cosgrave's nominees to the senate, veteran Sinn Féiner and Dublin businessman; Denis McCullough, the former President of the Supreme Council of the I.R.B. and piano tuner; George Lyons, a close associate and disciple of Griffith; and Michael Tierney, then a young academic at University College Dublin.[37]

On 24 June, Hughes wrote to McGrath inviting him to another meeting with the Standing Committee.[38] McGrath replied in the negative stating that the National Group believed that no useful purpose would be served by any proposed conference with an ineffectual Standing Committee:

> ... We would like to point out and to emphasise that our grounds of disagreement are based on dissent from the policy of the Executive Government and scarcely concern the Standing Committee of Cumann na nGaedheal, the function of the latter body being apparently merely to acquiesce in whatever decision in regard to policy the Executive arrives at of its own volition. Your Standing Committee appears to have neither inclination nor power to influence such executive decisions.

... All this has been very regrettable and has to a very considerable degree produced the cleavage and the differences, the causes of which you now invite us to discuss, as well as shaking the confidence of the Organisation generally and the people at large in the intention of the present Executive Government to pursue a policy in harmony with the ideas which we all understood the late President Griffith and the late General Collins to stand for.

In view of the foregoing reasons we can see no satisfactory result likely to be arrived at by a conference with your Standing Committee on matters of Executive Policy, and therefore, we must decline to accept your invitation.[39]

Hughes, replying on behalf of the Standing Committee, naturally took umbrage at the slight McGrath delivered to his committee but his rebuttal failed to refute McGrath's criticisms beyond claiming, rather lamely, that they were false.[40] That the party organisation, and indeed the party inside the Dáil, was bereft of political clout in matters of policy was wholly true. That Cumann na nGaedheal had abandoned the policy of Griffith and Collins was altogether a more contentious proposition and depended on one's interpretation of both men's political and ideological legacies. Griffith's doctrinaire protectionism, while still having the sympathy of a large section of the parliamentary party and the majority of the organisation, had been overturned by the elite at the April 1923 Convention.[41] Griffithite protectionism was replaced with a milk-and-water policy of selected and limited tariffs in Blythe's April 1924 budget, and after 1926 by the Tariff Commission which was dominated by the Department of Finance appointees and therefore prejudiced towards free trade in its lengthy deliberations.[42] Collins' interpretation of the treaty was complex if not utterly confusing and therefore offered no guidelines. In public he had advocated constitutional advancement, in private he was believed by some of his intimates, or he had allowed them to believe, that his stepping stones would lead to a republic by whatever route was most propitious.[43]

McGrath's stinging rebuke of the Standing Committee's impotency served only to embolden their efforts to have the party organisation's wishes heard in cabinet and translated into policy. Despite the ministers' posturing at the General Executive Council meeting of 13 May 1924, the government continued to ignore petitions from its party organisation. The revision and reduction of payments to old age pensioners in September 1924, once again aggravated government/organisation and government/party relations. Under the provisions of the Old Age

Pensions Act 1924, a uniform reduction of one shilling had been with-
held from the old age pension and a further revision of individual
recipient's means was to be completed by 5 September 1924, with
those deemed to have independent wealth adequate for their upkeep
to have their pension further reduced or withdrawn completely.
Hughes wrote a letter of protest to Blythe on 17 September, on behalf
of the Standing Committee:

> As matters stand our members everywhere regard the present revi-
> sion of payments as most inopportune, having regard to the prevail-
> ing poverty, the bad season and the coming by elections. I am to
> add that the Coiste Gnotha [Standing Committee] are at a loss to
> know whether, in arriving at such administrative decisions, the min-
> isters responsible take any account of the political effect produced,
> and of the possible consequences on the stability of the State of con-
> tinuous public displeasure.
>
> Without at least an adequate explanation and some forecast
> of measures designed to relieve economic depression, the Coiste
> Gnotha will find it a difficult problem to make good on behalf of
> the Government in the 5 by-elections now pending.[44]

In essence it was a conflict between the needs of the nascent administration trying to reduce expenditure and requirements of party politics
and in such matters the Executive Council seemed determined to plot
an administrative course without reference to electoral or political considerations. When Blythe eventually made his reply he simply invoked
the doctrine of the British treasury which demanded budgets must balance.[45] However, the attempted intrusion of the party into the realm of
policy clearly irked Blythe greatly, and in the original draft of his reply
to Hughes he vented his vitriol:

> ... I think the state of mind which your letter indicates reflects the
> state of mind which is responsible for a good deal of harm in this
> country. For example, as in the case of the Old Age Pensions, the
> Government after very careful consideration decides on certain
> measures as the best and most practical to deal with a difficult situa-
> tion: the majority of the members of the Oireachtas having heard
> the arguments and having agreed with them, vote for the measure
> and it becomes the law of the land. It is then surely the duty of a
> political organisation, by explaining to the people the reasons
> which have made this measure necessary, to endeavour to convince

them of the need for it and to reconcile them to the acceptance of it. Instead of this I find that Cumann na nGaedheal and its Branches, so far from trying to realise the position and appreciating the needs of the case, has joined in the ignorant and irresponsible chorus of criticism.[46]

Blythe's letter, betrayed a 'put up or shut up' attitude toward the party organisation in relation to policy which his fellow ministers shared but for obvious reasons chose not to vocalise. Blythe viewed the party as a propaganda machine at the disposal of the Executive Council in much the same way as the parliamentary party was viewed by the government simply as lobby fodder. The party organisation was at Hughes' invitation being used as a means for redressing the grievances supporters were encountering as they interacted with the new state's reforming bureaucracy. Blythe and his department were however unmoveable and refused to offer an accommodation or even a moratorium despite facing five by-elections. The continuation and maintenance of peace, stability, good government and a balanced budget were deemed by the Government as sufficient to retain majority electoral support.

At a meeting of the Standing Committee on 10 October chaired by Eoin MacNeill, President of the Cumann na nGaedheal party, and attended by Cosgrave, O'Higgins, FitzGerald, Blythe and the Minister of Industry and Commerce, Patrick McGilligan, the Standing Committee presented its *Statement of Views* policy paper to the Executive Council. The statement represented an assertion of aggressive nationalism which was proprietorial, anglophobic, belligerent and sectarian:[47]

…administrative life of the country remained almost as before, by reason of the dominant position in public and social affairs which the possession of political mastery had, in the course of centuries, given to an alien ascendancy…those who created the present regime and those who resisted it as long as they could, our interest as well as our raison d'être compel us to side with the popular claims. The brief of Cumann na nGaedheal is for the common people of Ireland, and what the common people want under the Free State is to abolish ascendancy, to undo the Conquest and resume the course of their national life as masters in their own land.

The power of the Organisation to hold the people's loyalty and, by gaining their support for its nominees, to secure the stability of the State, depends upon its efficiency, through the Government of its election, in giving reasonable satisfaction to the needs and hopes of its supporters. The question imposes itself whether it has been able to give them such satisfaction. The answer is undoubtedly – no. the [sic] Organisation's influence on Government policy and its power to effect patronage has been negligible, if not, nil. In parts of the country it is openly recognised that to be connected with Cumann na nGaedheal is in most cases a handicap and in many cases a complete bar to appointments, preferments or even a fair deal in Land or Compensations. It is unnecessary to demonstrate that the Organisation does not correspond in numbers, enthusiasm or finance to what might be expected of the political Organisation behind the first native Government for centuries. It has been described as moribund and, as an election machine, it is certainly weak.[48]

Drawing on memoranda Hughes had solicited from the organisation in the country, the document went on to outline the reasons for discontent and apathy in Cumann na nGaedheal. Despite unheeded calls for relief of unemployment and the alleviation of hardship caused by the extremely wet season, the government's economic policy was generally deemed to be sound with large revenues and low expenditure. The slow distribution of land and collection of debts under the 1923 Land Act was a major source of grievance: 'The only tangible result of the Land Act [1923] in most places was that the legal, military, and police organisation of the new regime was employed, in the collection of arrears of rent and rates, in a more abrupt and vigorous fashion than before experienced.'[49] It was felt that the administration of the Land Commission had not changed under the new regime and a deputation was to be sent to the Minister of Agriculture to complain. It was also asserted that members of the Cumann na nGaedheal party had been discriminated against in their claims despite having their papers in order. One western Deputy wrote 'It is impossible to make the people believe that there is not some "old gang" running the Land Commission and in league with the old gang left in the country.'[50] Appointments remained the 'sorest question of all'. Those who had fought for independence had 'not done well out of victory' while the

> pro-British ascendancy who lost the fight have done disproportionately well and got a new lease of life from the Free State. The civil servants are the Government and there is a distinct uneasiness throughout the whole country because of the fear that vital Irish interests are in the hands of those men whose allegiance does not lie in Ireland.[51]

The document suggested that the organisation should be allowed to develop, in consultation with ministers, 'a comprehensive policy of national advancement calculated to meet the needs and aspirations of the country'. Not having governmental responsibilities, it was argued, the organisation could develop policies which would not be realised immediately, but subsequent governments could draw on as a policy bank. Concluding, the statement issued a threat masquerading as a caveat to the government '... As correspondence just received by registered post from North Mayo will show, the failure to meet these criticisms satisfactorily may involve the dissolution of the Organisation, which would be followed by a policy of despair.'

Even the desiccated minutes of the meeting that followed the presentation of *Statement of Views* convey the febrile mood of the Standing Committee. Criticism was aimed at officials, especially in finance, who were categorised as alien, and anti-Irish. Johnny Collins, a brother of Michael Collins, claimed that officials who were English, were dictating policy and were actively retarding administration. Michael Tierney in a spirited speech claimed 'Retrenchment and collection of debt at the point of the bayonet were the features by which the Government was best known.' In responding to such sentiments, Cosgrave, Blythe and O'Higgins recited in harmony the treasury incantation of fiscal equilibrium against which they claimed to be powerless to act. The point was made during the exchanges that followed that what the Standing Committee wanted was only the removal of one or two key men. Attempting to temporise on the issue, O'Higgins disingenuously claimed that it would be pleasing to get rid of unpopular officials

> ... and dismiss them because they had not an Irish outlook but article 10 of the Treaty is the barrier, and with one eye on the Minister for Finance and another on Newspaper criticism of the Pension List, we must consider the amount necessary to pay off, for instance, the court staffs.[52]

Johnny Collins retorted that the 'country would pay'.

Following the joint meeting of the Executive Council and the Standing Committee on 10 October, it was agreed the policy sub-committee should meet with Hogan, Blythe and McGilligan to discuss proposals on policy embodied in the financial report.[53] The meeting with the three ministers took place on 20 October and was attended by Jenny Wise Power, Denis McCullough, Michael Tierney of the policy sub-committee in addition to Seamus Dolan, Cosgrave's parliamentary secretary and Frank Crummey of the Standing Committee. The main thrust of the policy proposal was the overturning of the existing administration of the Department of Finance which was founded on British treasury practices, and further to demand the elimination of Finance's dominance over other departments within the administration. It also called for the recently established Civil Service Commission – consisting of senior civil servants and responsible for recruitment to the new administration – to be replaced by one independent of the Finance Department and directly responsible to the Executive Council and the Dáil which would '... have charge of the entire recruitment, control and Organisation of the Civil Service.' The fiscal officer of the Department of Finance would be put on a similar footing to the permanent secretaries of other departments 'who will not be bounded by British traditions, but [be] an Irishman of loyal associations, in whom the country can have confidence.' An advisory board was to be established independent of departmental officials who would advise the Minister on fiscal policy, and a committee of experts was to be established to reconsider the present system of national accountancy which it deemed to be out of date. It was a naked attack on the influence of the Finance Department and more especially on the Ministers and Secretaries Act and the Civil Service Commission, both enacted earlier in 1924, both inspired by senior civil servants, and both underpinning the supremacy of the Finance department in the civil service hierarchy.[54] The establishment of the Civil Service Commission was of enormous long-term importance, ensuring that recruitment to the Free State's bureaucracy would be on merit not patronage. Cumann na nGaedheal's Standing Committee craved for a spoils system, which it might influence through the Dáil or by applying pressure on the Government directly, to enhance its own prestige and power and to try and ensure that new recruits to the civil service would be coloured with an acceptably aggressive brand of nationalism. The elite found themselves caught in a tug-of-war between their party and the civil service.

The deliberations of the policy sub-committee and the ministers came to naught. On 3 November the General Executive Council released a statement on policy which simply reiterated the existing constitution of the party and avoided any specific reference to the reorganisation of the Department of Finance.[55] The abandonment of the Standing Committee offensive followed the resignation of McGrath from the Dáil on 29 October, and eight National Group deputies two days later. The National Group's action pushed Cumann na nGaedheal and the new state into an electoral crisis. With the nine National Group resignations, the total number of outstanding by-elections came to 14. All were former Cumann na nGaedheal seats and all were vacant at a time of considerable hostility toward the government. Furthermore the organisation was confronted at local level with the possibility of divisions in the constituency organisations where National Group deputies commanded personal allegiance. Cosgrave called the first five by-elections in November, a 'mini-general election' and adjourned the Dáil on 7 November until the 18th of the month to facilitate electioneering. In both Cork elections and Donegal, Cumann na nGaedheal defended its seats successfully. In North Mayo the seat was lost following a belated and half-hearted contest waged on behalf of Michael Tierney who entered the contest just two weeks before polling. However, it was the Dublin South constituency which produced the most surprising result with Seamus Hughes losing what had been the safest Cumann na nGaedheal seat in the country to Sean Lemass.

The November by-elections augured badly for Cumann na nGaedheal. The next nine by-elections would be crucial not only to the stability of the Government, but also to the legitimacy of the new state. Cumann na nGaedheal won 63 seats at the 1923 general election and held on to them at all subsequent by-elections to November 1924. The secession of the National Group reduced Cumann na nGaedheal to 54 seats in the Dáil. However, the party was augmented by two Cork deputies, taking the Cumann na nGaedheal whip in June 1924 – Richard Beamish of the brewing family and Andrew O'Shaughnessessy, both of whom had stood as members of the Cork Progressive Association in August 1923.[56] The November by-election results reduced Cumann na nGaedheal once again to 54 seats and brought Sinn Féin from 44 to 46 seats. The electoral logic of the situation equated to a potential constitutional crisis. If Cumann na nGaedheal lost all nine seats to the anti-treatyites, as seemed quite possible, then Sinn Féin would hold more seats in abstention than the Government of the Free State held inside the Dáil.

The ministry, taking its lead from O'Higgins, used the by-election debacle in South Dublin as a means of undermining Hughes, the Standing Committee and the party organisation as a whole. A new Executive Organising Committee was formed but it was a thinly disguised version of the government consisting of four cabinet ministers, O'Higgins, Blythe, Eoin MacNeill and Patrick McGilligan, along with three extern ministers Fionan Lynch, Patrick Hogan, and J.J. Walsh.[57] Walsh was placed in charge of the Executive Organising Committee, and took over responsibility for the by-election campaigns for the nine seats vacated by the National Group. Walsh was an organiser *par excellence* who brought to bear a brand of efficiency learned in the British civil service and any of the half dozen or so revolutionary and cultural societies he had participated in during the previous 25 years. One of the first decisions of Walsh's committee was the demotion of Hughes and his replacement by Liam Burke, a schoolmaster at Castleknock College, as Chief Organiser on a higher salary in December 1924.

Walsh, again at O'Higgins' suggestion, designated various appointees of his committee to canvass and collect money from vocational groupings including businessmen, stockbrokers, medics and lawyers.[58] By establishing a better working relationship with the business community and professions it was hoped that individuals who had remained aloof from revolutionary Sinn Féin and Cumann na nGaedheal could be turned into active as opposed to passive supporters of the new regime. The loss of the South Dublin by-election was in part blamed on the apathy and disinterest of the business and professional community in the capital's most wealthy wards. Walsh attributed this to the idea that many of these groups saw election contests as a continuation of revolutionary Sinn Féin's private Civil War.[59] However, O'Higgins' real motive lay in moving the party away from revolutionary nationalism with its ardent militarist republican and anglophobic overtones. Consequently, the embracing of the business and professional elites served his dual purpose of reforming Cumann na nGaedheal into an even more conservative nationalist party and at the same time marginalising unreconstructed revolutionaries within it. Beyond this the securing of finance from private donors and business interests further reduced the party's dependency on its organisation for funding, and therefore removed another medium of influence from its grasp thereby reinforcing the elite's autonomy.

Walsh turned around the Cumann na nGaedheal's organisation and its finances. He inherited a staggering deficit of £11 612 from the Standing Committee most of which was run up in the 1923 general election as a result of poor accounting, the election agent's profligacy, petty fraud and incompetence at headquarters. By targeting business and professional elites the new committee raised £5000 in the course of the by-election campaign.[60] Walsh demanded and received weekly reports and receipts from a small army of election workers and 20 full-time organisers in the seven constituencies.[61] Cumainn numbers also increased dramatically from 275 to 430 during the course of the four-month campaign.[62] Walsh was also temporarily able to access patronage previously unavailable to Hughes and the organisation. He ensured that relief schemes appeared in contested constituencies with the desirable effect of winning over support to Cumann na nGaedheal.[63] The effect on the electorate and party organisation of such schemes was described in a letter from M.F. Connolly, Secretary of the Attymas Cumann na nGaedheal cumann in North Mayo, immediately after the by-elections:

> Two of our best townlands, Graffy and Cartron vote in Bofield and they have been responsible for the increase in Free State votes cast there – 47 in Nov [1924] to 101 now. Further, we have now a membership of 186 (heads of households) in our Cumann which in 1924 we had only 65, in spite of all our efforts to increase that membership and in spite of the fact that the majority of the people of the parish was opposed to the Bolshies [Sinn Féin and the I.R.A.]. The relief works were responsible for the change. In townlands where I could get no one to assist before, I could muster a band of willing workers and I have succeeded in getting the young fellows on our side. Nearly 200 of them marched in procession here to celebrate Prof. Tierney's victory. Mr Tierney himself witnessed a little of that enthusiasm here on election day.[64]

Whatever influence Walsh was able to exert over his fellow extern minister James A. Burke, the Minister of Local Government and Health, in facilitating the distribution of relief works in contested constituencies, he had less success within the Executive Council itself. Walsh attempted to persuade Blythe to call a halt to collecting income tax arrears during the campaign because it was a 'grievance of big business people – drapers etc... [and]... this position is likely to cost us thousands of votes.'[65] In response Blythe bluntly stated that he '... did not think there is ground for general complaint.' Likewise, O'Higgins was not prepared to pander to the vintner's protestations about the composition of the committee on Intoxicating Liqueur. O'Higgins seems to have come under pressure to alter his stance and the minutes of the Executive Organising Committee record 'After considerable discussion Mr O'Higgins said that it was not possible to change the personnel of the committee...'[66]

Despite these setbacks, Walsh's strategy ensured that seven of the nine seats remained in Cumann na nGaedheal hands and that the government retained its overall majority of the elected representatives within the state. The tactics Walsh employed and the initiative to place him in charge of the Executive Organising Committee had their origins in the Executive Council but the principle author, proponent and benefactor of this strategy was O'Higgins not Walsh.[67] In placing Walsh, the loudest advocate of protectionism and Irish-Ireland principles, at the head of the Executive Organising Committee, O'Higgins was able to usurp Hughes and the Standing Committee and the party organisation without exposing himself as being the enemy within the elite of the revolutionary old-guard.

Walsh did, however, prove that Cumann na nGaedheal could mount a successful campaign, utilising cumainn and paid organisers, while at the same time aggressively targeting professional and business interests as sources of support for the party. His management of the campaign and the development of formal organisational links with business and professional elites anticipated Fianna Fáil's much more successful enterprises with *Comh-Comhairle Átha Claith* later known as *Taca*.[68] Under Walsh's direction the Cumann na nGaedheal party managed to maintain 440 cumainn into mid-1926: though Walsh falsely claimed publicly that twice this number existed.[69] But despite these efforts and results, the party organisation failed to either sustain growth or realise the economic and electoral promise the March 1925 by-election campaign had seemed to augur. Walsh, like Hughes, failed to access patronage on a scale which could sustain growth and maintain support. He (not unlike Hughes) saw the party and his appointment as President of it in 1925 as a vehicle for personal aggrandisement. His friend, Liam de Róiste, noted of Walsh on a visit to Cork in January 1925 soon after his new appointment to the Executive Organising Committee:

> As to JJ: he is jubilant these times; is 'boss of the situation', according to himself, since he became chief of the organising executive of Cumann na nGaedheal. 'Tis a turn about' said he, 'from where I was last year, All the boyos (meaning thereby the Executive Council) are tamed now.'[70]

The hyperbole of a visit to his native Cork did not reflect accurately the state of politics in Dublin. With the crisis over the party quickly became less important in the concerns of government. In 1926 Hughes moved from the party to the State's first radio station 2RN where he became chief announcer. By the end of the same year the Standing Committee had met only once prompting Richard Mulcahy to argue that the party organisation was in terminal decline.[71] Walsh wanted to use the party as a means of exerting pressure on the government to implement a more aggressive tariff policy. To this end he ensured that representation at the annual Árd Fhéis reverted to the Sinn Féin practice of nominating two representatives from each cumann in March 1925: providing for a maximum attendance of 880 delegates.[72] Conventions became more representative of the grassroots treatyites, ensuring both a much more sympathetic hearing for a protectionist policy and also a platform from which to apply pressure on the Executive Council.

The 1926 convention resulted in a very public assault by Walsh on free trade and most especially on his fellow extern the Minister of Agriculture, Patrick Hogan.[73] At a meeting of the National Executive elected by the 1926 convention on 22 February 1927, Walsh placed a motion demanding that the government adopt a more rigorous tariff system. At Walsh's invitation, Liam de Róiste attended and spoke in favour of his motion, but during the course of his delivery de Róiste was interrupted and attacked by both Hogan and Blythe. Blythe argued that de Róiste was appealing to sentiment and, furthermore, that the support of the National Executive for the motion would be tantamount to a vote of no confidence in the government. De Róiste believed that the majority of those present would at the very least back tariffs on agricultural produce and, evidently fearing defeat, the ministers sent for Cosgrave 'to save the situation'. Having made his point, Walsh withdrew his motion to the consternation of de Róiste who could not understand why Walsh would not put the issue to a vote.[74] Walsh resigned in September 1927 ostensibly over the issue of protection.[75] Mulcahy in the early 1960s recalled of Walsh:

> … at that particular time he was very strongly entrenched in his interests with people like the Central Branch and he had a fine group of business people around him and J.J. [Walsh] was very strong with them and he had as much capacity to be a success as Lemass had in handling these people.[76]

Walsh did claim during the course of 1926 to have the financial backing of business interests to establish a breakaway protectionist party: though he failed to deliver on the promise.[77] However, Mulcahy was wrong in identifying the Central Branch of the party as the locus of such a support base. The Central Branch had first been established in 1923 as a debating society where treaty supporters could gather to hear learned papers and discuss politics. It had lapsed during 1924, and was only re-established at the end of 1926, once again as a 'deliberative body' but without the involvement of Walsh.[78] By 1931 it had a membership of over 200 businessmen, professionals and senior politicians.[79] However, its relationship to the party was designed to prevent it placing pressure on the elite. It existed independent of the old party structure which managed to limp on in the late 1920s – National Executive, Standing Committee and the annual Árd Fhéis – and therefore could not apply institutional pressure on the elite within the party through the annual convention. However, it did serve to bridge the gap between the new political order and business and professional elites within Irish society without threatening, as the party organisation had done during 1924, executive autonomy. In this sense the Central Branch reflected O'Higgins' desire for a new post-independence nationalist party which would embrace the elites within Irish society whatever their former political pallor – unionist, parliamentary nationalist, or hitherto bystander – while avoiding some of the risks of having another institutionalised lobby within the party. The treatyite focus on local and national elites, through the Central Branch and more informally through contacts between local deputies and ministers, developed in part because of the need to circumvent the party organisation which could threaten a highly autonomous executive which was itself a hangover from the revolutionary period.

It should be mentioned here, briefly, that the treatyites did enjoy a second wave of organisational expansion during the first year of Fine Gael/United Ireland's existence in 1933–34. Fine Gael organised 448 affiliated branches, theoretically independent of the Blueshirt wing of the party which had a membership in April 1934, according to the organisation's own statistics, of 40–48 000.[80] As in 1924, in 1934 the party, or at least the Blueshirt wing of the organisation, attempted to dictate policy to the leadership, by proposing at the August 1934 Convention that a rent and rates strike should be initiated in protest against the Fianna Fáil government's decision to collect annuities during the economic war with Britain. The controversy which followed led to the resignation of General Eoin O'Duffy, President of Fine Gael, and a series of splits in the Blueshirt movement over the next two years which accelerated its decline along with the Fine Gael organisation. By March 1935 the number of affiliated Fine Gael branches had fallen to 108.[81] Once again, as in 1924, in 1936 the Fine Gael elite this time headed by Dr T.F. O'Higgins, Kevin's brother, damped down the dynamic elements of its party organisation.[82]

The most aggressive attempt to exert pressure on the elite, in the autumn of 1924, was to be the last. The influence and importance of the members of the organisation's Standing Committee was temporarily enhanced between March and November 1924 because they were attempting to broker the reunification of Cumann na nGaedheal and in the process stave off both an electoral and constitutional crisis. The issue of treatyite unity, that is to say the reintegration of the National Group and mutinous officers, was therefore the subtext of the wrangles over the public service between the organisation's Standing Committee and the elite. The central question which faced the elite in 1924 was whether it was prepared to sacrifice the independence of the public service for the unity of the treatyite party. That the public service would win out over treatyite reunification was at no point a certainty. In early September Cosgrave entered into secret negotiations with the National Group with a view to reuniting the party. As discussions progressed during the month, Cosgrave indicated to McGrath that the officers who mutinied in March could be reinstated in the army and also opened the question of removing 'anti-Irish elements in positions', which meant senior civil servants and especially those in Finance.[83] By the end of the month Cosgrave had agreed an agenda with McGrath, and the veteran Irish-American politician Judge Daniel Cohalan acting as honest broker, which was to be put before a unity conference of Cumann an Gaedheal and the National Group. Its provisions included the establishment beyond all question, by peaceful, progressive and persistent steps, the reunification; bringing into the one constitutional movement all citizens of good-will; while reflecting faithfully the people's will. The final five clauses read:

(a) The Government of the day to be responsible definitely to the Organisation for policy.
(b) Removal as far as possible of all anti-Irish elements in positions and encouragement of those with Irish-Ireland views.
(c) Decisions of Government to be put into operation irrespective of opposition from Permanent Officials.
(d) Educational [the Introduction of a history into schools showing the reasons for the acceptance of the treat[84]].
(e) Replacing of Army men with records and ability who have been demobilised and resigned and the establishing of a real National Army.[85]

These clauses, with the exception of the last, represented the substance of the Standing Committee's demands in its *Statement of Views* delivered a week later. Cosgrave, while not accepting them without qualification, was prepared to put them forward as the basis for discussion towards achieving unity.[86] What precisely Cosgrave had in mind remains unclear. However, it is fair to assume that no unity deal could be struck or sustained with the National Group without compromising either the civil service or the army or indeed both. That Cosgrave even temporarily contemplated a compact on these grounds indicates the fluidity at this time of his thoughts on the fidelity of state institutions.

In September–October 1924, it would appear Cosgrave was prepared to put the probity of the new state's institutions on the negotiation table in the interests of party unity. At his final meeting with McGrath on 2 October Cosgrave rejected all the proposals for unity he had helped author, and behaved, according to McGrath, as if he had never seen them before.[87] His withdrawal from his original position, 24 hours before the unity conference, is inexplicable in the absence of further evidence. McGrath for his part suspected O'Higgins' intervention once again which had proved decisive during the mutiny crisis of March. At the final meeting all Cosgrave would promise to do was to nominate a new Minister of Defence (he had held the portfolio since March) but with no assurance that the new minister would accept the mutinous officers back into the army. The fact that Cosgrave suggested to McGrath that J.J. Egan, who was one of O'Higgins' protégé's within the parliamentary party, become a compromise Minister of Defence, lends some credence to the assumption that O'Higgins was applying pressure on Cosgrave: if indeed he was not dictating the policy he was putting forward.[88] Cosgrave's failure to give a concrete assurance led to the collapse of the negotiations.[89] The National Group, however, waited until the Standing Committee's proposals in the *Statement of Views*, and those of the policy sub-committee were rejected outright before resigning at the end of October.

The treatyites could conceive of their party as a means of holding on to power as the 1925 by-elections demonstrated, and they had experienced very real competitive party politics prior to Fianna Fáil entering the political arena. This raises the question of why the treatyite elite chose not to build a substantial party organisation during the late 1920s and for that matter again after the early Blueshirt period of Fine Gael? The answer is to be found in a deep mistrust of mass politics, and a controlling party organisation impinging upon executive autonomy. The experience of 1924, and indeed of Walsh's tenure as President of the Cumann na nGaedheal organisation and still later during the Blueshirt fiasco, all seemed to reinforce the treatyite elite's experience during 1922 when the Extraordinary Sinn Féin Árd Fhéis of February and May, called to decide on the treaty, had been nobbled and packed by the anti-treaty IRA. The inclination thereafter was to be suspicious of delegating responsibility for policy to an institution as easily manipulated as a party convention.

From September 1922, the treatyite elite did their best to ensure that their party organisation would be emasculated and play as small a part in the governance of the state as possible. O'Higgins, and for that matter Cosgrave, saw the elite's contract as being one between the executive and the electorate, or the nation as they preferred, and not between the executive and the party. Impulses to organise either coming from within the party, or indeed as a matter of political survival as in the 1925 by-elections could not be ignored, but they could be controlled by ensuring that patronage or for that matter any other source of power and influence was kept away from the corrupting hands of party officials, or those like Walsh, who might seek to build a lobby from within the party. In this sense the recruitment of elites through a none-party organisational structure like the Central Branch appealed to the Cumann na nGaedheal leadership. It linked the party and the regime to other elites within Irish society without giving such an institution recourse to an Árd Fhéis where it might, if mobilised, try and influence the executive.

The treatyite elite's responses to problems of organisation was to disengage where possible. There was, at least in the late 1920s, a failure of anyone to come forward and harness the party for the use of the elite. This may in part have been due to a lack of talent. Both O'Higgins and Walsh proved themselves brilliant party handlers, albeit towards their own ends, and both left the political scene during the summer of 1927: O'Higgins being assassinated in July and Walsh resigning three months later. Even that most obsessive of organisers, Mulcahy, failed to rise to the challenge and under the safe stewardship of John Marcus O'Sullivan, Minister of Education (1926–32), the party organisation was allowed to tick over but was not encouraged to expand. The experience of the early Fine Gael and the Blueshirts of organisational boom and bust simply impressed lessons learnt in 1922 and 1924, that mass politics would be subversive and even dangerous to the elite's will. But from 1925, as the treatyites were the first to prove with a series of organisational innovations commonly attributed to Fianna Fáil after 1926, a dynamic party organisation was not a wearisome adjunct, but an essential part of competitive Irish politics.

What was on the face of the matter an intra-party row in 1924 had, potentially at least, profound ramifications for the new state and indeed the establishment of a stable Irish democracy. The contribution of a professional civil service and army to the survival of democracy in independent Ireland cannot be overstated. It is difficult to see how power within the new state could have been transferred peacefully within a decade of the civil war if careers in both the army and civil service had been inexorably linked to the fortunes of political sponsors in the Executive Council and government party. The creation of a meritocratic and apolitical public service, as J.J. Lee has observed without exaggeration, 'verged on the miraculous'.[90] It was the most enduring achievement of the treatyite regime but it did not come about without challenge or risk, and it ultimately cost the treatyite party its unity in 1924. Maryann Valiulis in championing the dissident wing of the treatyites, apparently because of their more aggressive brand of nationalism, inadvertently supports the very group which would have undermined the meritocratic values of the new administration and the fidelity of its institutions. Valiulis is correct in suggesting that the shift in orientation in 1924 ensured that the centre-ground of Irish revolutionary nationalism was ceded to the anti-treatyites and eventually capitalised on by Fianna Fáil. However, whether the adoption of a more aggressively nationalist policy alone would have altered the electoral fate of Cumann na nGaedheal remains a moot question.

Prager's *Masada* thesis that the Cumann na nGaedheal in office sacrificed political interests exclusively to the needs of the state's institutions fails to take full cognisance of complex state–party–executive relations. During 1924, the interests of the three converged and their relationship became critical as the treatyite elite found itself torn between party and administration. An irrevocable division among the treatyites was resolved in favour of O'Higgins' moderate broad-church nationalism to the exclusion of a more aggressive revolutionary nationalism which had in part wrapped itself in the militarist republicanism of the mutineers and demanded a spoils system in both the army and the civil administration as part of its settlement with Cumann na nGaedheal. It seems probable that under duress from O'Higgins, Cosgrave was forced to break with the National Group and face the electorate by contesting nine treatyite seats where the constitutional stability of the state would be challenged. That the new administrative order survived the convulsions of 1924 was dependent not on an immutable dedication to apolitical institutions among the treaty elite in Government, as not only McGrath and Cosgrave proved, but on the ascendancy and dominance of Kevin O'Higgins after the army crisis. With regard to the state's administration O'Higgins was not

above bending rules or pulling a political stunt, whether it was a matter of attempting to place his mistress, Lady Hazel Lavery, in the
Phoenix Park by having her husband appointed Governor-General,[91]
or even on occasion by attempting to have old allies placed within the
civil service against the expressed orders of the cabinet.[92] In the course
of 1924, the interests of the new administration had the good fortune
to coincide with the drive against the unreconstructed revolutionaries
O'Higgins was engineering in the regime. Seamus Hughes writing
anonymously in a newspaper column in October 1924 on the government's refusal to use the patronage of the state for party purposes,
commented 'No doubt their [the government's] action is splendidly
Utopian, but it is not politics.[93] In reality it was O'Higgins' counter-
revolution hiding behind the ideal of an administrative Utopia.

Notes

1 The author would like to acknowledge the generous support of the British
   Academy during the researching and writing of this chapter.
2 James A. Burke memoir (A) in possession of Professor David W. Harkness,
   Emeritus Professor, Institute of Irish Studies, Queen's University, Belfast;
   James A. Burke memoir (B) in possession of Michael McCormack, London.
3 Ronan Fanning, 'Britain's Legacy: Government and Administration', in
   P.J. Drudy (ed.), *Ireland and Britain since 1922: Irish Studies 5* (Cambridge,
   1986), p. 51; Lawrence W. McBride, *The Greening of Dublin Castle: The
   Transformation of the Bureaucratic and Judicial Personnel in Ireland 1892–1922*
   (Washington D.C., 1991), p. 310.
4 J. Horgan, 'Sean Lemass: A Man in a Hurry', in P. Hannon and J. Gallagher
   (eds), *Taking the Long View, 70 Years of Fianna Fáil* (Dublin, 1996), pp. 38–9.
5 W. Moss, *Political Parties in the Irish Free State* (New York, 1933), ch. 2;
   C. Murphy, 'Party Organisation: Fianna Fáil How it Works', *Léargas*, vol. 12
   (March, 1968) pp. 10–3; C. Murphy, 'Party Organisation: Fine Gael How it
   Works' *Léargas*, vol. 14 (May 1968), pp. 5–7; for an account of the shambolic
   mess of Fine Gael Headquarters at the beginning of the 1977 general election
   see S. O'Byrne, *Hiding behind a Face: Fine Gael under FitzGerald* (Dublin, 1986),
   p. 4.
6 T. Garvin, *The Evolution of Irish Nationalist Politics* (Dublin, 1981), p. 146.
7 R. Fanning, *Independent Ireland* (Dublin, 1983), p. 101.
8 Masada is the hill-top fort in South East Israel where in 73 AD the Jewish gar-
   rison committed mass suicide rather than surrender to besieging Romans.
9 J. Prager, *Building Irish Democracy in Ireland: Political Order and Cultural
   Integration in a Newly Independent Nation* (Cambridge, 1986), p. 159; J.J. Lee,
   Ireland: Politics and Society (Cambridge, 1989), p. 82; R. Fanning, *Independent
   Ireland* (Dublin ,1983), p. 101.

10   Maryann Gialanella Valiulis, 'After the Revolution: The Formative Years of Cumann na nGaedheal', in A. Eyler and R.F. Garratt (eds), *The Uses of the Past: Essays in Irish Culture* (Delaware, 1988), pp. 131–42.

11   *Ibid.*, p. 142.

12   T. Garvin, 'Nationalist Elites, Irish Voters, and Irish Political Development: A Comparative Perspective', *Economic and Social Review*, vol. 8, no. 3 (1977), pp. 172–7; J.J. Lee, *Ireland: Politics and Society 1912–85* (Dublin, 1989), p. 82; Maryann Gialanella Valiulis, 'After the Revolution: The Formative Years of Cumann na nGaedheal', in A. Eyler and R.F. Garratt (eds), *The Uses of the Past: Essays in Irish Culture* (Delaware, 1988), pp. 131–42; R. Fanning, *Independent Ireland* (Dublin, 1983), p. 101.

13   Preliminary Statement of Policy by the Cumann na nGaedheal Policy Sub-Committee September 1924, University College Dublin Archive, hereafter UCDA, Desmond FitzGerald papers P80/1104.

14   For an exposition of the unaccountable political culture of the revolutionary Dáil government see P.S. O'Hegarty, *The Victory of Sinn Fein*, (Dublin, 1924), pp. 51–52.

15   Liam de Róiste Journal, 10 Sep. 1922, Cork Archive Institute hereafter, CAI, U271A Book 46.

16   For examples of anti-treaty coercion at cumann level see Liam de Róiste Journal 16–17, 21, 28 Jan. 1921, CAI, de Róiste Journal Book 42, U271A.

17   Minutes of special meeting of the general and election committee 7 Sept. 1922, UCDA, Cumann na nGaedheal minute books P39/1/1 hereafter minute books.

18   Address by Mr Kevin O'Higgins, Minister for Justice, Irish Free State, to the Irish Society at Oxford University, 31 October 1924, UCDA, MacNeill papers, LA1/F/305, p. 7.

19   For a full and detailed discussion of the pact general election see M. Gallagher, 'The pact General Election of 1922' *Irish Historical Studies*, XXI, (1979).

20   For accounts of police and army mutinies see C. Brady, *Guardians of the Peace* (Dublin, 1974), pp. 55–64; Statement by General Seán MacMahon to the Army Inquiry, 1924, UCDA Mulcahy papers P7/C/14.

21   See D. O'Sullivan, *The Irish Free State and the Senate* (London, 1940), pp. 181–2.

22   Conference between Executive Council and the Standing Committee 3 Dec. 1923, UCDA, Cumann na nGaedheal party minute books (hereafter minute books) P39/1/1.

23   For an evaluation of the party organisation after the 1923 general election see Diarmuid O'Hegarty, Secretary to the Executive Council, to William Cosgrave 24 Oct. 1923, UCDA, MacNeill papers LA1/F/252. Copy circulated to every member of the Executive Council.

24   Seamus Hughes to Richard Mulcahy, 25 Feb. 1924, UCDA, Mulcahy papers, P7b/59(118–121).

25   Seamus Hughes to Arthur Griffith, 28 July 1922, UCDA, Mulcahy papers, P7/B/29 (69); Collins to Cosgrave, 6 Aug. 1922, UCDA, Mulcahy papers, P7/B/29(66–7); see also John M. Regan 'Michael Collins: the legacy and the intestacy', in Gabriel Doherty and Dermot Keogh (eds) *Michael Collins and the making of the Irish State* (Cork and Dublin, 1998), pp. 117–27.

26   *Irish Times* 3 Apr. 1924; 'Why The National Group Resigned' n.d. November 1924? in the *National Issue* Supplement to the *Nation* (Milroy papers in the possession of Mr Conor Kenny, Galway).

27 Molesworth Street, adjacent to Kildare Street, is the location of the head-quarters of the Freemasons in Ireland.

28 'Why The National Group Resigned'.

29 Resolutions for the Annual Conference of Cumann na nGaedheal 24 Feb. 1924, UCDA Mulcahy papers P7b/59.

30 Minutes of the General Executive Council 4 March 1924, minute books P39/1/1.

31 Revolutionary Sinn Féin's relationship with agrarian radicalism in the west remains an area worthy of further research. For a personal view which emphasised an unwillingness to see the Sinn Fein party influenced by agrarian radicals in county Roscommon see 'Memories of my life: Kevin O'Shiel', *Irish Times*, 23 Nov. 1966.

32 *Roscommon Herald*, 16 Feb. 1924.

33 *Ibid.*, 19 Jan. 1924.

34 A report of a Cumann na nGaedheal meeting held in Elphin, County Roscommon in March 1924 noted: '...Amongst the correspondence read was instructions [sic]to our secretary to forward to the Secretary of the Land Commission particulars of all grazing ranches in the parish that are needed for distribution.' *Roscommon Herald*, 8 Mar. 1924.

35 The motion read 'That this meeting demands that in future when legislation is intended on matters that stir popular feeling that a real effort be made to sound the public through the Organisation as to what views are held on controversial points and if the Government have to adopt unpopular measures under pressure of necessity that an adequate explanation be furnished through the T.D.s to their Constituency Committees, of the reasons for such measures.' Cumann na nGaedheal Standing Committee circular 13 May 1924 (Milroy papers).

36 *Ibid.*

37 Minutes of the General Executive Council of Cumann na nGaedheal 30 May 1924, UCDA, minute books P39/1/1.

38 Hughes to McGrath 24 June 1924, UCDA, FitzGerald papers P80/1100.

39 McGrath to Hughes 25 June 1924, *ibid.*

40 Hughes to McGrath 7 July 1924, *ibid.*

41 Mulcahy's Diary 18 May 1923, UCDA, Mulcahy papers, P7/B/322.

42 Hughes claimed that if the Executive Council had not given in to the demands within the party for protection that the party would have split, 3 May 1924, *Irish Catholic Herald*.

43 Tobin related that Collins said to him 'I swore an Oath to the Republic and I'm going to keep that Oath Treaty or no Treaty.' Mulcahy's notes on an interview with Cosgrave, Mulcahy, Tobin, Dalton, Thornton, O'Malley. In the President's Office, Government Buildings, 25 June 1923, UCDA, Mulcahy papers P7/B/195.

44 Hughes to Blythe 17 Sept. 1924, UCDA, Blythe papers P24/453.

45 Blythe to Hughes 19 Sept. 1924, *ibid.*

46 His initial fit of pique having subsided, Blythe penned a less barbed concluding paragraph: '...I think that when the Government faces the facts of a difficult situation and decides on measures which receive the approval of the elected representatives of the people in the Dail, it is entitled to look to well informed and responsible citizens for support and encouragement.' The second letter drafted was sent to Hughes on the 26 September. Draft letter from Blythe to Hughes 19 Sept. 1924, *ibid.*

47 *Statement of Views of Coiste Gnotha* [Standing Committee] *Relative to the Political Aspect of the Present Situation.* 10 Oct. 1924, minute books P39/1/1.
48 *Ibid.*
49 Minutes of Cumann na nGaedheal standing committee 10 Oct. 1924, UCDA, Cumann na nGaedheal minute Books, P39/1/1.
50 *Ibid.*
51 *Ibid.*
52 *Ibid.* Article 10 of the Treaty required that 'The Government of the Irish Free State agrees to pay fair compensation on terms not less favourable than those accorded by the Act of 1920 to judges, officials, members of Police Forces and other Public Servants who are discharged by it or who retire in consequence of the change of government effected in pursuance hereof.' The provisions did not cover special constabularies such as the Auxiliaries and the Black and Tans.
53 Minutes of Policy Sub-Committee 16 Oct. 1924, UCDA Mulcahy papers P7/C/99.
54 Blythe defended the personnel of his department as 'Irishmen of loyal associations' and refused to discuss further the personnel of his department. As to the suggestion that the officials controlled policy Blythe commented with characteristic directness 'The ministers are not bloody fools.' Lee, *Ireland*, pp. 105–6; Joint meeting of Policy Sub-Committee and Ministers re Economic Policy 20 Oct. 1924, UCDA, Mulcahy papers, P7/C/99.
55 Statement of policy by the General Executive Council of Cumann na nGaedheal 2 Nov. 1924, UCDA, Mulcahy papers, P7b/60 (136).
56 *Irish Catholic Herald*, 12 July 1924.
57 Minutes of the Standing Committee 28 Nov. 1924, minute books P39/1/1.
58 Minutes of the Executive Organising Committee 16 Dec. 1924, minute books P39/1/1.
59 Minutes of special meeting of the Standing Committee 27 Nov. 1924, minute books P39/1/1.
60 Minutes of the Cumann na nGaedheal Annual Convention 13–14 May 1925, UCDA Mulcahy papers, P7b/60/98.
61 General Secretary's Report to Annual Convention of Cumann na nGaedheal 13 May 1925, UCDA Mulcahy papers P7b/60/98.
62 General Secretary's Report to Annual Convention of Cumann na nGaedheal 13 May 1925, UCDA Mulcahy papers P7b/60/98.
63 In county Roscommon it was announced at a Cumann na nGaedheal meeting at the end of January that the Government inspector would have three to five hundred men employed repairing bye-roads. *Roscommon Herald*, 31 Jan. 1925.
64 M.F. Connolly to Secretary of the North Mayo Constituency Committee, 25 Mar. 1925, UCDA Tierney papers, LA30/308(65).
65 Minutes of the Executive Organising Committee 13 Feb. 1925, minute books, P39/1/1.
66 *Ibid.*
67 Special meeting of the Standing Committee 27 Nov. 1924, minute books, P39/1/1.
68 For an insider's guide to the origins and development of *Taca* see Kevin Boland, *The rise and decline of Fianna Fáil* (Dublin, 1982) pp. 96–9.

69 Walsh claimed, apparently for propaganda purposes, that the organisation had grown to 797 cumainn in his presidential address to the 1926 Cumann na nGaedheal Convention. Both Garvin and Prager have taken this as an indication of Cumann na nGaedheal's response to the formation of Fianna Fáil in May 1926. However, Liam Burke, a more trustworthy source and the party's Chief Organiser, put the size of the organisation at 440 cumainn at the same convention. Garvin, 'Evolution', p. 146; Prager, *Building*, p. 210; Report of the Annual Convention Cumann na nGaedheal 11–12 May 1926 (Athlone, 1926), p. 3, p. 21: interview with Mrs Ena Crummey, niece and personal secretary to Seamus Hughes 1922–7, secretary at Cumann na nGaedheal party headquarters 1927–33, Dublin, 28 June 1991.

70 Liam de Róiste Journal 27 Jan. 1925, CAI, De Róiste Papers, U271A, book 52.

71 Mulcahy's speech to the Árd Comhairle of Cumann na nGaedheal, 14 Dec. 1926, UCDA, Mulcahy papers, P7b/61 (60–6).
Report of the Annual Convention Cumann na nGaedheal 11–12 May 1926 (Athlone, 1926), pp. 22–5.

72 Minutes of the Executive Organising Committee 30 Mar. 1925, and 21 Apr. 1925 (U.C.D.A. Cumann na nGaedheal Party minute books P39/1/1).

73 Report of the Annual Convention Cumann na nGaedheal 11–12 May 1926 (Athlone, 1926), pp. 22–5.

74 Liam de Róiste diary, 22 Feb. 1922 CAI, U271a, Book 54.

75 Walsh even went as far as to solicit protectionist candidates to run against his own party in the June 1927 general election. See Sean Milroy to J.J. Walsh 24 Apr. 1927, Milroy papers; *Irish Times* 6 Sept. 1927; Cosgrave to Walsh, 7 Sept. 1927 (CAI, Walsh papers U355).

76 Transcript of conversation between Senator Michael Hayes and Mulcahy 22 Oct. 1964, UCDA, Mulcahy papers, P7/D/78.

77 Liam de Róiste Journal 25 June 1926, CAI, U271A, Book 54.

78 Walsh was not a member of officers' board or committee of the Central Branch in 1926–7, despite being the president of the party. Cumann na nGaedheal Central Branch list of officers and committee can be found on its letterhead. UCDA, Mulcahy papers, P7b/67/10.

79 List of members of Central Branch 1931, UCDA, Blythe papers, P24/619 (b).

80 The size of Blueshirt membership remains a highly contentious issue. The April 1934 return is an optimistic estimation of membership compiled by County Directors given to exaggeration and a General Secretary (Commandant Ned Cronin) given to organisational inflation. The movement by mid 1934, *may* have had a nominal membership of 48 000, but its active membership was about a quarter of that number. Fine Gael/United Ireland monthly bulletin, no. 2, Feb. 1934 copy in MacEoin papers; Strength return of League of Youth (Blueshirts) April 1934 UCDA, Blythe papers, P24/ 671(a).

81 Minutes of the Standing Committee of Fine Gael-United Ireland 14 March 1935 UCDA ,Fine Gael party minute books P39/Min/2.

82 For an account of the 1934 O'Duffy split see Maurice Manning, *The Blueshirts*, (Dublin, 1987), pp. 146–78; With regard to the suppression of the Blueshirt movement by the Fine Gael executive see T.F. O'Higgins to Richard Mulcahy 14 Oct. 1936 (UCDA, Mulcahy papers, P7c/47 (26)). This file contains a considerable amount of material relating to the 1936 division.

83 Joe McGrath to Judge Daniel Cohalan, 13 Oct. 1924, American Irish Historical Society, New York, Cohalan papers, Box 10 file 1.

84 The full educational clause was not included in the original document and the clause included is the one reproduced by Liam Tobin in a published statement 'Why the National Group resigned' n.d., Dec. 1924 (Milroy papers).

85 Joe McGrath to Judge Daniel Cohalan, 13 Oct. 1924, American Irish Historical Society, New York, Cohalan papers, Box 10 file 1.

86 Report on Negotiations September 1924 reproduced in 'A history of the Irish Republican Army Organisation as Revealed in Captured Documents,' Department of Defence document, Sean MacEoin papers, uncatalogued, consulted at the Franciscan Archive, Killiney, Dublin, now housed in UCDA.

87 *Ibid.*

88 *Ibid.* For an example of O'Higgins' appreciation of Egan in the Fifth Dail (September 1923–May 1927) see Kevin O'Higgins to Frank MacDermot 24 June 1927, NA, Frank MacDermot papers 1065/1/3.

89 Joe McGrath to Judge Daniel Cohalan, 13 Oct. 1924, American Irish Historical Society, New York, Cohalan papers, Box 10 file 1.

90 Lee, *Ireland,* p. 107.

91 Sinead McCoole, *Hazel: A life of Lady Lavery 1880–1935* (Dublin, 1996), p. 138.

92 O'Higgins attempted to have an old Leix friend Joseph Lynch placed in the Department of External Affairs in April 1923, disobeying an earlier cabinet decision not to make political appointments. O'Higgins to FitzGerald, 14 Apr. 1923, UCDA, FitzGerald papers, P80/431; Ronan Fanning, *The Department of Finance* (Dublin, 1978), p. 63.

93 *Irish Catholic Herald* 11 Oct. 1924.

4
The Enigma of Fianna Fáil: Party Strategy, Social Classes and the Politics of Hegemony

Richard Dunphy

During the 1997 general election campaign in Ireland, the deputy leader of Fianna Fáil, Mary O'Rourke, told a seminar on unemployment organised by the Irish Congress of Trade Unions that her party had more in common with the Labour Party on the question of unemployment than it had with its prospective coalition partners, the Progressive Democrats. Flatly rejecting the Progressive Democrats' proposals to shed 25 000 jobs in the public sector, she projected Fianna Fáil as the defender of the public sector.[1] Her remarks were, of course, a classic example of Fianna Fáil tactics and rhetoric . By 'muddying the waters' of those who sought to portray the election as a contest between a centre-left rainbow coalition and a centre-right Fianna Fáil–Progressive Democrats alignment, she emphasised Fianna Fáil's ability to face both 'left' and 'right' simultaneously. The statement indicated to the trade union movement that Fianna Fáil, which has continued to win more working-class votes than the Labour Party and Democratic Left combined, understood the economic concerns of both the unemployed and public sector worker components of its cross-class electoral bloc. Thereby setting limits to the extent to which that cross-class electoral bloc would be endangered by the pursuit of orthodox economic liberalism.

The political instincts displayed by Mary O'Rourke were honed during the first two decades of the country's independence when the foundations of Fianna Fáil's always dominant and at times hegemonic role in Irish political life were established. Fianna Fáil's achievement during those early decades was the deployment of a political strategy which enabled it to supersede the tensions within a class bloc composed of potentially fissile elements. This ensured its passage to power, by placing opponents on a more or less permanently reactive and

67

defensive footing. But just what type of party did emerge as the dominant political force in the Ireland of the 1930s and ever since? The 'enigma' of Fianna Fáil has been evident in its apparent success in eluding attempts by political scientists at classification according to existing typologies of political parties. In this chapter I wish to examine the Fianna Fáil enigma by raising some questions about the nature of the party during those formative years, the importance of party strategy, and the relationship of parties to social class.

These are questions which have been explored in my recently published study of Fianna Fáil,[2] a work greatly influenced by what the Italian political theorist Antonio Gramsci had to say about the study of political parties. Gramsci cautions that any attempt to construct the history of a political party which consists of a 'simple narrative of the internal life of a political organisation ... how it comes into existence, the first groups which constitute it, the ideological controversies through which its programme and its conception of the world and of life are formed' may result in 'a history of certain intellectual groups, or even sometimes the political biography of a single personality'.[3] The 'vaster and more comprehensive framework' he commends instead, would focus on the mass of people who have given the founders of the party their 'trust, loyalty and discipline. Or criticised them 'realistically' by dispersing or remaining passive before certain initiatives. Even this does not signify merely active members of the party: it is not sufficient when constructing a party's history to focus solely on party congresses, votes, and so on. Rather one needs to 'take some account of the social group of which the party in question is the expression and the most advanced element. The history of a party, in other words, can only be the history of a particular social group'.

Two other things are striking about Gramsci's analysis. First, his insistence that as any social group is not isolated, but locked in co-operation and competition with others, then

> the history of any party can only emerge from the complex portrayal of the totality of society and State (often with international ramifications too). Hence it may be said that to write the history of a party means nothing less than to write the general history of a country from a monographic viewpoint, in order to highlight a particular aspect of it.

And second, that one should strive not to be distracted by 'mystic enthusiasm' for 'petty internal matters' from the overall picture of how effective a party has been, in both positive and negative terms, in bringing certain social changes about and preventing others from taking place. Obviously, the schema outlined above sets the historian of any political party ambitious and complex tasks. In particular, there was not enough attention focused on the 'international ramifications', either in terms of the international context in which Irish economic development of the time took place, or in terms of cross-national comparative analysis of the type of political organisation and system of political power which emerged with Fianna Fáil (to which I will return later). Gramsci's considerations may, however, enable us to move beyond the limitations of three of the dominant characteristics of so much of the published writings on Irish political parties and twentieth-century Irish politics in general. First, the 'heroes of Irish history' approach which concentrates on the personal qualities and relative merits of individual leaders and sometimes elite groups, abstracted from social context. Second, the tendency to consider internal party disputes and even inter-party disputes, including those over constitutional and nationalist issues, is again devoid of social context. Third, the paucity of consideration hitherto given to the relationship between party strategies and party cultures and modes of organisation on the one hand, and the salience of economic and social interests, disputes and issues on the other, when explaining the rise of Fianna Fáil to a dominant position in Irish political life.

My study of the early decades of Fianna Fáil implicitly contains six fundamental theses or propositions. The first is that the rise of Fianna Fáil to political dominance during the first few decades of the life of the new state can best be understood by the application of the concept of political hegemony. I have argued that during the 1920s and 1930s Fianna Fáil was first and foremost the political representative of the interests of the emergent national bourgeoisie. The genius of the party lay in its ability to project the interests of that social class as 'universal', in the process building an enduring cross-class electoral bloc which included urban workers, small farmers, those dependent on welfare payments, and so on. Naturally the composition of this electoral and political bloc changed as the social structure of the country changed, and as the balance of political forces in the field changed. From the mid-1940s until the early 1960s, for example, and again since the late 1970s, the party can be said to have lost a hegemonic role. During the 1980s and 1990s it has suffered serious erosion of its electoral support and a relative weakening of its place in Irish society. Nevertheless, it remains the country's biggest political party and retains stronger cross-class support than any other party. It also retains political instincts and a culture of exercising power which are rooted in that earlier period.

The concept of hegemony used in this Gramscian sense implies more than just the claim that Fianna Fáil successfully built a catch-all electoral base. A first and obvious philosophical point of departure is the argument that social classes with distinctive (and sometimes antagonistic) interests do exist and that class analysis – which seeks to deepen our understanding of political actors by 'teasing out' the dialectical relationship between their discourses, strategies, actions and struggles and social class divisions – is valid. Not of course everyone agrees, and in Ireland in particular there has long been an antagonism born of the overwhelmingly conservative nature of the intellectual culture as well as the weakness of an urban, industrial working class towards any attempt to analyse Irish politics in class terms. For example, Brian Girvin[4] has argued in the course of a review of my recent work 'the appeal of the party [Fianna Fáil] was based on class consciousness' – whereas I actually argue that the appeal of the party rested on a hegemonic party strategy which took advantage of the relative weakness of class consciousness on the part of subordinated groups, while recognising the necessity to secure their adherence to a particular capitalist developmental model. Girvin ascribes to me the crudest form of vulgar Marxism – that social class membership determines electoral behaviour – before dispensing with any further necessity to engage with class analysis on the grounds that Irish electoral statistics support the assertion that 'class rarely carries into electoral politics'.[5]

Political hegemony implies that Fianna Fáil rose to power in the 1930s because of its success in bringing about a unison of political and economic aims which enabled it to seize the intellectual and moral leadership of a developing society. The party was thus able to give effect to the hegemony of the national bourgeoisie over a series of subordinate classes. It was able to pose various questions around which its struggle for political dominance took place – such as the introduction of protectionism, the Economic War with Britain, the quest for national sovereignty which culminated in the 1937 Constitution, and the construction of a model of cultural and religious homogeneity. Fianna Fáil was able to achieve this because the national bourgeois project was presented convincingly as dynamic and modernising. It was contrasted with a welfarism devoid of any clear strategy for economic growth which characterised the Irish Labour Party of the time, and with a Cumann na nGaedheal/Fine Gael economic strategy which had benefited minority social classes and groups and seemed devoid of any potential for generating further growth. In other words, political, intellectual and moral leadership was rooted, crucially, in economic leadership.

The second fundamental thesis underpinning my work on Fianna Fáil is that once we employ the concept of political hegemony within a Gramscian framework which highlights the importance of economic factors, we are challenged to deconstruct and 're-read' certain constitutional and nationalist discourses. The point here is most certainly not to argue that nationalism or republicanism is 'irrelevant' or even of 'secondary' importance. On the contrary, it is necessary to acknowledge the power and force of nationalist and republican ideology in explaining the party's appeal. But a key distinction between the new Fianna Fáil party and those they left behind in the rump of Sinn Féin was that the nationalism of the former was never just an abstraction; rather, it was tied to a concrete economic and political project which satisfied to a significant degree the material aspirations of key social classes. The 'pragmatism' which allowed Fianna Fáil to escape from what Richard English[6] has called the solipsism of anti-treaty republicanism reflects the fact that Fianna Fáil's republicanism was rooted in the material needs of the national bourgeoisie. The republicanism of the IRA and other such groups in the 1930s and 1940s was rooted in their fantasies, and not the needs and interests of only social strata or class.

My next three propositions all reflect the belief that it is necessary to eschew the vulgar Marxist tendency towards economic reductionism typified by the assumption that history has predetermined the roles allocated to political and economic factors in an omnipresent class struggle. And, further, by the belief that only a combination of treacherous leadership of the working-class movement and Machiavellian cunning on the part of the class enemy can explain why the 'good guys', the proletariat, keep losing. In place of this romantic leftism, we need to understand and explain the behaviour of political actors, such as parties, dialectically. That is to say by focusing on the range of tactical and strategic choices available in any given situation, the ways in which interrelationships between the economic, the social, the cultural and the political spheres condition and help define the field of possibilities, and the role of individual agency.

Hence the importance of focusing on party strategy. I have argued that what critically distinguished Fianna Fáil from its rivals during the 1920s and 1930s was that Fianna Fáil decisively broke with the lack of attention given to political strategy by the old Sinn Féin movement. Thus we need to study the ways in which a successful party such as

Fianna Fáil both sought to piece together a bloc of social and political forces capable of propelling it into office and ensuring the partial success of its economic and political project. Then, as its policies brought significant changes to the social and cultural environment, it strove to keep its rivals on the defensive by constantly 're-inventing' the equilibrium within the ranks of its constituency in ways which allowed the interests of the dominant social class or social groups to which it was wedded to prevail *only up to a critical point*, short of placing in jeopardy the cross-class alliance which Fianna Fáil had constructed. This line of reasoning also helps us understand the hard line taken towards trade unions and striking workers during the 1930s and 1940s. The espousal of welfarist measures and wooing of sections of the labour movement during the same period and after do not represent contradictory zigzags from right to left, but form a dialectical whole.

This leads me to my fourth proposition which is the necessity of focusing on the importance of internal debates and divisions within the party – and of attempting to relate these to the dynamics of social change. It is precisely by studying such differences and attempting to locate them in a social context – admittedly often a difficult task given the absence of satisfactory documentary evidence – that we gain a deeper understanding of how extensive or limited have been the changes which a party in power has brought about in society, and how successful or otherwise it has been in making the right strategic choices which guarantee its own continued dominance. Thus, it is a major mistake to treat Fianna Fáil in power as an undifferentiated monolith, striving, as it were, to thwart the onwards march of Irish labour as if according to some invisible but perfectly understood game-plan. This, I would argue, is the impression one gets from Kieran Allen's recent study *Fianna Fail and Irish Labour*,[7] which is representative of romantic leftism.

A further challenge facing the student of politics who seeks to focus upon the evolution of a political party is to attempt to relate a party's internal culture, types and styles of organisation, and of course its *ideology*, to the wider social context. Thus, it is necessary to pay attention to such questions as the role of charismatic leadership and the extent to which the adoption by Fianna Fáil at its foundation of the old IRA network and style, rather than the old Sinn Féin organisation, influenced its subsequent evolution; the question of party discipline and the ways in which debate and dissent were managed; the role and extent of clientelism; the question of paternalism and the relationship here between mutually overlapping and perhaps reinforcing ideological codes inspired by republicanism and Catholicism; and the relationship between the party's own culture and the culture and mores of the society which was emerging under Fianna Fáil in the 1930s and 1940s. This list could be extended considerably. The important point here is, however, that questions of party culture and structure are intensely political questions and cannot be discussed in isolation from questions of party strategy and the broader social and political picture. Finally, my study was guided by the belief that it is at least as important to focus on what a party such as Fianna Fáil actually does in office as on what it says; on attempting to understand whose interests were served, and whose interests frustrated, by its policies as on how it perceived its motivations; and on the extent and limitations of its achievements as on the goals it set itself.

Political scientists have seemingly long been confounded by the task of locating Fianna Fáil within any of the typologies of political parties which are usually produced within the discipline, and particularly those which attempt to categorise parties along an ideological spectrum or which categorise parties according to the circumstances of their origins. This, in turn, has hindered analysis of Fianna Fáil in a comparative framework, and above all in a comparative European context. I have argued that a tendency on the part of commentators to fall prey to the 'mystical sway of Irish political language'[8] and a too-glib acceptance of the notion that the civil war cleavage on its own explains the party allegiances of most Irish voters have reinforced the idea that Irish politics is *sui generis*.

The political scientist Klaus von Beyme has identified nine major party groups or 'spiritual families' which are present in the western European context: liberal and radical parties, conservative parties, socialist and social democratic parties, communist parties, Christian democratic parties, agrarian parties, ecology parties, regional and ethnic parties and right-wing extremist parties.[9] Von Beyme argues that Fianna Fáil belongs to the 'family' of conservative parties. Yet, whilst one would agree that Fianna Fáil shares certain characteristics of conservative parties – not least its nationalism, commitment to capitalism, and a socially conservative or paternalistic ethos – this classification obscures important distinctions between Fianna Fáil and other conservative parties relating to its popular origins, and its remarkable cross-class electoral support with a consistent appeal to the poorest classes and social groups in Ireland. Alan Ware, quite rightly, takes issue with von Beyme on this point, but, however, falls back upon the old argument about Irish exceptionalism. Concluding, Ware argues that Fianna Fáil falls outside a comparative framework in the same way as 'the Icelandic Women's Alliance':[10] which it may be safe to conclude is about the only thing Fianna Fáil might have in common with the Icelandic Women's Alliance!

Three political scientists with considerable expertise in the field of Irish politics – Michael Gallagher, Michael Laver and Peter Mair[11] – have produced a classification of western European political parties based on the following factors: shared 'genetic' origins, such as those having mobilised in similar historical circumstances or to defend similar interests; links which have been forged across national frontiers; and the pursuit of similar policies. On this basis they classify parties into ten 'party families' – social democrats, communists, greens, and 'new left' parties on the Left; Christian democrats, secular conservatives, liberals, agrarians and neo-fascists on the Centre and Right; and regionalists and nationalists. Obviously, this is very similar to von Beyme's schema. Gallagher, Laver and Mair, however, argue that Fianna Fáil is best understood as belonging to the secular conservative family – which they describe as 'distinguished from the Christian democrats by a more strident anti-socialist rhetoric as well as by the absence of traditional links with organised religion'.[12] On the face of it this is an extraordinary claim. Of course, political parties do change over time, and it may be argued that Fianna Fáil is more 'conservative' and 'secular' now than it was 60 or 70 years ago. Although competition for working-class electoral support and the logic of coalition formation in Ireland has perhaps meant more intense clashes between Fianna Fáil and the Labour Party down the years than between Fine Gael and Labour, it would be difficult to sustain the proposition that Fine Gael – which the authors classify as Christian Democrat – has been less given to anti-socialist rhetoric. Indeed, as I have argued, Fianna Fáil has on occasions displayed an ability to sow the seeds of ideological confusion on the left by portraying itself as 'socialist' when it felt an advantage was to be had.[13]

More seriously, the classification of Fianna Fáil as 'secular conservative' obscures the historically close relationship between the party and the Roman Catholic Church. Examples of this during the 1930s, 1940s and 1950s include, of course, the special status accorded to the Church in the 1937 Constitution: and indeed the consultation of the bishops during its drafting. The enactment of legislation to give effect to Roman Catholic teaching on family law and censorship, and the enlistment of the bishops' support for the Fianna Fáil government's agricultural policies during the 'Emergency'.[14] Fianna Fáil made full use of the integrative effects of Roman Catholic teaching to the extent that Erskine Hamilton Childers, one of the few protestants in the early leadership, became alarmed at what he interpreted as an anti-protestant ethos within the Government.[15] In the late 1940s Childers expressed the concern that members of Fianna Fáil had hinted to him that 'a Protestant was unlikely to be appointed to the Ministries of Justice, Health, External Affairs, Education, and probably Social Welfare'.[16] Indeed, even to this day, the erosion of the political influence of Roman Catholicism and the rise of a liberal and moderate secular agenda probably causes more tensions within the electoral constituency of Fianna Fáil than that of any other party.

It seems possible that Gallagher, Laver and Mair, having accepted the definition of Fine Gael as a Christian democratic party because of its membership of the European People's Party, and ruled out 'liberal', 'agrarian' or 'neo-fascist' as adequate or accurate descriptions of Fianna Fáil, have been left with the secular conservatives as the only remaining centre-right 'family' to which the troublesome Fianna Fáil can be squeezed into. The problems of classifying Fianna Fáil in this way have led many scholars to abandon attempts at analysing the party in a comparative European context at all, preferring instead to search for comparable parties in 'Third World' countries, particularly those which might be described as 'post-colonial'. The concept of populism has frequently been put forward as one which might throw more light on the nature of the party, viewed in this context. For example, one commentator responding to my book has argued that Fianna Fáil is a 'classic populist party' such as arise in many underdeveloped countries and has suggested a comparison with Latin American populism, quoting with approval Jorge Castaneda's description of Mexican populism as 'a compromise between limited political will to impose reform from above, and limited capacity to fight for reform from below'.[17] There is undoubtedly much substance in this analysis, and references to Fianna Fáil's 'populist political agenda'[18] are not unusual. But populism is a notoriously difficult concept to define, and too loose or careless an application of the term to Fianna Fáil – particularly if the Latin American or 'Third World' comparisons are taken too far – may in the long run raise more questions than answers.

Peter Calvert[19] has argued that Latin American populism is above all characterised by three things:

1. An assertion that the people are always right.
2. A broad non-ideological coalition of support.

3. A charismatic leader, often lacking any specific ideological commitment.

Right away it is possible to see that an uncritical attribution of this
schema to the Irish context would obscure or distort two aspects of the
Fianna Fáil phenomenon. First, the emphasis on a lack of ideological
profile considerably underplays the strength and complexity of Fianna
Fáil's nationalist ideological discourses. Second, the above schema,
were it applied to Ireland, would also underplay the importance of the
party in Irish politics and the strong identification of the party with
the nation. For Fianna Fáil did not preach that 'the people are always
right'; rather, that the people had no right to do wrong and that the
party, representing the spirit of the nation, had the mission of calling
the people back to their senses whenever they strayed from the path of
the righteous. At first sight this might seem extraordinarily arro
gant and implicitly authoritarian. But in actual effect, once the transition was made from solipsism to an acceptance that, short of a
renewed civil war, 'existing political realities' were here to stay, the
party–nation identification may have enabled Fianna Fáil to face peri-
ods of defeat and opposition with fortitude and may have proven less
destabilising to Irish democracy that the sort of populist credo one
encounters in societies where the institutions of civil society are less
well-developed.

Moreover, we still have to address the question of the nature of the
policies pursued by a political party whose interests were served by
those policies, and which social groups/classes the party sought to
mobilise. Margaret Canovan has argued that the Mexican example
of 'the catch-all party, an all-embracing non-ideological organisation
that integrates many different and potentially conflicting groups and
sections of the people' is in fact atypical of Latin American populism,
and that

> in most Latin American countries a party that is radical in the sense
> of seeking to redistribute wealth and power may gain support from
> more than one class, but could hardly be catch-all to the extent of
> the P.R.I. [Party of the Institutional Revolution in Mexico] because
> there would be too many vested interests opposed to it. Most Latin
> American populist parties, therefore, have not exactly been populist
> in the sense of appealing to the *whole* people; rather, they have been
> coalitions of different groups among the *common* people – those not
> members of the elite.[20]

In other words, the class nature of a party and the social profile of its support and appeal may be obscured if we simply assume that populism is an undifferentiated category.

Brian Smith has recently argued that populism is best understood as a 'style of leadership rather than an ideology'.[21] As such, populist parties do not form a new type of party distinct from, say, nationalist or Christian Democratic parties; rather, it may be the case that a populist leadership style is deployed in different contexts by parties which reflect a range of ideological positions and might be held to serve the interests of different combinations of social groups. For Smith, the essence of the populist style of leadership is that

> it seeks to mobilise people regardless of class by denying the existence of class and of any class-based ideology. Populism tries to mobilise all interests under a single conception of the national interest ... [It] is thus a way of presenting a view of society that stresses homogeneity rather than diversity ... Leaders specifically aim to prevent the development of a consciousness of conflicting interests. The methods used include building support on the basis of rewards rather than ideological conviction, and expressing contradictory policy positions incoherently.[22]

By identifying the denial or suppression of social diversity and class and other forms of social antagonism as the essence of a populist style, Smith is able to conclude that 'populism is inevitably conservative, since it seeks to prevent alternative perspectives to the status quo developing'. Whilst it is perhaps true that a populist style contains within it the seeds of stagnation – for precisely the reasons given by Smith – it should not be forgotten that a key ingredient of the strategy of a successful populist party may be the projection of that party as dynamic, modernising and developmental, and of its opponents as conservative and addicted to the status quo. I have argued that this was true of Fianna Fáil.

In a similar vein to Smith, Canovan has singled out what she refers to as 'politicians' populism', and defines as a 'technique that can be used in a very wide variety of circumstances'. Canovan argues that

> On occasion this vague, unifying 'politicians' populism' has been raised to the status of an explicit ideology in claims that 'the people' are a single entity, that supposed divisions among them are unreal, and that one leader or one party can stand above maliciously divisive

politics and represent them all. While this kind of claim can be used by an established Government to justify its monopoly of power, similar appeals are often used by outsiders in competitive political systems. Politicians (so the argument goes) squabble among themselves over unreal issues and create divisions where none need exist. What is therefore needed is a party that will set aside both doctrine and selfish interest and put the *people* first.[23]

It can be readily seen that many of the characteristics of the populist style of leadership referred to by Smith and by Canovan do indeed apply to Fianna Fáil. For example, the projection of the party from the outset as a national movement rather than a party or sectional force; the counter-balancing of the party's alleged sympathy with the 'common people of Ireland' and even the 'working man' with strong hostility towards any autonomous labour or trade union organisation which dared to advocate 'selfish class interests'; and the deployment of the integrative ideologies of nationalism and Catholicism to stress the homogeneity of the partitioned southern Irish state. Indeed, as Paul Bew has put it, 'Fianna Fáil has been the chief long-term beneficiary of Irish partition, luxuriating in a culture in which others could be denounced for their "Unionist" or "Freemason" sympathies'.[24] Or, he might have added, their 'unpatriotic' socialist views as evidenced, for example, by membership of 'alien', British-based trade unions.

Smith also argues that in '... some countries, the structure of post-colonial society lent some support to this way of viewing the political world, particularly in those that did appear to be devoid of significant class distinctions simply because economic underdevelopment had prevented classes from emerging fully.'[25] Certainly the Ireland of the 1920s and 1930s scarcely appeared to be devoid of significant class distinctions – the bitter class struggles of the 1920s involving tens of thousands of striking urban workers and land labourers; the conflict of interests between the emergent national bourgeoisie who sought the development of the home market behind protection and the export-oriented sections of the bourgeoisie; the conflict between the new urban classes and the so-called 'ranchers' which was one of the factors behind the emergence of the Blueshirt phenomenon in the 1930s; these are all evidence of that. But Smith's point is nonetheless salient. The political and numerical weakness of an urban working class, the lateness and partial and dependent nature of industrialisation, and the sway which national and constitutional issues exercised over the political agenda in the post-civil war period all militated strongly against the emergence of successful challenges to the celebration of alleged social homogeneity. So too did the way in which emigration served to drain the ranks of both the poor and disaffected and the critical intelligentsia.

That said, it was not inevitable that a populist style of leadership would facilitate the rise to political hegemony under democratic conditions of a political party in the Ireland of the 1930s, nor that the party would be Fianna Fáil. If we accept what Smith has to say, then a populist style is compatible with a range of ideological and strategic attempts to construct a cross-class political bloc. The task of understanding why Fianna Fáil has proven to be so successful must surely involve us in an examination of the ideological and strategic choices of the party and its opponents; and, beyond that, of the relationship between party strategy, social structure and economic development. References to populism, therefore, do not necessarily take us to the heart of the question 'what type of party was/is Fianna Fáil?' We must also be careful least the classification of Fianna Fáil as a 'populist party' serves to locate any comparative analysis of the party in an exclusively 'Third World' or post-colonial arena.

There are centre-right parties elsewhere in Europe with which Fianna Fáil may be usefully compared. However, such comparative analysis is not always helped by attempts to 'force' the party into particular frameworks. We must also treat with caution the argument that Irish political alignments are somehow unique within Europe and that the country is really a 'Third World' one, as far as making sense of its parties is concerned. It may be more useful to concentrate on analysing Fianna Fáil's ideology, its political strategy, the nature of its class profile, and the effects upon the social structure of its occupancy of governmental office.

Girvin has alluded to the possibility that a useful comparison might be drawn between Fianna Fáil and the French Gaullists.[26] Certainly there are obvious, or at least superficial, similarities: both organisations were created and led from the beginning by complex and charismatic individuals; both espoused a strongly nationalist ideology, although the nationalism of de Gaulle was arguably more inclusive and less sectarian than that of de Valera;[27] both, to some extent, attempted to transcend the Left–Right divide, appearing as all things to all voters. But there remain huge differences between Gaullism and Fianna Fáil, relating to the differing social structures, political environments, political strategies and institutional effects of their exercise of power. France, by the time of the rise of Gaullism to power in 1958, was a far more industrialised society than Ireland in 1932, with a much stronger and more politically organised working class. Gaullism during the Fifth Republic was faced by an electorally strong and militant, if sectarian and Stalinist, working-class party – the French Communist Party – and Gaullism itself had a less variegated social base than Fianna Fáil. Indeed, the principal challenges which Gaullism had to watch for tended to come from petty bourgeois movements of the far right. The different political environment also meant that different strategic concerns faced the two parties: after all, Gaullism's predecessors in power during the lifetime of the Fourth Republic had displayed a strong commitment to economic planning and state intervention to remodel French capitalism, and the post-1958 period saw more of a continuation (and possibly acceleration) of existing economic policies than an attempted break with perceived orthodoxy.

The institutional effect of the two parties also differs significantly in many respects. In terms of party organisation, although the Gaullists did import American-style techniques of campaigning – such as the systematic use of advertising and opinion polls during the 1960s – it was neither the largest nor the most disciplined and best organised party in France and, in relative terms, did not match Fianna Fáil's success in building a party machine. Its degree of dependence on a single individual also proved to be greater than Fianna Fáil's. Partly, this was due to the very different political institutions shaped by the two parties in power. Whereas de Gaulle famously ushered in a presidential system of rule in which political parties were partially displaced, and the president himself stood somewhat aloof even from his own party, Fianna Fáil helped to consolidate a parliamentary democracy in which parties and party loyalties were absolutely central. The enormous emphasis which Fianna Fáil placed on building a disciplined and centralised electoral machine also helped ensure that personal rivalries would not threaten the unity and centrality of the party.

A stronger case for comparison with Fianna Fáil in the European arena is surely the Italian Christian Democratic party (Democrazia Cristiana or DC). Both parties came to power in relatively underdeveloped societies in which industrial development was partial, distorted and dependent. Both recognised the importance of modest welfare concessions to the poor and the marginalised and sought to transform relations of economic dependence into relations of political dependence – the DC to a much greater degree than Fianna Fáil. Both engaged in the politics of patronage and clientelism, although again the system of *partitocrazia*[28] constructed by the DC would go far beyond the wildest dreams of the most ambitious Fianna Fáil machine politician. Both constructed cross-class movements which were not classically 'conservative' but which rapidly gained the support of the bourgeois strata in the absence of any creditable right-wing alternative. Indeed, both played a major role as 'midwives' of new or more dynamic bourgeois strata during their early years in power, although the means chosen – protection for Fianna Fáil, and free trade for the DC – could not have been more different. Both came to enjoy a fruitful relationship with a section of the trade union movement which helped boost their 'popular' image and appeal during times of rapid economic and social change. Both benefited politically from the effects of emigration (and in the case of Italy, migration). Both operated in political environments in which the external constraints were omnipresent, although this was much more consciously a factor in postwar Italy – often described as an arena of the Cold War in miniature. Both deployed strongly integrative ideologies – in Fianna Fáil's case Irish nationalism, in the Italian DC's case anti-Communism – backed up by the social and cultural weight of the Roman Catholic Church.

There are also notable differences. The DC's long and unbroken period in power contrasts with a healthier functioning of multi-party democracy in Ireland, and the degree and extent of party penetration of the state apparatus and of the state sector of the economy achieved in Italy – as well as the degree and nature of corruption and clientelism – far surpasses the Irish experience. In Ireland, the external environment – in the form of old antagonisms towards Great Britain and the question of partition – reinforced the nationalist incentive to vote for Fianna Fáil; in Italy, the external environment – in the form of the perceived Soviet menace and an effective American veto over the inclusion of the powerful Italian Communist Party in Italian governments – for a long time rendered the formation of any other government other than one led by the DC risky if not unthinkable. The degree of social and cultural homogeneity was far greater in Ireland; in Italy, vast regional differences both in the levels of economic development and in the development of the institutions of civil society were if anything reinforced by the effects of the long decades of DC rule. All of these differences obviously have to be taken into account in attempting to address the issues of party strategy, party culture, and the relationship of parties to social classes which were mentioned at the outset.

Nevertheless, it is surely the case that Donald Sassoon's description of the DC as 'a composite party: a coalition of traditional Catholics, young technocrats, populists and other disparate groups all united under the banner of Catholicism'[29] is not without resonance in the case of Fianna Fáil – especially if one was to replace 'Catholicism' with 'Catholic nationalism'. The lesson is that if one begins to deconstruct some of the categories used in comparative analysis, then it becomes clear that a centre-right formation such as Fianna Fáil is not without parallel. There are insights to be gained about its formative decades by looking at other parties in lesser developed countries and not only in a 'Third World' or post-colonial context.

In this chapter I have made explicit the assumptions behind my approach to the study I have applied to Fianna Fáil and have argued that the methodology adopted highlights the importance of paying attention to the constant interactions between party strategy, environment, and social classes. The rise of Fianna Fáil to a hegemonic role in Irish politics during the first two decades of its existence helped define the nature of party competition in Ireland. That rise was facilitated by key strategic choices made by competing social and political forces – choices which were themselves conditioned, never determined, by factors such as the class structure of Irish society, the partial and dependent nature of industrialisation, and the cultural triumph of integrative ideologies of nationalism and Catholicism. I have also argued that comparative analysis with similar – but of course never identical – political movements in Latin America and elsewhere in Europe can add to our understanding of the achievement, and crucially the limitations, of Fianna Fáil. Of course, Fianna Fáil has changed significantly since the early decades – as has every political party – but the early decades remain the period to which historians and political scientists seeking to understand the enigma of this hugely successful political party – at once uniquely Irish and yet with so many echoes and parallels elsewhere – will return. As Angelo Panebianco, seeking to challenge hitherto prevailing explanations for party change, puts it: 'no institution can...entirely escape from its past. No matter how extensive the renewal of leadership, change in the organisation, or "succession of ends" may be, many traces of the organisation's "genetic model" remain visible.'[30]

Notes

1   Quoted in *The Irish Times*, 27 May 1997.
2   R. Dunphy, *The Making of Fianna Fáil Power in Ireland, 1923–48* (Oxford, 1995).
3   A. Gramsci, *Selections from Prison Notebooks* (London, 1982), pp. 150–1.

4 B. Girvin, reviewing *The Making of Fianna Fáil Power in Ireland, 1923–48*, in *West European Politics*, January (1997), pp. 183–6.
5 *Ibid.*
6 R. English, ' "Paying no heed to public clamor": Irish republican solipsism in the 1930s', *Irish Historical Studies*, vol. xxviii, no. 112 (1993), pp. 426–39.
7 K. Allen, *Fianna Fáil and Irish Labour, 1926 to the Present* (London, 1997).
8 R. Dunphy, *The Making of Fianna Fáil*, pp. vii–viii.
9 K. von Beyme, *Political Parties in Western Democracies* (Aldershot, 1985), p. 3.
10 A. Ware, *Political Parties and Party Systems* (Oxford, 1996), p. 23.
11 M. Gallagher, M. Laver and P. Mair, *Representative Government in Modern Europe* (New York, 1995), pp. 181–208.
12 *Ibid.*, pp. 191–2.
13 R. Dunphy, *The Making of Fianna Fáil*, p. 130.
14 *Ibid.*, p. 226.
15 Undated letter to MacEntee, n.d. c.1945, UCDA MacEntee Papers P67/269.
16 Letter dated 11 February 1948, UCDA MacEntee Papers P67/298.
17 P. Kirby, 'Fianna Fáil and the Roots of Power', *The Irish Times*, 6 September 1995.
18 The quotation is from Paul Bew, reviewing my study of Fianna Fáil in *Irish Political Studies*, vol. 11 (1996), pp. 194–5.
19 P. Calvert, *The International Politics of Latin America* (Manchester, 1994), p. 130.
20 M. Canovan, *Populism* (London, 1981), p. 276.
21 B.C. Smith, *Understanding Third World Politics* (Basingstoke, 1996), pp. 202–3.
22 *Ibid.*
23 M. Canovan, *Populism*, pp. 261–2.
24 P. Bew, in *Irish Political Studies*, p. 194.
25 B.C. Smith, *Understanding Third World Politics*, pp. 202–3.
26 B. Girvin, in *Western European Politics*, p. 185.
27 S. Hazareesingh, *Political Traditions in Modern France* (Oxford, 1994), p. 273.
28 An Italian term denoting the wholesale colonisation of the public sector and of state agencies by political parties, which ruthlessly exploit the potential of the public sector in terms of awarding jobs and benefits to their supporters.
29 D. Sassoon, *Contemporary Italy: Economy, Society and Politics since 1945*, 2nd edn (Harlow, 1997), p. 7.
30 A. Panebianco, *Political Parties: Organization and Power* (Cambridge, 1988), p. 261.

5
Socialist Republicanism in Independent Ireland, 1922–49

Richard English

Irish socialist republicanism is important for three main reasons. First, the forces implicit within it, namely a nationalism drawing sustenance from ethnic and religious roots, and a socialism heavily influenced by the thought of Karl Marx, are arguably the most important in modern history. In independent Ireland in the period 1922–49 they can be studied in detail on a small canvas. Such an approach can yield greater precision than is possible at the level of abstraction or of global generalisation. Second, while socialist republicanism has never sustained a position of dominance within the Irish nationalist tradition, its adherents have wielded considerable influence over Irish republicanism and, through this, over the development of Irish politics. This has been true at several crucial moments in the twentieth century: the establishment of Fianna Fáil hegemony in independent Ireland during our period, the 1916 Easter Rising before it, and later during the emergence of the Northern Ireland civil rights movement during the 1960s. On none of these occasions have the ambitions of socialist republicans even neared completion. Indeed, it is more plausible to argue that in each case their activities rendered even less likely the achievement of their goals. But their influence has been significant in driving Irish politics in new directions, even though these directions have not been those which they intended. Third, the socialist republican tradition is important because it has produced some of Ireland's most talented dissident intellectuals. James Connolly is the most famous, but in the years 1922–49 Peadar O'Donnell, George Gilmore and Frank Ryan are examples of those who merit attention from historians keen to feel the rich texture of modern Irish intellectual life.

What was the socialist republican argument? Essentially it was this: that the struggle between the oppressed nation (Ireland) and the oppressor nation (England) is necessarily interwoven with the struggle within Ireland between those classes oppressed by capitalism and those which benefit from it. Why? England's control over Ireland – colonial or neo-colonial, depending on the period in question – is sustained with the purpose of economic exploitation. The means of such exploitation is the capitalist system and, therefore, while England controls Ireland it will ensure the sustenance of that system. Those classes which benefit from capitalism thus have an economic imperative to support some form of subservient political connection with England; those classes which suffer under capitalism (the working classes, urban and rural) have an equally compelling economic motivation to be separatists. So, the argument went, if you want to establish socialism in place of capitalism in Ireland then you have to end English rule, and if you want to end English rule then the only truly reliable forces on which to depend are those with an economic compulsion to see the struggle through: namely, the working class or as James Connolly put it '[the] incorruptible inheritors of the fight for freedom'.[1] The two causes, that of class and that of nation, are necessarily interwoven; or to borrow another epigram from Connolly: 'The cause of labour is the cause of Ireland, the cause of Ireland is the cause of labour. They cannot be dissevered.'[2]

According to socialist republicans, therefore, true republicanism was driven by an anti-capitalist dynamic. As the 1930s Republican Congress movement declared: 'a Republic of a united Ireland will never be achieved except through a struggle which uproots capitalism on its way.'[3] The attempt to build a republican campaign by uniting classes which had competing interests was bound to fail. As Peadar O'Donnell – early-twentieth-century IRA leader and irrepressible zealot for the socialist republican cause – put it in 1927: 'It is about time we heard the last of the childish talk of uniting all classes to free the country. Such balderdash is ages out of date.'[4] O'Donnellite politics differed vitally from those of Eamon de Valera, with the latter emphasising the importance of justice between all classes and the deliberate avoidance of a class programme. A telling recollection of O'Donnell's (about a conversation he had had with de Valera while the latter was President of the Republic of Ireland) captures the gulf between the two men, and also something of O'Donnell's charmingly impish style:

'You've got to remember, Dev', said O'Donnell '…that damn nearly a million Irish people left there while you were Taoiseach.'

'Ah, be fair now', de Valera replied '... if you had been in my place there'd have been emigration too.'

To which O'Donnell responded, 'Yes, Dev, that's quite true, if I had been in your place there'd have been a great many people who would have left the country. But they would not have been the same people!'[5]

To those of O'Donnell's inclination, de Valera was not a true republican because the forces he represented were capitalist forces and stood, therefore, across the true path to the republic. Thus, the world created by de Valera once Fianna Fáil came to power could not, in socialist republican terms at least, have been truly republican. Indeed, according to socialist republicanism, true republicans were those who recognised the class struggle lying at the heart of the campaign to free Ireland from English rule. Figures from the Irish nationalist Valhalla – whether Civil War anti-Treatyites, 1916 rebels, Fenians, Young Irelanders or United Irishmen – were claimed as having been true republicans because of their recognition of this class-struggling dynamic. This produced problems. When viewed from the less indulgent perspective of the historian, the claim of continuity between United Irishman Theobald Wolfe Tone, for example, and Civil War martyr Liam Mellows looks rather hollow. So, too, do claims that James Fintan Lalor, or the Fenians, lie in a cosy ancestral line waiting to be claimed by twentieth-century socialist republican descendants whose views are, in fact, in each case dramatically different.

The deployment of heroic figures for propagandist purpose is unsurprising. In this case it is also unconvincing. And the difficulties which the republican left faced in building an historical pedigree reflected the many obstacles it encountered in winning the minds of its would-be adherents. Peadar O'Donnell's engagingly poignant latter-day observation that 'I never was on the winning side in any damn thing ever I did'[6] underlines the fact that while the republican left has significantly affected political life in Ireland, the ambitious goals of its revolutionary project have never even neared completion. The career of pre-independence socialist republican, James Connolly, reflected the problems which his post-1922 disciples would experience. His participation in the 1916 Easter rebellion – a gesture sitting awkwardly with his earlier philosophy – marked the degree of desperation which he had come to feel during the First World War. Rather than representing the triumph of his socialist republican ideology, his 1916 involvement reflected the inadequacy of his central argument when set against the actual Irish people's attitudes and actions.[7] Connolly discovered the hollowness of his claim that the working class were the incorruptible inheritors of the fight for Irish freedom. But the socialist republicans who came after him failed to recognise this. Indeed, the revolution which 1916 inaugurated was interpreted by those socialist republicans who were to inhabit the emergent Irish state as having validated rather than refuted the logic of their political philosophy. Peadar O'Donnell's explanation of the emergence of the independence movement provides a telling example: 'It was as Connolly's Union that the Irish Transport and General Workers' Union gripped the country. The Irish political struggle came under a new light. Out of the ranks of workers and peasants the Irish Republican Army grew.'[8]

If there is a confusion here between membership of a class (the working class) and adherence to a political philosophy (socialist republicanism) then it is one which has proved surprisingly persistent. Leftist republicanism possesses a continuing allure for some observers. Indeed, there are still scholars who adhere to a Connollyite approach to Irish politics. W.K. Anderson has, for example, recently written:

> There is no doubt that Connolly's greatest and most enduring legacy to Irish socialism lies in his recognition that the struggle for national independence was an inseparable part of the struggle for socialism, and that by combining the forces of socialism and nationalism both would be strengthened.[9]

And there are still those who hold that the years of the Irish revolution offered the possibility of a radically oriented social revolution. Typically, here, one finds the argument that the rank and file with militant inclinations was betrayed by pusillanimous, conservative leadership during the revolution, and that had those on the radical left built the correct kind of revolutionary workers' party then things might have turned out very differently.[10] It is, of course, important to consider the full range of possibilities inherent within a set of historical circumstances. But recent research has demonstrated emphatically that anti-capitalist class conflict was not the central dynamic of the Irish revolution.[11] Indeed, the picture which emerges is complex rather than monocausal. The forces behind the revolution included: Gaelic and Catholic idealism; Catholic revanchism, assertiveness and sectarianism; specific educational influence; a number of possible socio-economic dynamics (by no means necessarily radical or relating to the working classes); the psychological and other direct rewards of revolutionary activity; and the absorption – from a variety of sources – of romantic nationalist assumptions. The striking feature about this list is how far many of these forces were capable of transcending class background. It is vital also to recognise the importance of variation, regional as well as individual, and any blanket explanation applied to the revolution as a whole is likely to smother the real nature of the conflict. Indeed, it is arguable that the best way of explaining the 1916–23 Irish revolution is to look at the particular ways in which individuals reached their decisions. Each of the forces mentioned above could operate differently upon individuals, and the interaction between these forces again varied from person to person among the revolutionaries.[12] But the politics of 'if only' remains an enduring phenomenon. Kieran Allen, for example, espouses that brand of Marxist argument which holds that if there were only a political alternative in Ireland 'that roots itself in the struggles of workers'[13] then the picture would be very different and that, in such circumstances, the Fianna Fáil hegemony which emerged between the 1920s and the 1940s would have been severely challenged.

The link between nationalism and economic interests need not have anything to do with socialism at all. Socialist republicans identified a key issue when they addressed the often overlooked question of the material basis to Irish nationalism. But they exaggerated the mechanical influence of economic interest and further assumed that pursuit of this road would lead to an anti-capitalist destination. Yet Fianna Fáil's success within Irish politics during the 1920s, 1930s and 1940s owed much to the party's ability to offer both nationalist symbolism and economic advantage to its supporters, and to weave deftly the two strands together. The problem is often one of misreading historical detail. One recent author has, for example, cited IRA leader Dan Breen as typifying a lower-class republicanism frustrated during the revolution.[14] But Breen's case in fact offers little comfort to socialist republicans. Peadar O'Donnell, who had an interest in presenting the most radical possible reading of the revolution, recalled Breen telling him that 'if in the 1919–21 period someone had talked of dividing up estates in his area, he would have had him shot'.[15] If the masses during the revolution were so radicalised then why did they vote for so conservative a party as Sinn Féin? The latter saw class struggle as disruptive of the national movement which they sought to foster between all classes, precisely the kind of approach which O'Donnell and his comrades abhorred.

Socialist republicans were at odds with the revolutionary experience which had produced the Free State. They assumed a connection between anti-capitalist social struggle and the national independence movement, and this left them as liable to marginalisation after 1922 as before it. Even within the republican movement itself independent Ireland's leftist republicans found themselves in the role of dissidents. The Irish republican movement in the 1922–49 period was overwhelmingly Catholic nationalist and was unwilling to make class struggle the defining feature of its campaign. The attempt to portray republicanism as a tradition which centred on class conflict was an attempt which rested on distortion.[16] Indeed, the foundation of socialist republican politics – their conception of the relationship between economics and nationalist commitment – was simplistic and doomed to disappointment. The relationship was more complex than the republican left's rather stringent ideology would allow, their crude economic determinism being too inflexible to respond to or account for the complex ways in which social dynamics moulded and drove attitudes towards nationalism. Middle-class ambition could direct people towards committed Irish republicanism every bit as effectively as could working-class instincts. And the working classes were not necessarily anti-capitalist anyway. This was true of Ulster unionist workers and also of those Irish nationalists in the working class who supported Fianna Fáil. The latter party's essentially conservative populism resonated more tunefully with working-class attitudes in independent Ireland than did socialist republican ideas.

Fianna Fáil's success is also illuminated by socialist republican failure in relation to the mechanisms of political power. De Valera's party scooped up authority by means of their pragmatic endorsement of majoritarian practice. Their rivals on the republican left preferred to remain in the extra-constitutional, purist margins. In independent Ireland reserves of strength were built up by those willing to build on the actual power of the state's structures, those willing to take political responsibility and to effect practical change. As one 1930s left-leaning republican, Sheila Humphreys, put it: 'There were a lot of people that thought [de Valera] was going slowly, but he was going somewhere – and they were happy with it.'[17] If their unwillingness to compromise with democratic structures weakened the republican left, so too their approach to other key aspects of Irish political life further impoverished their position. During the early part of the century the politics of land was vital to anyone aiming to determine the agenda of Irish nationalism. The socialist republican hero James Connolly had virtually nothing to say about the subject, and successors such as Peadar O'Donnell implicitly preferred, as had Connolly before them, a nationalisation strategy with no likelihood of success in rural Ireland. Religion also proved a problem. Socialist republicanism stumbled up against the charge of being unchristian, and therefore un-Irish, from Roman Catholic nationalists without any effective way of combating the allegation. The republican left failed significantly to address the ways in which religious attachment determined political allegiance in Ulster. The notion that religion was really a device manipulated by the bourgeoisie to ensure continuing working-class division is implausible to all but republican zealots: and even the occasional literary critic.[18] But the idea that the radicalisation of Ulster politics would result in an alliance between the Protestant and Catholic working classes persisted in republican circles. It was a misconception which reappeared disastrously in the minds of later civil rights enthusiasts during the 1960s. In fact, the Protestant working class proved less likely to respond to that particular crisis by allying with their Catholic fellow workers than by joining loyalist paramilitary organisations and killing them.

The socialist republican attitude to politics in Northern Ireland was revealing. Peadar O'Donnell, for example, recognised that economics played a part in determining Irish partition:

> Partition arises out of [the] uneven development of capitalism in Ireland; sentiment won't remove it. But there is an evenness in the exploitation of the working class and small farmers North and South, and common ground can be found there for the destruction of the state machines North and South. To fight against any such team-work a hectic effort is being made to raise religious antagonisms.[19]

Here, typically, O'Donnell mingled the acute observation that economic realities helped shape different politics in different parts of Ireland with a rigid adherence to socialist republican orthodoxy. The latter might have been shaken by the former, but not in O'Donnell's mind. This is something which later commentators have sometimes emulated by recognising that divergent economic development lay behind partition, but maintaining nonetheless a rigid all-Ireland orthodoxy. In the case of socialist republicans in the early years of the independent Irish state, such an approach involved an evasion of the crucial challenge which Ulster represented for republican thinking. As Henry Patterson observed in his excellent study of socialist republicans,

'On the issue of Protestant Ulster, social republicanism had failed utterly to escape the iron cage of nationalist assumptions'.[20]

The argument that class unity could transcend confessional allegiance, and the conviction that the tensions between Protestant workers and Protestant employers could produce a fissure which would allow republican radicalism to flourish, proved equally illusory in this period. Socialist republicans failed to grasp that economics might indeed help to determine the attitude of working-class Protestants in Ulster, but in a non-republican direction. Having acknowledged that different kinds of capitalist development in Ireland had helped to produce partition, and in particular noting the importance of Ulster's concentration of British-style urban workers, the republican left failed to make the leap necessary to realise that this compromised their own theory of Irish unity. If workers in Ulster were impelled by economic considerations to respond to the national question then, for the bulk of Protestants at least, it was a case of deciding that their economic interests were better served through embracing rather than rejecting the English connection. Peadar O'Donnell's suggestion that northern Protestants had no opposition to the IRA's existence but were simply impatient with the IRA's idea that they could achieve Irish unity through violence,[21] reflects his and for that matter his colleagues' spectacular misunderstanding of Ulster Protestant attitudes.

The European context of these years was one of considerable turbulence involving threats to liberal democracy from the right and from the left. The Irish republican left stressed the fascist threat posed in Ireland, and the 1930s witnessed significant conflict between socialist republicans and the Blueshirt movement, with the forces of the state caught somewhere between them. What are we to make of this contest? The most comprehensive scholarly treatment of the Blueshirts[22] reckons them to have been an aberration in Irish political history, albeit an influential one. They emerge as having had a complicated relationship with fascism: undoubted fascist traces existed, but the rank and file offset some of the more fascistic inclinations of sections of the leadership. Indeed, like the republican left, and like the republican movement from the 1916–23 Irish revolution, the Blueshirts in part represented a response to boredom and offered a powerful sense of identity. They were important in that they challenged prevalent political conceptions in the post-Treaty period, but those whose primary loyalty was to party (Fine Gael) rather than to shirt were the group which prevailed. On this reading the Blueshirt movement as a whole was at most partially fascist, its fascist strains being backed only by a minority.[23] Blueshirt intellectuals drew much sustenance from Catholic teaching: where Pope Pius XI's 1931 encyclical, *Quadragesimo Anno*, opposed (among other things) the socialist response to economic problems, the Irish republican left looked frequently to Marx.

As Patrick Byrne, one of the Joint Secretaries of the 1930s Republican Congress, argued with typical ebullience, he and his Congress colleagues 'never stopped talking about Marx, Lenin, Engels and the others. We openly discussed Marx, and wrote about him ... We all regularly quoted Marx.'[24] Other evidence supports this Marxist debt, one which combined with a range of Irish historical influences.[25] One feature of the approach exhibited by these people was their conviction that persistent explication of their Marxist-influenced world view would result in its widespread acceptance. William McMullen, who was involved in the Republican Congress, held 'the belief that the labour or socialist message only required to be repeated often enough, to find acceptance by an increasing number, until the stage was reached when it would hold sway and we would be on the way to the socialist millennium'.[26] Socialist republicans held that they were swimming with the historical tide. In the words of the Communist Party of Ireland in 1933, 'History is on the side of Ireland's struggle. The capitalist system is collapsing.'[27] They were confident that they had identified the essential radical instincts of the Irish masses. Consider Peadar O'Donnell's claim that, while he was merely trying to lead people in a direction which was 'natural' for them, his opponents were attempting to steer the masses away from their real interests and instincts. Referring to the 1931 campaign against the left in Ireland, he argued that 'the Irish bishops were playing havoc with the rural minds which would naturally, if left free to themselves, sympathise with those they were being incited to destroy'.[28]

But the conflict with the Blueshirts also points to other crucial aspects of socialist republicanism in these years. One concerns violence. The threat to free speech identified by the pro-treaty side in this period was indeed an important threat to liberty, and Blueshirt insistence on preserving the right to free speech deserves to be taken more seriously than the republican left allowed. In 1932 Frank Ryan and Peadar O'Donnell both took a strong stand opposing the right of their opponents to speak freely: Ryan argued : 'No matter what anyone said to the contrary, recent events showed that while they had fists, hands and boots to use, and guns if necessary, they would not allow free speech to traitors'. And in a similar vein O'Donnell: 'The policeman who put his head between Mr Cosgrave's head and the hands of angry

Irishmen might as well keep his head at home'.[29] It is worth recalling that ten years earlier, in 1922, Peadar O'Donnell had called for Labour leader Tom Johnson to be forcibly ejected from Ireland and such episodes should be considered when one contrasts the preservation of Irish parliamentary democracy during the early years of the new Irish state with socialist republican ambitions. Moreover, early twentieth-century socialist republican attitudes to violence were as confused as they were menacing. Formally eschewing the idea that physical force should be central to the republican struggle, they in practice endorsed vanguardist violence as a key republican method in 1916, between 1919 and 1923, and again during the early years of Irish independence.

For while socialist republicans perceived themselves as existing automatically on the side of international struggles against tyranny and oppression, the picture during these years was in fact far less clear than this self-image would suggest. The celebrated case of Frank Ryan points the way here. Ryan's career in fighting against fascism in the Spanish Civil War was ironically followed by a period when he was indulged by the Nazis, who embraced him with a view to his being of use to them during the Second World War. He had become a conspicuous figure, with his involvement in Spain having become so famous that it had been noted by observers as divergent as Eric Hobsbawm and the Pogues. And his case illustrates many of the key themes involved in socialist republicanism. A belligerent physical force republican, Ryan felt both that the national and social struggles within Ireland were intertwined, and also that Irish republicanism was at one with international campaigns against tyranny and in defence of freedom. His preparedness to consider a liaison role between the Nazis and de Valera hardly backs up the second of these convictions. And the logic of his being involved with the Second World War Germans at all owed nothing to class struggle and far more to what was a truly central dynamic of Irish republicanism: implacable and violent opposition to England. One recent author has mistakenly attributed to me the view that Ryan's presence in Germany during the Second World War 'clinches the argument of radical republicanism's inherent lack of progressiveness'.[30] In fact my argument was that this episode demonstrated not their inherent lack of progressiveness, but rather their lack of inherent progressiveness – a very different point indeed.[31] The Second World War indeed provided a powerful test of loyalties. The impressively austere George Gilmore, a key figure in the republican left during those years, was himself committedly anti-fascist; but his reading of Irish attitudes immediately prior to the Second World War hardly coincided with the view that Irish republicanism naturally formed part of an internationally progressive alliance: 'I saw a war coming and I knew that all the more republican elements in the Dáil or outside it would tend to back the Germans'.[32] Indeed, some Irish republicans were openly pro-German during the Second World War,[33] and some Irish communists also showed a certain sympathy towards Hitler during the conflict.[34]

The 1922–49 period witnessed the establishment of post-revolutionary Ireland and, as such, it presented huge problems for the socialist republican dissident minority. A sub-species of Catholic Irish nationalism – whatever their protestations to the contrary – they were hamstrung by the fact that the Irish revolution which they so cherished, and on which they built so much, had led to a state so inimical to their own ambitions. In founding a new state, the ex-revolutionaries who assumed power in the 1920s, 1930s and 1940s defined the authentic political community in terms of the – sometimes Anglophobic – pursuit of distinctiveness from Britain, and in terms of religious and cultural triumphalism and revanchism. Each of these components of the new state's identity undercut the republican left's preferred definition of the nation in terms of class. The essentially conservative nature of both pro- and anti-treaty cultures left socialist republicans in the position of a largely powerless cult. Millenarian revolutionaries adrift in the world of post-revolutionary mundanity, their critique of the world can be seen as hopelessly inadequate: their view of history, of the class–nation relationship, of the mechanisms of political power, of land, religion, political violence and Ulster unionism were all ill-focused or distorted. Their ideas were self-sustainingly circular – opponents were merely held to be either class enemies or people who had yet to be freed from some form of false consciousness – but they were also ultimately self-defeating when set against the realities of Irish experience.

Why then has the tradition persisted? It still has committed adherents at the end of a century which has provided ample evidence of its bankruptcy. In part, the continuing appeal of the tradition lies in the fact that it asks some very important questions. The republican left interrogated romantic nationalist assumptions with a sometimes surprising degree of iconoclasm: leading IRA socialist George Gilmore's reference to Patrick Pearse as a 'backward-looking romantic'[35] serves as a telling example. Rather than accepting nationalist sympathies as a political given, socialist republicans attempted to explain attitudes towards nationalism in relation to economic and social realities. 'As we have again and again pointed out' – argued Connolly in his classic *Labour in Irish History* – 'the Irish question is a social question.'[36] A certain glamour still attaches to the republican left of the post-Connolly period who adopted a similarly restless and inquiring approach. And if the argument has seemed to offer a way of unravelling the mystery of nationalism, then its exponents have often been charismatic, intelligent and compelling. Some have reached significant cult status: neither Peadar O'Donnell nor George Gilmore reached the standing of James Connolly, but both enjoyed guru status during the generative period of the Northern Ireland civil rights initiative in the 1960s. And, as noted, glamour attaches also to people such as the colourfully distinctive leftist republican Frank Ryan.

But a proper understanding of the roots of Irish republicanism in the twentieth century cannot be achieved through the essentially mono-causal explanation attempted by these economic determinists. Serious explanations must recognise the varying interaction of numerous forces: the tension in modern Ireland between Anglophobic marginality and unavoidable Anglocentrism; the persistence of meaningful sectarian self-definition on the part of both Catholic and Protestant communities; the impact of the economic background on the political ambitions of people of a variety of classes; the appeal of a simplifying, emotionally satisfying physical force politics (or anti-politics). Socialist republicans practised a form of solipsism: self effectively became the only thing really existent, with the world beyond the cult not being considered truly valid. This helps to explain its self-sustaining appeal, for it enabled adherents to dismiss the majority of Irish people as not being politically authentic. A particular image of the working class was defined as the true Irish nation, and awkward realities were dismissed from view. The early years of independent Ireland, however, saw parliamentary democracy and capitalism prove popular and durable, and saw the definition of national identity in Ireland remaining ethnic, religious and xenophobic rather than focused on class struggle.

This brings us back to the wider picture of twentieth-century historical experience. In Ireland as in so many other places, liberal democracy and capitalism have endured despite taking forms which even Francis Fukuyama would recognise to be profoundly imperfect. In Ireland the imperfections were compounded by the constriction and chauvinism involved in ethno-religious affiliation and in various kinds of xenophobic and intercommunal hostility. Socialist republicans might serve as exemplars here of a wider intellectual pattern, for their dissident dissatisfaction with the existing order demands a certain sympathy and their restless interrogation of common assumption commands respect. But, as so often with compelling dissident visionaries, their proposed alternative to an unsatisfactory present was distinctly unconvincing.

Notes

1   J. Connolly, *Collected Works i* (Dublin, 1987), p. 25.
2   J. Connolly, *Collected Works ii* (Dublin, 1988), p. 175.
3   *Republican Congress,* 5 May 1934.
4   *An Phoblacht,* 24 December 1927.
5   O'Donnell, speech in Belfast, 7 April 1984.
6   *Ibid.*
7   R. English, *Radicals and the Republic: Socialist Republicanism in the Irish Free State 1925–1937* (Oxford, 1994), pp. 15–29.
8   *Workers' Republic,* 26 August 1922.
9   W.K. Anderson, *James Connolly and the Irish Left* (Blackrock, 1994), p. 41.
10   For a recent example, see C. Kostick, *Revolution in Ireland: Popular Militancy 1917 to 1923* (London, 1996).
11   R. English, *Radicals and the Republic,* pp. 1–65; P. Hart, 'Class, Community and the Irish Republican Army in Cork 1917–1923', in P. O'Flanagan and C.G. Buttimer (eds), *Cork: History and Society – Interdisciplinary Essays on the History of an Irish County* (Dublin, 1993), p. 971; P. Hart, 'The Geography of Revolution in Ireland 1917–1923', *Past and Present,* vol. 155 (May 1997), p. 163; J. Augusteijn, *From Public Defiance to Guerrilla Warfare: The Experience of Ordinary Volunteers in the Irish War of Independence 1916–1921* (Blackrock, 1996), p. 360.
12   For the reconstruction of one leading IRA man's experience, see R. English, '"The Inborn Hate of Things English": Ernie O'Malley and the Irish Revolution 1916–1923', *Past and Present,* vol. 151 (May 1996), pp. 174–99.
13   K. Allen, *Fianna Fail and Irish Labour: 1926 to the Present* (London, 1997), p. 13.
14   C. Kostick, *Revolution,* pp. 31, 49.
15   J.P. McHugh, *A Study of An Phoblacht: Irish Republican Thought in the Post-Revolutionary Era 1923–37* (UCDA MA thesis, 1983), p. 34.
16   P. Walsh, *Irish Republicanism and Socialism: The Politics of the Republican Movement 1905 to 1994* (Belfast, 1994), pp. 35, 45.
17   Interview with the Sheila Humphries, Dublin, 26 February 1987.
18   D. Lloyd, *Anomalous States: Irish Writing and the Post-Colonial Moment* (Dublin, 1993), p. 19.
19   *An Phoblacht,* 7 February 1931.
20   H. Patterson, *The Politics of Illusion: A Political History of the IRA* (London, 1997), p. 75.
21   R. English, *Radicals and the Republic,* p. 138.
22   M. Cronin, *The Blueshirts and Irish Politics* (Dublin, 1997).
23   Cronin suggests the term 'potential para-fascist' to depict the group's simultaneous opposition to the autocracy of Fianna Fail and the IRA, and to the

prospect of a genuine fascism typified by Eoin O'Duffy (M. Cronin, *Blueshirts*, p. 65).

24 Patrick Byrne to the author, 12 April 1988.

25 R. English, 'Reflections on Republican Socialism in Ireland: Marxian Roots and Irish Historical Dynamics', *History of Political Thought*, vol. 17, no. 4 (Winter 1996), pp. 555–70.

26 W. McMullen, untitled ms. (n.d.), McMullen Papers, in the possession of Joyce and Terry McMullen, Belfast.

27 Cork Workers' Club, *The Irish Case for Communism* (Cork, n.d.), p. 39.

28 Peadar O'Donnell to Cape, 24 February 1933, Jonathan Cape Archives, University of Reading.

29 Both comments made at the same meeting in Dublin on 10 November 1932; quoted in R. English, *Radicals and the Republic*, p. 109.

30 E. Staunton, 'Frank Ryan and Collaboration: A Reassessment', *History Ireland*, vol. 5, no. 3 (Autumn 1997), p. 50.

31 R. English, *Radicals and the Republic*, pp. 245–51.

32 *Ibid.*, p. 273.

33 See, for example, *War News*, 22 March 1940.

34 M. Milotte, *Communism in Modern Ireland: The Pursuit of the Workers' Republic since 1916* (Dublin, 1984), pp. 183–5.

35 G. Gilmore, *The Irish Republican Congress* (Cork, 1978), p. iii.

36 J. Connolly, *Collected Works i*, p. 183.

6
The Unpopular Front: Catholic Revival and Irish Cultural Identity, 1932–48

Susannah Riordan

Cultural nationalism in independent Ireland has found few sympathetic historians. Exceptions include Margaret O'Callaghan's challenge to the F.S.L. Lyons 'battle of two civilisations' thesis, in her masters thesis 'Language and Religion: The Quest for Identity in the Irish Free State 1922–31' published in part in *Irish Historical Studies* in 1984 as 'Language, Nationality and Cultural Identity in the Irish Free State 1922–27: The *Irish Statesman* and the *Catholic Bulletin* Re-Appraised'. Here, O'Callaghan argues that 'Irish-Ireland' cannot be regarded as a fully-developed cultural bloc which set itself up in opposition to an equally coherent Anglo-Irish culture. The war of words over the rightful place of the Irish language and the Roman Catholic religion in the life of the nation were, rather, symptomatic of a society striving to give cultural expression to its newly won independence.[1] Similarly, Patrick Maume's critical biography of Daniel Corkery argues that his subject's criticisms of Synge and his fellow Anglo-Irish writers, and his ultimate rejection of all Irish writing in the English language as inauthentic, were based on an original creative impulse to promote the expression of a distinctive Irish voice.[2] In analysing the intellectual roots and the evolution of Corkery's ideas, Maume's work, like O'Callaghan's, suggests that the quest for intellectual forms of self-expression was not confined to Irish liberals.

On the whole, however, this theme has not been pursued into the period of Fianna Fáil's ascendancy, during which time the activities of the board constituted under the Censorship of Publications Act, 1929 became increasingly excessive. While it may be argued that literary censorship directly affected the lives of few citizens, it may also be seen as symptomatic of a society pursuing intellectual and cultural self-sufficiency with all the determination its government adopted in pursuit of the same goal in the political and economic arenas. Terence Brown's analysis is not untypical:

> The 1930s if anything deepened the conservatism of Irish life...To cultural and religious protection at their most draconian in the censorship policy was added the official encouragement of an essentially rural society dominated by the social, cultural and political will of the farmers and their offspring.[3]

The image of Ireland in the 1930s as being intellectually and culturally stagnant – and the impression that this was regarded as a misfortune only by a small group of disillusioned and alienated writers such as Sean O'Faoláin and Frank O'Connor – is one which there has been little attempt to reconsider. In particular, while Irish socialist and communist thought have been subjected to considerable analysis, there has been a tendency to dismiss the impact of another intellectual movement which offered a challenge both to the rhetoric of a Catholic and Gaelic nation and to the reality of a democratic and capitalist state – that of Vocationalism or Catholic social theory.

Following the publication of the papal encyclical *Quadragesimo Anno* in 1931, which reinforced and developed the teachings of the encyclical *Rerum Novarum* published forty years earlier, Catholic social theory became increasingly influential on the writing of Irish Catholic lay and clerical thinkers.[4] In the long term, and at its most optimistic, Catholic social theory was concerned with preventing class conflict by promoting the replacement of existing state structures with forms of representation based on vocational groupings. In the interim, Catholic social theorists aimed at minimising state control in several aspects of national life – for example, the economy, agriculture, social services – in the interest of a more popular and organic approach. The essential goal, in theoretical terms, was set out by Edward Sheehy in 1937, when he denounced the international organisation of 'popular fronts' and called instead for the formation of an 'unpopular front':

> a hypothetical body of men whose first consideration would be the well-being of society in all its parts, the liberty, not the licence, of the individual, the richness of that society, its homogeneity, integrity, that depend, to my mind, on the supplanting of a materialist code of values by a spiritual code.[5]

The main political influence of vocationalism may be found in the social provisions of the 1937 Constitution, and in the means of election to the Senate. In addition, Catholic social theory may be seen as intruding twice on the political history of the Irish Free State: once by its partial adoption by the Fine Gael party and Blueshirt movement – in differing degrees of enthusiasm and indeed understanding – and for the second time with the presentation and out-of-hand rejection of the Report of the Commission on Vocational Organisation in 1943. In very broad terms, therefore, the popular historical interpretation of the movement has been that it was fascistically inclined, ultimately ineffectual and essentially the mental plaything of group of a small academic and clerical elite.

The purpose of this chapter is twofold. Firstly, it seeks to suggest that the history of Irish Catholic social theory is worthy of a more extensive analysis both in terms of its intellectual content and its popular appeal. In part, this has already begun with the pioneering work of J.J. Lee. He argues that the negative reaction of civil servants to the Report of the Commission on Vocational Reorganisation might be interpreted as representing an institutional lack of intellectual initiative rather than self-evident craziness on the part of the drafters, and so draws attention to the desirability of reexamining Catholic social theory from this perspective.[6] Discreet studies, such as Lee's own work on the Commission, and Diarmaid Ferriter's unpublished dissertation ' "A Peculiar People in Their Own Land": Catholic Social Theory and the Plight of Rural Ireland', while supporting the view that ultimately vocationalism had little impact on social policy, also draw attention to the degree to which the language of Catholic social theory permeated political and social discourse.[7] This chapter seeks to pursue Catholic social theory into the realm of cultural discourse and, more specifically, into the debate over censorship and the broader issue of Irish literature in the English language. Its second purpose: to draw attention to a hitherto unrecognised factor in the cultural debate of the period; that is to say, the contribution of a loose phalanx of thinkers influenced by Roman Catholic social theory. The neglect of this aspect of the issue is in part due, it would appear, to the failure to recognise the usefulness of what Brian Kennedy rightly describes as 'an underutilised source of facts, observation and commentaries'.[8] That is, those cultural journals which followed a middle path between the rabid paranoia of the *Catholic Bulletin* and the patient and persistent reasonableness of *The Irish Statesman* and *The Bell*.

Such journals constitute the main source for this chapter. They include the *Irish Ecclesiastical Record*, written mainly by and for priests; the two Jesuit publications *Studies*, which was academic in tone, and the *Irish Monthly*, a somewhat more mainstream literary periodical; and the *Irish Rosary* which, while tending towards an obsession with Masonic influences and a vitriolic style reminiscent of the *Catholic Bulletin*, regarded itself as leading a Catholic cultural crusade under the slogan 'There's Reason in *The Rosary'*. These journals had in common a self-conscious Catholic intellectualism which made them the main medium for contributors who assumed the desirability of encouraging the independent nation's development in accordance with Catholic social theory and wished to publicise their thoughts on putting that goal into practice. These included prominent theorists, such as Michael Tierney and the Rev. E.J. Coyne, and men of letters, such as Riobárd O Faracháin and Aodh de Blacam, as well as less well-known clerics, academics and members of the wider intellectual community.

The articles discussed in this chapter are for the most part from the decade 1932 to 1942 and are treated thematically rather than chronologically. It is therefore necessary to state that there was no significant development of the ideas discussed between those dates. Though reference has been made to cultural 'debate', the term is slightly misleading insofar as it was rare for either the Catholic social theorists on one hand, or contributors to the letters page of *The Irish Times* or *The Bell* on the other, to engage each other's arguments directly. Both tended to generalise, and indeed to parody positions which they wished to undermine. Between 1936 and 1938 the short-lived journal *Ireland To-day* published articles on Irish culture which reflected both Catholic social theory and a more liberal agenda, but this experiment was not repeated. Contributors to the journals which are discussed here frequently give the impression that there was no opposition to their views worth acknowledging and that they are merely giving their opinion on the best means to achieve a goal on which the Irish nation had agreed. This chapter is therefore largely impressionistic, reflecting the degree to which the contribution of Catholic social theory to Irish cultural identity was fragmented, individualistic and purely theoretical.

In the early 1930s, however, the mood of many theorists was buoyant, suggesting an assumption that the teachings of *Quadragesimo Anno* were not merely ideals but predictions of imminent world change. The existing social systems, capitalism and communism, which were based on a materialist ethic which regarded the distribution of wealth as the prime objective of society, were seen as being not merely practically redundant but intellectually outdated. Catholic social theory contained a strong element of nostalgic mediaevalism – vocational representation was intended to be an approximation of the guild system. One parish priest explained that world history had been essentially on the wrong track since the Reformation – which began the replacement of spiritual with materialist values – and denounced the Whig interpretation of history for which 'the whole story of man-kind had been a Jacob's ladder leading to that noblest of ages – the age of material prosperity and mechanical invention ... It was pure determinism and denial of free will but it was in perfect harmony with the tendencies of the age.'[9] As the Second World War appeared to give ample evidence of the failure of materialist social systems, the subject was approached with renewed vigour. In 1941, John Marcus O'Sullivan, the former Cumann na nGaedheal Minister for Education, pointed out that capitalism and communism both 'reject the spiritual factor in human life and worship the same gods – economic values are supreme. To us they stand for – though not in equal degree – a gravely distorted and false view of life and human nature. Thus ideology gives way to ideology, but humanity wanders further into the desert: mirages are no safe guides.'[10]

Such articles, it should be noted, were written from the perspective of analysing unsophisticated, if superficially attractive, foreign heresies rather than that of dissecting the Irish body politic. The tone of intellectual superiority may be seen as a propagandist rhetorical device, but the treatment of erroneous ideologies is preventative, not diagnostic. The assumption that Catholic Ireland had not significantly deviated from pre-Reformation spirituality was an underlying feature of all the writings considered here, but its most prolific and enthusiastic adherent was James Devane. In a symposium in the *Irish Rosary* in 1941 on the topic of Ireland's failure to put catholic social theory into practice – a rare occasion of deviation from that journal's apparent policy of national self-congratulation – Devane attempted to cheer up the readers. He argued:

> Nor has our failure been near so great as the failure of our common civilisation in Europe. Our Civil War was but a children's squabble compared with the anarchy in Spain and Russia. There is class jealousy here but it is not worth mentioning compared with the class war in liberal Europe. There is no gross inequality of wealth here compared with that which existed in plutocratic Britain and America. There is no worship of wealth here like that so common in Anglo-American society. At the heart and in the depths our people are sound.[11]

In the following year he set out the reasons for his satisfaction:

> Here in Eire you have a nation that is different from [other
> Christian] states. You have a state that is personified in a religion,
> and a religion that is incarnate in a people; a society that with its
> superficial and inessential glosses like steam engines, electric lights,
> motor cars and photographs, is a recussitation of a mediaeval
> polity; more catholic than many a mediaeval polity for there is no
> conflict between Church and State, no Thomas à Becket, no
> Frederick Barbarossa; a people that is more Catholic than Rome of
> the Popes or the Papal states for many hundreds of years; a society
> that is judged by every test, whether of public profession, ceremo-
> nial or ritual, or these formidable statistics of pilgrimages, retreats,
> confraternities and daily offices is the most Catholic country in the
> world.[12]

As Devane's reference to a common European civilisation indicates,
such reflections were not intended merely to bolster a feeling of complacency and self-righteousness in neutral and isolated Ireland as it
watched the outside world suffer the inevitable consequences of its
materialist impulses. On the contrary, they were intended to reassure
those who might have doubts about Ireland's readiness to take up the
challenge to which the Catholic press frequently referred. That was, in
the words of the editor of the *School and College Yearbook* – the professional journal of the Association of Secondary Teachers, Ireland, which
was deeply influenced by Catholic social theory – Ireland's future role
as 'a force in the rejuvenation and re-Christianization of a post-war
Europe.'[13] This preoccupation on the part of the Catholic press was
noted by Conor Cruise O'Brien in 1945:

> In this context Ireland's importance is clear; she contains the prin-
> cipal deposits of faith from which the great powers may be influ-
> enced towards catholicism, or at least away from Materialism ... We
> cannot judge the Catholic Press correctly unless we keep the
> 'theopolitical' background in mind. We must think of these papers
> as weapons in a world battle, the latest phase of the counter-refor-
> mation and not as 'reflections of Irish Catholic opinion' which they
> certainly are not.[14]

However, from 1932, when contributors to the Catholic press began
to announce the inevitability of social change, to the immediate

postwar period there was one aspect of Irish spirituality about which contributors were far from complacent. This was the artistic expression of Irish Catholicism and in particular Ireland's contribution to Catholic literature. After all, whereas theorists required the cooperation of state institutions to bring about social and economic reorganisation, they could hope to influence producers and consumers of art and literature directly. The main target of the Catholic critics was literary realism, which they portrayed as the product of social materialism with all its intellectual errors. Their main aims were the development of an alternative literature which reflected Catholic spirituality in a way that was both authentic and artistically excellent, and the creation of a reading public which appreciated and demanded such literature.

In the early 1930s some contributors portrayed these developments as an automatic result of the social change which was on the verge of being realised. One writer in the *Irish Monthly* in 1932 noted that there was 'abundant evidence that a fundamental change in our civilisation is imminent' and predicted that this would result in the abandonment of 'the bestiality of the so-called realist and pseudo-psychological in literature and art, the cruder sensationalism of the literature of the Gertrude Stein and James Joyce school and the grosser productions of Epstein in art' and return to writings and art infused with Catholic spirituality. In short, there would be 'a second and greater Renaissance'.[15] Similarly, the editor of *Comhthrom Feinne*, the magazine of the Students Representative Council at University College Dublin, which reflected the vogue of Catholic social theory and its practical expression, Catholic Action, among students, predicted that 1932 would be a year of crucial importance on a global scale, adding, 'being optimists, let us hope for another Renaissance'.[16]

This appears to raise an obvious question: if great art was a natural by-product of Catholic spirituality, why had Ireland failed to produce a significant artistic or intellectual expression of her near-pristine faith? The problem was apparent to the theorists who offered historical explanations for it but were nonetheless concerned. Devane, that stalwart defender of the soundness of the Irish Catholic heart, was less sanguine about the mind:

> When ... I wander through this old Irish land, with fifteen hundred years of Christian civilisation behind it, and find little music, art or letters made by the Catholic mind, then do I feel that something is lacking, that I am looking at a beautiful girl with the form and carriage of a woman and the mind of a child.[17]

Some years previously, in 1937, the editor of *The Irish Rosary* had complained that

> the predominant difficulty of a cultural magazine which aims to be a witness to the Truth arises from the very nature of such a magazine – the setting forth of the reasons and rightness of things when people lack the education and culture that seek for the reason and rightness of things and are interested only in sentiment and emotions about things.[18]

A symposium in *Studies* in 1938 considered the advisability of including scholastic philosophy in the school curriculum in order to address the perceived intellectual underdevelopment of Irish Catholics. The proposer, Arthur Little S.J., claimed of Irish children that 'they hold the faith on authority that is in fact valid, but they lack a grasp of those natural truths that prove the reasonableness of accepting that authority.' They were consequently ill-equipped to answer attacks on their religion which were based on reason. Reaction was varied. The Bishop of Galway believed that children got as much of the substance of Christian philosophy as they could absorb. He opposed exposing them to metaphysics 'with all the difficulties and objections, and all the crazy errors that have ever been pronounced'. However, Rev. Edward Leen and Rev. Father James (Professors of Philosophy at the Holy Ghost Father's Missionary College Kimmage Manor and University College Cork, respectively) thoroughly approved of the motion, the latter adding, 'no one is more vividly conscious, I hope, than I am of the exalted spiritual destiny of our country. Ireland should not only live the Faith but should also find a worthy intellectual expression of it.'[19]

The necessity for educating the Irish people to fulfil their spiritual destiny was a frequent topic of discussion in the periodicals. It appears also to have been, perhaps belatedly, recognised by teachers' organisations, judging by the regularity with which references to this subject appeared in their publications. The Irish National Teachers' Organisation argued in their 1947 pamphlet, *A Plan for Education*, for the teaching of philosophy in secondary schools since

> in this age of conflicting social and economic theories, when the very basis of our civilisation – the Christian tradition and the philosophy which grew out of it – is being attacked by strange heresies, it is essential that our young people should be given a grasp of unchanging philosophical principles.[20]

Greater moral education 'would help to eliminate class hostility by a transfer of the emphasis from the material to the spiritual' and 'Ireland could again be a beacon to a world that had lost its way... Ireland could again give an example to the world of a right way of living, the Christian way, the Irish way.'[21] Michael Tierney and Rev. E.J. Coyne were contributors to the *School and College Yearbook*. Coyne warned that

> the social reorganisation of which we talk so much will, I fear, never be realised until educationists the world over refuse to be dominated by the *zeitgeist* and swept along in the current of 'progress' and 'achievement' and insist, on the contrary, that education should give the key-note to social change, not social change to education.[22]

Educational change was required, not merely for future social advances, but, as Little had argued, in order to counter present dangers to Irish Catholic culture. One of the most pressing dangers was what *A Plan for Education* described as 'the agents of informal education' – the media – which were 'developing a new culture, generally alien and debased, which threatens to engulf our civilisation and culture and almost to introduce a new morality.'[23] Catholic social theorists had long been, in their way, as wary of and as preoccupied by, the effects of alien cultural influences as any bishop who ever denounced 'the dance hall, the bad book, the indecent paper, the motion picture, the immodest fashion in female dress – all of which tend to destroy the virtues characteristic of our race.'[24] There were significant differences however. In the first place, the theorists tended to portray the attraction and the danger of such influences as being intellectual rather than carnal. In 1932, the Rev. James MacLoughlin had warned that

> if our people are now, as a result of the greater diffusion of education, becoming intellectually more stimulated and more receptive of new ideas, it would be a tragedy to allow the wrong people to be their teachers. It is the Church that has moulded European thought and the European culture in which we share. And it is only the Church (though not necessarily only the clergy) which can supply the teaching in ethics, social matters and history by which we can hold on to that culture.[25]

Five years later, Cornelius Lucey, the future bishop of Cork noted that there was 'something seductive about the written word. Those who

read it come almost unconsciously to make its ideas their own...
Hence whoever can control the reading matter in a community can
control, too, the minds and emotions of the citizens.'[26]

In Ireland, the threat posed by the literary expression of undesirable
ideas was particularly pressing. In the first place, Ireland lacked an
orthodox Roman Catholic national literature. There was, therefore, little alternative to reading matter which reflected foreign conditions.
That is, the conditions of a materialist, secular world and, due to historical connections, a common language and geographical proximity,
this meant ultimately the literature of the Anglo-American liberal-
democratic culture.[27] Secondly, while an increasing number of Irish
writers who were Catholic born and educated – Sean O'Faoláin and
Frank O'Connor being obvious examples – were coming to prominence, they were by no means providing an acceptable intellectual
expression of the Catholic faith. To begin with, their works were falling
foul of the literary censors, and were thus, according to the wording of
the Censorship Act, defined as being 'in...general tendency indecent
or obscene'.

The main significance of literary censorship in this context is the
extent to which it served to divide the liberal and the Catholic intelligentsia, that is individuals who were equally concerned with the development of a national literature, however their views on the social
duties of the author might conflict. Among the opposition, there
appears to have been a continuation of the attitude taken by Yeats,
whose remark that 'every educated man in Ireland hates the Bill'[28] suggests that his definition of an educated man was one who hated the
Bill. When, as editor of *The Bell*, Sean O'Faoláin took over leadership of
the anti-censorship cause, he attempted a reassuring redirection of the
campaign: 'In theory the thing is sound. (We are all in favour of
Censorship in theory and in principle.) It is nationalist by definition. It
was imposed on us "democratically". In practice it has become a silly
shameful joke.'[29] However, the degree of support for this approach is
questionable. In 1945, an article in *The Bell* which pointed out that
while the Irish practice was to be deplored there was an argument for a
sensible and well-regulated censorship called down the wrath of Sean
O'Casey and George Bernard Shaw, among others, in a symposium the
following month.[30]

On the other hand, while there is little direct evidence that individuals among the contributors to the Catholic journals were uneasy
about the board's prohibitions, it is not unfair to suggest that a ratio-
nal defence of some specific cases would have been a considerable

challenge. However, censorship was an issue rather like the ban on divorce or the revival of the Irish language: it may have had little impact on the average member of the public, but it was a mistake to appear publicly to have anything but absolute enthusiasm for it.

This was reflected in responses to the Senate motion proposed on 18 November 1942 by Senator Sir John Keane 'that in the opinion of Seanad Eireann, the Censorship of Publications Board...has ceased to retain public confidence and that steps should be taken by the minister to reconstitute the Board'.[31] In the first place, the senators themselves showed almost uniform hostility. When Keane proposed to read from banned works Senator William Magennis, the chairman of the Board, successfully moved that the passages quoted from not be recorded since 'otherwise we will have some of the vilest obscenity on our records, and the Official Reports can be bought for only a few pence.'[32] The debate lasted four days due to the number of senators who wished to speak against the motion. Only one speaker other than Keane appeared to favour liberalisation of the Board's practices and even the seconder of the motion made it clear that he opposed the motion and was merely facilitating debate. Keane was prevented from withdrawing his motion so that the matter could go to a division.

A similar desire to be seen to be on the respectable side of the debate was to be exposed in press coverage of the event. The editorials of both the *Irish Press* and the *Leader* expressed reservations about the practices of the Board, yet both appeared reluctant to be seen to side with banned writers. The *Irish Press* assured its readers that the Board was composed of 'men of education who have read widely. When four such men agree that a book should be prohibited it can be taken that there are good reasons for the prohibition.'[33] The *Leader*, which dedicated a long editorial to criticising the practices of the Board and recommending the establishment of an Appeal Board, nonetheless attacked its opponents as 'the strongly *seoinín* elements who hate everything here that has not a counterpart in England' and the 'mainly self-interested groups of pseudo-intellectuals'.[34]

The idea that the activities of the censorship board accurately reflected Irish mores, and that those who opposed them were somehow un-Irish had been a recurrent theme in the Senate debate. For example, Senator Kehoe argued that

> the moral standards in the Ireland of today and in the Ireland of the past, whether people like it or not, are based on one particular standard, that is the religion we profess...We hear about authors of

repute. Authors of repute from what point of view? From the point of view of world standards, which, mark you, are not the standards of Ireland.[35]

The editorials of the *Cork Examiner* and the *Irish Times* drew attention to the inconsistency of a position which insisted that Irish morals were superior to those of other peoples and yet suggested that they needed legal protection. The *Cork Examiner* suggested that it would be better 'to strengthen the moral fibre of the people, rather than go on persuading them that they are better as a race and nation than their neighbours and that contact with the outside world is undesirable'.[36] More brutally, the *Irish Times* asked 'whether the people of Ireland are genuinely the honest, high-minded, demi-angels of tradition, or debased troglodytes who must be driven willy-nilly into decency by boards?'[37]

This was a question which contributors to the Catholic cultural journals occasionally attempted to answer, largely through the assertion that censorship was not intended to deprive prurient citizens of their favoured reading matter but to protect decent Irish people from accidental exposure to moral danger. Stephen Brown S.J., founder of the Central Catholic Library, and a regular contributor to *An Leabharlann*, the professional journal of Irish librarians, on the subject of immoral literature, explained that the purpose of censorship was to give 'salutary warning' to 'the ordinary citizen who … is not looking for obscenity'.[38] Aodh de Blacam elaborated: Irish readers required to be warned against the content of certain books because of the 'huge market for vile writing in a land nearby'. By virtue of their large base sale abroad, certain books recommended themselves to the Irish public which, on their own merits, would never be read. He concluded, 'I would rely on public opinion, if it were Irish public opinion, to defend us, but why should we allow Irish public opinion to be overwhelmed by foreign laxity?'[39]

Irish writers whose works had been banned, or were otherwise regarded as objectionable, were frequently portrayed in the Catholic press as enemies of the Irish way of life. Whereas protestant writers could be dismissed as irrelevant to the nation and even treated as sincere if misguided, Catholic born writers who fell into these categories were regarded as being traitors. A correspondent in the *Irish Press* neatly summed up the position in response to the foundation of the Irish Academy of Letters, a body widely, and with some justification, regarded as being primarily concerned with the abolition of censorship. It was a title under which 'a few renegades to their race and religion join hands with off-shoots of the former Alien Ascendancy (who may be in good faith) in getting up a cry of accusing us [Irish catholics] of being enemies of freedom'.[40]

To some vocationalists, these writers were a significant social problem in themselves and a detraction from Ireland's position in world Catholicism. Their proliferation needed to be explained and prevented from reoccurring. This was one aspect of the concerns expressed about the adequacy of Irish education. Speaking at Blackrock College Union, John Charles McQuaid gave prominence to the problem when he listed the fears of the teacher 'lest any of ours be false to the graces of his education in the sins of social laziness; lest anyone later be found among the self-constituted intelligentsia of pagan movements, literary and artistic; lest any, being tricked by a catch-cry, become the tool of unquiet agitators'.[41] Nor was McQuaid alone in ranking pagan literature amongst the worse social ills. Writing to congratulate de Valera on his new constitution Edward Cahill, the Jesuit intellectual, expressed regret that no provision had been made for compulsory denominationalism in education. The reason why he considered this omission ill-advised was that 'there is a very simple phenomenon which "strikes one in the eye" and needs explanation. This is the fact that *Catholic* Ireland of the 20th century has given and still gives the world a seemingly endless stream of apostate and semi-apostate writers...Our *non-denominalisation* is I believe somewhere very near the root cause.'[42]

Expressions of the distaste for these writers illustrate the point that battle was being joined for the minds, as well as the hearts, of catholic readers. In 1932, the year in which the Irish Academy of Letters was founded, a correspondent in the *Irish Rosary* assured readers that the Academicians' works 'are really belated additions to a school of thought which is becoming discredited in high intellectual circles, who take more account of the value of the thought expressed than of the beauty of the style misapplied to the exposition of what is corrupt and disgusting.'[43] The *Irish Rosary's* editor also dismissed the Academy: 'Irish letters cannot be represented by merely dirty books, by clever blasphemies or by borrowed Russian realism.'[44] In 1935 Fr. M.F. Gaffney protested against the first Irish production of O'Casey's *The Silver Tassie*:

Dublin is to have an opportunity of drinking deep from The Silver Tassie. But I think Dublin is a little too wise in 1935 to put its lips to a cup that may possibly have been filled from a sewer...It is a vigorous medley of lust and hatred and vulgarity...If this dramatic dose turns out to be too bitter and a revulsion takes place, the Abbey Theatre will not be in the same position as it was when Mr Yeats called in the policemen to quell the Playboy troubles before we were born. For … the Abbey theatre has now to reckon with a vigorous intellectual force which is not alien to the authentic spirit of the Irish people.[45]

Despite the tone of these contributions, the writers were not primarily concerned with ferreting out such obscene or indecent publications as had not been drawn to the attention of the censors, but with warning the faithful against the less obvious perils of all works which propagandised or reflected non-catholic ideals. Works from deliberate anti-catholic propaganda, through Shaw and Freud to discourses on diverse subjects including fortune-telling and cubism, might appear harmless or neutral to the layperson but were contrary to Catholic teaching and thus tending to undermine faith and morals. Undiscriminating readers whose experience lay for the greater part with works which were not written from an explicitly orthodox perspective were in danger since, in the words of Stephen Brown:

at the very least such readers will drink in notions of the conduct of life and of morals wholly at variance with Christianity or subtle propaganda for one or other of the -isms and -ologies which are contending for the mastery of men's minds. In most of what he reads the supernatural order is ignored, when belief in it is not sneered at as a survival of by-gone superstition, or again some false philosophy is assumed or some view of history is taken for granted.[46]

The particular culpability of apostate Irish writers was that they were exposing their readers to such dangers, while their birth and education made it impossible for them to plead that they were ignorant of the consequences. Another Jesuit, Patrick J. Gannon, took a conciliatory stance in one article, attempting to recall Irish writers to their duty:

It seems fairly clear that already a chasm, both wide and deep, has been dug between the Church and a section of our 'Intelligensia', to use a convenient but somewhat vague term; and the chasm is widening and deepening. For the moment I am not concerned with the question of responsibility but of fact, and the fact is tragic enough to call for serious investigation. I propose in this article to give some personal reflections which may help to clear the air

a little. For though there are some fundamental differences of outlook which cannot be easily reconciled, the growing alienation
arises still more from mutual misunderstanding.

Gannon defended the Catholic Church against the accusation of being
hostile to art and literature and, although he believed censorship was
justified by the teaching of Christ – 'woe to that man by whom the
scandal cometh!' – he continued: 'even for those "advanced", "progressive", "enlightened" minds which are too "emancipated" to regard
these words as divine, they must surely enunciate a truth that on social
grounds alone must be maintained. It is a council of social prudence to
protect the people, as far as may be, from the corrosive influence of
corrupt literature.' Gannon did not dispute the talents of those whom
he addressed, but felt that 'altogether it is a sorry business to see
so many men of undoubted gifts employing these to misdirect their
fellow-men':

> Surely our Catholic literati are held to a serious responsibility…
> Least of all men can be ignorant of the influence of the written
> word. Life and death are in the power of the tongue, still more in
> the power of the pen – life and death for individuals, nations, whole
> cultures. Even if they grow deaf to the message of the Heavens
> which proclaim the glory of God, they must feel obligations to
> mankind, and therefore, are bound to weigh well every word they
> hammer out on their typewriters.[47]

The more sophisticated Catholic social critics went beyond pointing
out the failings of the practising Catholic literati and attempted to set
down guidelines for the development of a genuinely Catholic national
literature. This was often outlined in purely negative terms; that is to
say, certain forms or styles of writing would be held up as an example
of what was manifestly *not* in accordance with such a philosophy. It is,
however, possible to pick out some features which were considered
essential. Firstly, and unsurprisingly, a degree of restraint was required.
According to Louis Walsh, 'we Catholics must make up our minds to
take our stand either with St. Paul or the World. Anybody who knows
anything about life knows that morality cannot be preserved if there
are to be no reserves and if everybody is to be free to discuss certain
aspects of Life and Sin with the freedom that your modern novelist and playwright demand. Modesty is as necessary a virtue as ever
it was.'[48] Yet it was not suggested that Catholic literature must be

completely sanitised. The fundamental difference between the Catholic writer and the writers of the materialist world was not the choice of subject matter but the treatment. It was accepted that if novels were to present a true picture of life they could not be without depictions of evil and crime. What mattered was that the reader should not be attracted by the evil that he or she was exposed to but should be uplifted and fortified against temptation.

The fatalistic tendency of some contemporary literature was particularly frowned on. Stephen Brown suggested that

> evil may be portrayed if that is done with high seriousness and in a Christian spirit, free from all connivance or complicity, and done, not in the tone of the preacher, still less in the spirit of the Pharisee, for of his erring fellow-mortal every man must say, 'There go I but for the grace of God.' At the same time moral evil is for the Christian writer not merely a social disease, a personal weakness or error; it is *sin* and must be recognised as such.[49]

Gannon argued that art and literature were 'achievements of the spirit, not of the body or the senses…They must spiritualise us, or they are renegades to their true allegiance; false to their primary loyalty.'[50] All these observations were reflected in Aodh de Blacam's projected outline of 'a truly great national literature' in 1935. This must consist of

1. Great, central, simple themes…
2. A treatment consistent with our own culture [using]…the full range of Catholic language, imagery, custom…in themes that are drawn from Catholic life: otherwise the treatment will be out of proportion, and almost certainly false.
3. Language must be subservient to thought and feeling, direct not allusive. And finally
4. There must be orthodoxy in moral standards; not for the sake of the appeal to an orthodox people, but because orthodoxy is a radical condition of greatness in every branch of art everywhere.[51]

Such discussions remained largely hypothetical, as the only Irish writers who appeared to satisfy Catholic standards were either dead or wrote in Irish. The *Irish Rosary*'s editor asked, 'now if there is to be an academy of Irish letters how can you blend George Bernard Shaw with a Catholic poet like Padraic O Conaire? How can you compare Liam O'Flaherty with the sacred ghostly Spirit of Joseph Plunkett?'[52]

Riobárd O Faracháin considered Plunkett to be in many ways Ireland's greatest loss. His poetry were works of

> Catholicism, not as a routine, not as the simple faith of the loyal poor, not the purblind Catholicism that puts its church in one pigeonhole, and its politics, its art, its economic theory each in its own; but a Catholicism acknowledged and served by intellect, heart and will; a faith that was an outlook, an outlook with the intensity of a vision, a vision that was a perennial inspiration.

Plunkett, Pearse and MacDonagh had briefly 'stayed the domination of false thought' and 'I say "stayed" for challenged it must be, and overcome; for the antinomies of a country which can awe the world with the sublimity of the Eucharistic Congress and nauseate it with "Ulysses" are as petrol and creeping flame, and the flame it is that consumes. But the flame has been creeping too long, and too often the timid have blown it back. We must make it a racing fire.'[53]

O Faracháin's main point, however, was to draw attention to the paucity of Irish catholic writing which made the loss of these poets a particular tragedy. However, a constant theme of such articles was a reassurance that Ireland was not without literary forbears, since she shared in a common European culture and her connections with that Catholic tradition must be embraced. It may be suggested that the assertion of an association with that tradition was a manifestation of an Irish cultural inferiority complex, or simply an attempt to annex a piece of intellectual high ground from which to launch further attacks on British culture and on the Irish writers who wrote for the British market. After all, according to Devane, 'the Christian in Ireland and in Europe is not the abnormal man. He is the normal man. He is in the classic line of European and of Irish culture and tradition. The Romantics are the new men – the racialists, the Marxists, asiatics, surrealists, cubists, the gaga men who ask us to accept their myths for truth.'[54]

Frequent allusion was made in the pages of *The Irish Rosary*, *The Irish Monthly*, and *The Irish Ecclesiastical Record* to the Catholic intellectuals and writers of other countries – Jacques Maritain and G.K. Chesterton being particular favourites. Controversy arose over whether Shakespeare was a Catholic or not. The majority who contributed to the debate in these journals agreed that his credentials were valid. Aodh de Blacam offered reassurance to those who might think 'that there is a dreadful air of evil in some of the plays, and that this is not the work of a

Catholic. The answer is, that Shakespeare was, indeed, dreadfully familiar with sin, but that he never forgot that it was sin. The plays show us the darkest things in life, and always the poet stresses the moral horror.'[55]

At times, the attempt to drag Ireland into Europe seems a little forced. In 1936 de Blacam was distressed by the favourable reaction of an Irish audience to a film which had portrayed crusaders in an unflattering light:

> Would we allow the soldiers of Ireland to be shown as evil livers? No, we would be loud and effective in our protests. What, then, are we to say of the historical sense of a Catholic people who applaud a similar slander of the Christian armies? Evidently we are so far from a Catholic view of history that we have no feeling for the Crusaders.[56]

Nonetheless, it is one of the factors which distinguishes this from more insular varieties of Catholic nationalism and justifies separate treatment. Occasionally it offered a relatively safe position from which to challenge aspects of such nationalism. Devane, among others, insisted that the difference between Irish and Anglo-Irish literature was not that of language. The emphasis remained on Catholicism rather than on nationalism based on any other precept.[57] John Marcus O'Sullivan rebuked those who seemed to find the essence and import of Catholicism in the fact that it was in conformity with the national genius.[58] The outspoken Michael Tierney argued that in Ireland rejection of materialism was often accompanied by the adoption of 'a pseudo-spiritual insular variety of the nationalism which for a century has torn the continent' and he offered as a third option 'a deliberate intellectual return to the concept of civilisation as dependent on religion and ever renewing itself from a revivified, enhanced, and lovingly preserved historical and artistic tradition.'[59] Tierney's article appeared in the *School and College Yearbook 1940–41* and reflects an apparent shift in emphasis among those Catholic social theorists who were concerned with cultural development from literature to education dating from the early 1940s. The expression of the desire to re-Christianize postwar Europe in teachers' journals has already mentioned, but the contemporaneous decline in discussions of literary matters in the Catholic press requires further explanation. Several factors may be relevant, not least of them paper rationing during the emergency which curtailed coverage of all aspects of national life in the journals.

In addition, articles on Catholic literary theory were frequently inspired by the activities of the anti-censorship lobby and after the 1942 Senate debate this impetus abated. O'Faoláin's editorials in *The Bell* continued their critique of Irish culture but tended to concentrate on what he perceived to be the effects of an established state culture, rather than engaging in dialogue on the direction it *should* take. In around 1943, O'Faoláin and Frank Duff of the Legion of Mary set up a group called 'Common Ground' but, despite mutual good will at the outset, the common ground appears to have been too narrow to sustain interest and the endeavour was short lived.[60] Eventually, emotionally exhausted by the fruitlessness of his campaign, O'Faoláin resigned the editorship of *The Bell* to Peadar O'Donnell. Also in 1943 the Commission on Vocational Organisation reported and Lee suggests that

> the hostility of the official mind may have lead to a hardening of some ecclesiastical attitudes that were reflected in attitudes to the 'Mother and Child Scheme'...It is also possible that the hostility to some extent disillusioned genuine idealists such as Browne and Coyne, and perhaps Dr Lucey also, and lead to a certain feeling of frustration that may be detected in their later pronouncements.[61]

It is possible that this disillusionment may have extended to a lack of confidence in the possibilities of cultural revival without a return to first principles in education.

However, neither the teachers nor the social theorists were in any position to influence the educational policies of the state or of the Catholic Church. In the constituent colleges of the National University of Ireland (NUI) academics had freer rein and there the Emergency period was marked by a renewed emphasis on traditional intellectualism which one historian of the NUI has labelled 'neo-Newmanism'.[62] Yet for Tierney, who became President of University College Dublin (UCD) in 1947, nothing short of rebirth would permit the National University to develop in accordance with Cardinal Newman's educational ideas.

In an article written for *Studies* which did not appear, Tierney attacked the atmosphere of Trinity College Dublin, but added that it was essential to realise that Trinity 'sprang from a source originally Catholic and did and even still to a certain extent does represent a perversion of the Catholic university tradition'. Trinity retained two crucial elements of the medieval university system; the intention of giving a religious and moral education, and, towards that end, the institution of residency. This, for Tierney, constituted the university ideal: 'a corporate body, perpetually endowed and self-renewing, and independent of all direct external pressure whether from government, local authorities, or even public opinion'. By contrast, the NUI sprang not from the medieval but from the redbrick tradition, founded by Utilitarians, of which the chief characteristics were secularism, non-residency and federalism. He suggested that Cork and Galway should be made independent universities while a new University of Dublin should be instituted (he disputed the right of Trinity college to this title) incorporating not only Trinity but one or more residential colleges for catholics. The various colleges could share a number of functions and all would have access to the facilities of which Trinity had such an abundance in comparison with UCD. When this plan came into effect, Dublin would be made 'into what it could easily become, one of the greatest and most influential university centres in the world'.[63]

As President of UCD, Tierney was largely responsible for the move to the present UCD campus at Belfield which was large enough to allow for the building of student residences. While there were good practical reasons for this development, it is tempting to associate it with Tierney's earlier expressed ambition. This may be stretching a point, but inspiration is a difficult thing to assess. Research into the broader aspects of Catholic social theory may yet indicate that it had a greater, if more subtle, influence on Ireland's secular development than is presently obvious.

Notes

1 M. O'Callaghan, 'Language and Religion: The Quest for Identity in the Irish Free State 1923–32', M.A. Thesis, UCD, 1981.
2 P. Maume, *'Life that is Exile': Daniel Corkery and the Search for Irish Ireland* (Belfast, 1993).
3 T. Brown, *Ireland: A Social and Cultural History 1922–1985* (London, 1985 ed.) p. 151.
4 J.H. Whyte, *Church and State in Modern Ireland 1923–1979* (Dublin, 1980) remains the most useful authority on the reception and influence of catholic social theory in twentieth-century Ireland.
5 E. Sheehy, 'The Unpopular Front', *Ireland To-day*, vol. 2, no. 4 (April 1937), p. 35.
6 J.J. Lee, *Ireland 1912–1985: Politics and Society* (Cambridge, 1989) p. 578 and *passim*.
7 J.J. Lee, 'Aspects of Corporatist Thought in Ireland: The Commission on Vocational Organisation, 1939–43', in A. Cosgrove and D. McCartney (eds),

Studies in Irish History Presented to R. Dudley Edwards (Dublin 1979). D. Ferriter, ' "A Peculiar People in Their Own Land": Catholic Social Theory and the Plight of Rural Ireland 1930–55', PhD thesis, UCD, 1996.

8 B.P. Kennedy, *Dreams and Responsibilities: The State and the Arts in Independent Ireland* (Dublin, 1990), p. 269.

9 Very Rev. John Johnson P.P., 'The Catholic View of History', *Irish Ecclesiastical Record,* vol. 49 (February 1937), p. 113.

10 J.M. O'Sullivan, 'Perversion of Values: On some Ideologies of Today and Yesterday II', *Irish Ecclesiastical Record,* vol. 57 (April 1941), p. 311.

11 J. Devane, 'Why we have Failed: A Symposium', *The Irish Rosary,* vol. 45, no. 10 (October 1941), pp. 724–5.

12 J. Devane, 'Irish and Catholic', *The Irish Rosary,* vol. 46, no. 4 (April 1942), p. 264.

13 Editorial, *School and College Yearbook 1940–1,* p. 9.

14 D. O'Donnell [Conor Cruise O'Brien], 'The Fourth Estate: The Catholic Press', *The Bell,* vol. 10, no. 1 (April 1945), p. 31.

15 G.C. Heseltine, 'A New Renaissance?', *Irish Monthly,* vol. 60 (June 1932), pp. 330–9.

16 Editorial [Niall Sheridan?], *Comhthrom Feinne,* vol. 3, no. 1 (January 1932), p. 137.

17 J. Devane, 'Culture and the Folk', *The Irish Rosary,* vol. 45, no. 12 (December 1941), p. 897.

18 'Many Happy Returns (?)', *The Irish Rosary,* vol. 4, no. 3 (March 1937), p. 162.

19 Rev. A.J. Little, 'The Case for Philosophy in Secondary Education', *Studies,* vol. 27 (December 1938), p. 532 and 'Comments on the Forgoing Article', pp. 543, 553.

20 I.N.T.O., *A Plan for Education* (Dublin, 1947), pp. 78–9.

21 *Ibid.,* pp. 17–18.

22 Rev. E.J. Coyne S.J., 'Educational Systems in our Brave New World', *School and College Yearbook 1940–1941,* p. 23.

23 I.N.T.O., *A Plan for Education,* p. 16.

24 Joint Pastoral of the Irish Hierarchy, 1927, cited in Brown, *Ireland,* p. 40.

25 Rev. J. MacLoughlin, 'Is Our Culture Threatened?', *Irish Ecclesiastical Record,* vol. 39 (February 1932), pp. 115–6.

26 Rev. C. Lucey, 'The Freedom of the Press', *Irish Ecclesiastical Record,* vol. 50 (December 1937), p. 584.

27 Daniel Corkery offered as one argument in favour of the restoration of the Irish language, the contention that under existing circumstances English literature was given a disproportionate and indiscriminate prominence in Ireland. He did not wish to deprive Irish people of English culture, merely to put it in perspective. 'What might we not learn from that great, if somewhat peculiar literature', he asked, if the revival of Irish conferred 'the power to keep that literature at arm's length, and of seeing it as *English* literature, one among many literatures.' D. Corkery, 'What is Wrong with Irish Culture?: A Symposium', *Irish Ecclesiastical Record,* vol. 46, no. 2 (February 1942), p. 93.

28 M. Adams, *Censorship: The Irish Experience* (Dublin, 1968), p. 49.

29 S. O'Faolain, 'Attitudes', *The Bell,* vol. 2, no. 6 (September 1941), p. 11.

30 M. Gibbon, 'In Defence of Censorship', *The Bell*, vol. 9, no. 5 (January 1945), and Symposium, *The Bell*, vol. 9, no. vi (February 1945).
31 There appear to have been several explanations for the timing of this rather fatalistic motion. The immediate stimumus was the banning of Eric Cross's *The Tailor and Ansty* which had not only offended the usual contributors to the letters page of the *Irish Times* but which, it was felt, might be used to mobilise the forces of cultural nationalism against the censorship. However, it also reflected Sean O'Faoláin's new approach and may have been related to the recent appointment of Senator William Magennis to chairman of the Board. The desciples of Yeats had also inherited his attitude to the Professor of Metaphysics at UCD, whom Frank O'Connor described as 'a notorious and unscrupulous politician'. F. O'Connor, *My Father's Son* (London, 1968) p. 143.
32 *Seanad Eireann. Parliamentary Debates: Official Proceedings*, vol. 32, 18 November 1942, col. 20.
33 *Irish Press*, 20 November 1942.
34 *The Leader*, vol. 85, no. 14, 31 October 1942.
35 *Seanad Eireann. Parliamentary Debates: Official Proceedings*, vol. 32, 18 November 1942, col. 39.
36 *Cork Examiner*, 20 November 1942.
37 *Irish Times*, 19 November 1942.
38 S.J. Brown S.J., 'Concerning Censorship', *The Irish Monthly*, vol. 64 (January 1936) p. 33.
39 Aodh de Blacam, 'Poison in the Wells', *The Irish Monthly*, vol. 65 (April 1937), pp. 279–80.
40 *Irish Press*, 22 September 1932.
41 *The Standard*, vol. 4, no. 39, 6 February 1932.
42 NAI, S9902, E. Cahill to E. de Valera, 8 May 1937.
43 Lord Ffrench, 'Quo Vadis', *Irish Rosary*, vol. 36, no. 8 (August 1932), p. 584.
44 'There is a Grey Eye that Looks Back upon Erin', *Irish Rosary*, vol. 36, no. 12 (December 1932), pp. 881–2.
45 *Irish Press*, 14 August 1935.
46 S.J. Brown S.J., 'But Why Catholic Reading?', *Irish Rosary*, vol. 45, no. 7 (July 1941), p. 523.
47 P.J. Gannon S.J., 'Literature and Censorship', *Irish Monthly*, vol. 65 (June 1937), pp. 434–45.
48 L.J. Walsh, 'Catholic Standards in Criticism', *Irish Rosary*, vol. 39, no. 3 (March 1935), p. 172.
49 S.J. Brown S.J., 'The Catholic Novelist and his Themes', *Irish Monthly*, vol. 63 (July 1935), p. 438.
50 P.J. Gannon, 'Literature and Censorship', pp. 439–40.
51 Aodh de Blacam, 'What do We Owe the Abbey?', *Irish Monthly*, vol. 63 (March 1935), pp. 199–200.
52 'There is a Grey Eye', p. 881.
53 R. O Faracháin, 'A Lost Revival', *Irish Monthly*, vol. 62 (July 1934), pp. 421–2.
54 J. Devane, 'The New Romantics', *Irish Ecclesiastical Record*, vol. 45, no. 3 (March 1941), p. 186.
55 Aodh de Blacam, 'A Dramatic Festival and After', *Irish Monthly*, vol. 63 (May 1935), p. 330.

56   Aodh de Blacam, 'A Church History for Everyman', *Irish Monthly*, vol. 64 (July 1936), p. 479.

57   J. Devane, 'The Faults of the Irish', *The Irish Rosary*, vol. 46, no. 3 (March 1942), pp. 197–8.

58   J.M. O'Sullivan, 'Perversions of Values: On Some Ideologies of Today and Yesterday', *Irish Ecclesiastical Record*, vol. 57 (March 1941), p. 247.

59   M. Tierney, 'Progress, Civilisation and Religion', *School and College Yearbook 1940–41*, p. 19.

60   L. O Broin, *Just Like Yesterday: An Autobiography* (Dublin, 1985), p. 152.

61   J.J. Lee, 'Aspects of Corporatist Thought', p. 346*ff.*

62   D. McCartney, *The National University and Eamon de Valera* (Dublin, 1983), p. 46.

63   M. Tierney, 'The University Question after 30 years', MSS article (UCDA LA30/207).

7

Social Catholicism and the Social Question in Independent Ireland: The Challenge to the Fiscal System

Finín O' Driscoll

Within the general configuration of nineteenth-century European developments among Roman Catholics, Irish Catholics did not face the same social, economic or political situation as their continental counterparts. Whereas other continental Catholics built up extensive and often elaborate practical and intellectual frameworks for the Christian organisation of their societies, Irish Catholics did not. In Ireland the political aspirations of the Catholic Church were intimately intertwined with the attainment of Home Rule government by the Irish Parliamentary party at Westminster.[1] This union of Church and the proto-state negated any need for a separate Catholic political party. Dominance of the national question in the nineteenth and early twentieth centuries ensured that the social question within a Catholic political context did not arise as a topic for discussion in the same way as it had in continental Catholicism. Ireland existed as a predominantly agricultural-producing country with a rural-based social structure in the nineteenth century. By the turn of the century this picture had changed significantly with the growth of urbanisation in Belfast, Dublin and Cork, which brought with it an intensification of modern urban social problems. Housing conditions, sanitation and conditions of employment were considered comparable to similar situations in Britain's main urban centres by some contemporary policy-makers.[2]

These new social questions came to dominate the urban social democratic discussion in Ireland for the first two decades of the new century. Moreover, despite the large land-purchase schemes introduced by the British administration in the 1880s and 1890s, the economic life of the small farm-holder or for that matter those who remained landless in the more remote regions of the west, tended to be just as precarious as it had been in the past. The turn of the century saw the increasing marginalisation of the small farmer and agricultural labourer in rural Ireland.[3] Within these new developments in Irish social conditions, the Irish churches now found themselves having to address some of the same problems that their continental counterparts had begun to come to terms with almost a century before. This chapter sets out to examine how the broad Catholic movement in Ireland, clerical and lay, dealt with the plethora of social issues that came to prominence in the period during and after independence. Although never manifesting itself as a separate political party, the force of social Catholicism had a wide-ranging impact on the intellectual and political life of independent Ireland. This chapter attempts to chart the scope of that impact, and to examine in particular how the social catholic movement came to question the government's fiscal policy in the 1930s.

Commentators at the turn of the century highlighted the need for the church to direct its attention to the growing social problem in Ireland. Filson Young in his 1904 study *Ireland at the Cross-Roads* held the Catholic Church responsible for 'a large proportion of the present misery of Ireland' with the view that the 'tall spires' acted as wasteful 'conductors of the people's energies'. Sir Horace Plunkett, the Unionist MP for South Dublin and founder of the Irish Co-operative movement, made the same criticism of the Irish church in his controversial work *Ireland in the New Century* stating that the Church presided with 'an entire lack of serious thought on public questions; a listlessness and apathy in regard to economic improvement which amount to a form of fatalism'. Contemporary historians have followed the same line of criticism. J.H. Whyte argued that Irish Catholicism at the beginning of the twentieth century, ' ... contrasted with many areas of the continent, where Catholics had developed a network of organisations with a social purpose: co-operatives, friendly societies, farmers' organisations, youth movements, adult education movements, trade unions.'[4] Emmet Larkin has also suggested that the Irish Church was 'ill-equipped, institutionally and intellectually, to meet the growing complexities of a rapidly changing society to which it was being introduced.'[5]

From the 1890s and into the early years of the twentieth century a group of clerics led by Dr Walter McDonald, Professor of Theology at St Patrick's seminary at Maynooth, began addressing the difficult question of the role of Catholicism in the face of such a rapidly changing social situation. In journals such as *The Irish Theological Quarterly* and through the six hundred or so local cooperative societies supported by priests, the movement for social Catholicism became both an intellectual and practical manifestation. The 1912 Lockout also had a profound impact on the development of social Catholicism. As the bishop of Cork, Corneilus Lucey, commented as late as 1949, 'the Big Strike shocked the Irish people to the consciousness that they had a social as well as a national problem to solve.'[6] Such sentiments were translated into practical efforts on the part of Catholic commentators. The hierarchy in their joint Lenten Pastoral on 22 February 1914 stated that there was 'a necessity for improved education for the labourer, skilled and unskilled' and recommended 'circles for social study, debate and work'.[7] The Lenten Pastoral concentrated minds and the succeeding years saw a proliferation of conferences, pamphlets and books concerned with Catholic social teaching. One of the earliest statements of the new agenda came from the young Jesuit scholar Lambert McKenna. In the concluding part of the series, *The Church and Social Work*, McKenna came out with his strongest demand for concerted social action among Irish Catholics. He highlighted the obligation for Catholics to come to grips with the fact that charity was no longer a viable solution to the problems encountered in modern society. Now McKenna maintained, that the emphasis of the Church's social endeavours and actions centred on the need to 'reconstitute the diseased and weakened organisms of society, the family, the city, the state'.[8]

This new social Catholicism differed sharply from the traditional response to social problems, that is the provision of charity. It concerned itself, in its technical sense, with the consequences of industrial problems and urbanisation. It represented the belief that it was possible and a matter of moral obligation to improve the social structure as well as to bring charitable relief to the victims of industrialism. There was no sense of fatalism inherent in this new Catholicism. Instead, it argued for the possibility of consciously directed change: though the kind of change desired might be more backward looking than progressive. Catholic social commentators also began to see the social question intertwined with the evolving nationalist question. The Catholic middle class and clergy saw in the Vatican's social teaching a viable alternative to worrying radical social demands of labour and a firm security against the rise of an anti-clericalist strands of socialism among the working class. The young Jesuit Edward Coyne, who later established himself as one of the most important commentators on Catholic thinking in Ireland, stated in his 1913 essay, 'The Necessity for Social Education for Irishmen'[9] that with the resolution of the Home Rule question, the new 'Parliament on College Green would introduce Catholic laws for a Catholic people'.[10] In April 1919, Rev Myles Ronan noted[11] in an article entitled 'Citizenship in the Irish

State' that 'Irish Catholics must necessarily apply Catholic principles to the Labour programme' in an attempt to improve the social problem.[12] These aspirations for a confessional state were further developed by a number of scholars at Maynooth. Among the early leading lights were Fr Peter Coffey, Professor of Philosophy, and Fr William Moran, Professor of Theology, who initiated a debate on the merits of what was termed the 'Distributist Solution' to the Irish social problem in 1919. For Coffey and Moran and other Catholic social commentators the creation of a new state and self-government would afford scope for social and economic experimentation along the lines of contemporary Catholic social thinking.

For the Maynooth group, Independent Ireland would be a land of plenty and opportunity and, in essence, they proposed a third way between capitalism and socialism which they styled as Distributism. Coffey put the press of the Catholic Truth Society to use and published two pamphlets in November 1920 on this 'third way'. Much of what he wrote had appeared in a series of articles that he had written earlier for the polemical nationalist periodical the *Leader*. The first collective work was entitled *Between Capitalism and Socialism* and was an attempt to broaden the appeal of Distributism to the general public. It dealt with the Catholic doctrine of property, capitalism and socialism. Coffey began his defence of Catholic social principles by stating that social Catholic teaching had a positive contribution to make to Irish society through advocating '...the diffusion of small ownership in land and capital; the encouragement of joint ownership and of co-operation in production and distribution'.[13] He maintained that the state had a number of duties: it had the right to control the economic forces of production and distribution, and it had the right to supervise and direct the economy so that it be exercised for the common good. The inequality of the capitalist economy was, he argued, impermissible, and future state intervention within an independent Irish economy was imperative. The state would take over any particular form or excessive quantity of productive wealth from its private owners. The private owner would in turn be compensated with the real capital value in government stock or bonds.

This system of state intervention would also involve allowing workers and farmers to borrow from the state to buy out companies or property and thus establish cooperative ownership. Coffey used the example of the massive land-purchase schemes introduced into Ireland at the close of the nineteenth century as existing proof that such a system of compensation could work. Furthermore, he proposed there would not be a rapid system of confiscation but instead '... a peaceful and orderly expropriation or confiscation of the surplus productive wealth that is held in the control of the few, and its gradual effective redistribution among the many – in other words, a policy of economic readjustment by gradual diffusion of moderate private proprietorship (through co-operative or group guild ownership, or by a variety of other reasonable devices).'[14] Coffey presumed that this policy of state intervention would bring about a new order in Church–State relations with the Church becoming the moral arbiter of such intervention since 'the moral teaching of the Church will always be available to help them [the state].'[15]

William Moran, Coffey's colleague, also articulated a defence of state intervention on theological grounds in the *Irish Theological Quarterly* to further the Distributist case. In a series of articles entitled 'Social Reconstruction in an Irish State' he reiterated Coffey's thinking. Like Coffey, he dealt with the three areas of capitalism, socialism and the state and their interrelationships. Moran considered first the question of capitalism. Its historical basis, he argued, lay in the Reformation, the French Revolution and the Industrial Revolution, all of which introduced the 'principle of unfettered individualism'. The Church, however, had stood firm throughout in its demand for the dignity and respect for all individuals. This 'unfettered individualism' led, he argued to the justification of the right to excessive property-ownership in the capitalist state. The right to private property must not, he continued, run against the common good since 'the individual's right to live implies, in ordinary circumstances, a right to a field of Labour, from which none can lawfully exclude him. This right to exploit by his Labour the bounty of nature is limited by the necessity of conceding a like right to his fellow-men.'[16] The conditions for the Distributist state were already in existence. Ireland, he remarked, had as yet undeveloped resources and the tradition of holding property was still strong among the people. He assumed that since 'such a frame of mind among the Irish workers is a condition of prime importance for the Irish social reformer of the future; it makes a settlement on the basis of diffused ownership a feasible proposition.' Moran continued:

> The Irish state must, of course, be the reformer; and the process of repossession or redistribution – in so far as the redistribution may be necessary – will be its most serious problem. Catholic theology recognises in the state a power called the *altum dominium* [ancient ownership]; and if our main contention throughout this paper is

well-founded, the Irish state will possess in its *altum dominium* sufficient authority for any reforms that may be necessary for the establishment of a Distributive State.[17]

Moran ended the series with a warning to those involved in social
reform. He urged caution and saw the need for social study among
both clerics and laity to resolve the problems of society based on firmly
Catholic lines. More importantly, he believed that the implementation
of such proposals could only come about when

> we get our own Government, since the alien Government will always
> exercise its *altum dominium*, not for the good of Ireland, but of
> England. 'If on the other hand, the Capitalistic system is allowed to
> become part of the constitution of a free Irish state, the difficulty of
> curbing the moneyed interests afterwards will be immensely
> increased. It follows that Irish social reformers, and the wage-earners
> of Ireland in particular, should so educate, organise and discipline
> their forces, as to be able to make social reconstruction on Catholic
> lines one of the chief planks in the platform of the first Irish
> Government.'[18]

Coffey and Moran continued to publicise their ideas on Distributism
through the *Catholic Bulletin*, the *Irish Ecclesiastical Record* and the *Irish
Theological Quarterly*.[19]

The 1921 Anglo–Irish Treaty secured the right to independent government for a 26-county Irish Free State. The new treatyite governments had the immense task of attempting to administer a country on
the brink of civil conflict throughout the first half of 1922. As the revolutionary party and its institutions disintegrated, and in an environment of increased lawlessness, social questions again took a secondary
place to a national question which might now be decided by civil war.
Coffey established a small study-group early in 1922 consisting of
Moran from Maynooth, Fr O'Flanagan of Marlboro St, Dublin, Mr Frank
Sweeney and Seamus Hughes, a former trade unionist with the ITGWU,
and the group published their ideas in a booklet entitled 'An Economic
Programme for the Irish Free state'.[20] In September 1922 Coffey published their monetary proposals in the *Irish Times* under the pseudo-
nym 'Scrutator'.[21] These articles were a synopsis of his ideas already
presented in the *Irish Theological Quarterly*: he argued that the government should take over the effective control of the nation's credit, so as
to 'exploit the national credit for the benefit of the Irish people', to

introduce a financial policy aimed at gradual deflation, to move away from the gold standard and to 'fix the values of the currency upon as many items and goods as possible'.[22]

Later, in October 1922, Coffey wrote to President Cosgrave[23] and advised the establishment of a commission 'to investigate the whole question of the principles and policy of credit-issue, currency and price-fixing, in its relation to the primary purpose of industry'.[24] On 25 October, Coffey presented to Cosgrave, 'A practical scheme for using the nation's credit to advantage' whereby the government could utilise the nation's credit to raise money for public work schemes such as housing. The returns, interest-free, would then be reinvested in more public schemes.[25] Even though the scheme intended solving the housing problem, the authors envisaged it would save the country's industries enormous tolls of interest; 'encourage industries whose advance is demanded in the national interest; and offset as required, at least to a large extent, the expansion or contraction of credit caused by the other banks and finance consumption as well as production, if it should be necessary in time of crisis'.[26] Cosgrave replied to Coffey that he 'need not refer to the fact that your scheme would require some detailed criticism. If I might say so without offence, it is the scheme of an amateur.'[27]

Coffey replied to Cosgrave's criticisms on 31 October:

> It comes to this in a nutshell: Will you make the Irish people as a whole pay what the parties intended to be benefited by the National Credit actually received (National Financing), or will you make them pay double and treble as much over again (in interest charges) to a section who monopolise the issue of the financial credit which enables the Nation to use its Real Credit?[28]

Cosgrave chose the latter course of action. This was the view of the civil servants in the Department of Finance too when Cosgrave circulated the memo. Patrick Hyland in a memo to Cosgrave warned 'in this transition period, and until we have made up accounts with England, I take it that our policy should be to proceed on conservative well-established lines; for one thing we cannot afford to frighten English finance'.[29] Thus, any attempts to see the new state entertain radical alternatives to the existing system were met with stiff and conservative opposition both from the Cosgrave government and the civil service. Neither did the hierarchy entertain any such financial radicalism. Coffey's efforts to petition Cosgrave resulted in his being officially silenced by the Hierarchy and the *Irish Theological Quarterly* was discontinued in 1922.

Alongside direct attempts to influence the policies of the government ran a far more successful attempt to establish a populist form of Catholic Action. Central to the pontificate of Pius XI was the idea of bringing Catholicism into a more active role in society. In 1925, he published the social encyclical *Quas Primas* in which he maintained that it was only the Church that could supply the principles and inspiration required for a just settlement of the social, political and economic problems that were besetting nations all over the world, and the document argued for the establishment of the 'Kingship of Christ on Earth'.[30] Interpreted in an Irish context, Catholics were encouraged to overcome the divisions of the civil war and unite under the one banner in order to achieve the goal of complete and unfettered national sovereignty through the leadership of the Kingship of Christ. A provisional Catholic Action movement along these lines was founded in the summer of 1925 under the direction of the Edward Cahill S.J., Professor of Church History and Lecturer in Sociology at the Jesuit College at Milltown Park.[31] The Catholic Action movement came into being on 29 April 1926 after a meeting of a group of 40 lay people and clerics in Dublin.[32] Those present included some members of Fianna Fáil the party such as Eamon de Valera, Sean Brady and Eoin O'Keefe. The meeting was also attended by members of Saint Vincent de Paul, notably, George Gavan Duffy the former Sinn Fein plenipotentiary at the 1921 treaty negotiations and a leading Dublin barrister in the mid-1920s, Arthur Clery and Sir Joseph Glynn. The organisation would be known as *An Cumann Caitliceach Náisiúnta* – or the The Catholic National Society. Its aims were to stimulate an intelligent interest in Irish problems – social, economic and political – from a Catholic standpoint and with particular reference to the papal encyclicals. To refute the fallacious systems of communism, capitalism and their attendant creeds. To advocate the application of Catholic social principles; and to further the idea of a unified and independent Ireland.[33] Membership was open only to students of University College Dublin so as to ensure that no graduates of the 'godless colleges' would be allowed to join.[34]

De Valera's involvement in the establishment of the Catholic National Society is a point of interest. It is widely accepted by historians that de Valera was a devout Catholic being 'both patriotic and loyally Roman Catholic but in a very independent way'.[35] De Valera's attendance at the meeting was due in part to his friendship with Cahill. However, this relationship was not based on any desire on de Valera's part to establish a Catholic social order in Ireland but rather out of an ulterior motive. De Valera had broken away from the fundamentalist republican Sinn Féin party some months before. The new anti-treaty Fianna Fáil party was at the time been planned and was eventually launched on 16 May 1926 at the La Scala Theatre in Dublin. In the run up to the launch, de Valera wished to learn more about Catholic teaching on political and social issues and the study-circle concept appealed as the best way to learn and allowed him to 'draw upon the resources of the Irish intellectual elite'.[36] According to John Waldron, one of those present, '...the Civil War had ended, leaving an aftermath of disillusionment. Minds which might have become cynical were attracted by the high ideals placed before them by Father Cahill, who was thus able to bring together on a common platform, men and women who had been in opposite camps in the Civil War.'[37]

The meetings of the *ad hoc* group continued for another six months, and eventually agreement on a common aim was found (without de Valera) and An Ríoghacht (the League of the Kingship of Christ) was established on 31 October 1926. At the first meeting, at the Ierne Hall, Parnell Square, Dublin, it was proposed by Eoin O'Keefe to form a definite Catholic Action society. Its main objects were:

(a) To propagate among Irish Catholics a better knowledge of Catholic social principles.
(b) To strive for the effective recognition of these principles in Irish public life.
(c) To promote Catholic social action.[38]

The main objective of An Ríoghacht, to study Catholic social principles, was strictly adhered to. Nevertheless, Cahill and the Ard-Comhairle of An Ríoghacht had drawn up *Notes on the Projected National Programme*,[39] a document with a far wider agenda. The movement argued that a number of areas such as forestry, fishing, manufacturing industry and the control of credit and currency were in need of careful and detailed economic planning to bring about the resurrection of the Irish state and the solving of the social problem. Education, however, was singled out as an area that needed fostering especially against statism, and it was demanded that the state should have no control of the educational system. The Programme envisaged that the new Catholic order would 'safeguard the inalienable rights of the [sic] parents to control the education of their children, subject in moral and religious matters to the guidance of the Church.'[40] Public morality would also come under the strict supervision of the Catholic Church. Irreligious and indecent literature would be banned from importation and the State would ensure 'a strict limitation and control of such public activities as tend to foster and promote an excessive craze after dissipation and excitement; such as the undue multiplication of race-meetings, cinema-shows, dancing houses, commercialised sports meetings etc.'[41]

The economic programme of An Ríoghacht stressed the importance of self-sufficiency. It also indicated that some of the ideas fermented by Coffey and Moran in the early 1920s had been taken up by some Catholic commentators. Its principle aim was to ensure that there be 'the widest possible diffusion of capital; the abolition of capitalistic monopolies especially the monopoly of credit, the curtailment of undue capitalistic control of industries and credit; and the gradual conversion of our present class of small independent owners of capital, especially of land.'[42] There would be a complete ban on the export of Irish financial credit. This in due course was to be followed by a ban on the 'undue expenditure of the energies and capital of the nation on unproductive and harmful activities such as racing, cinema shows, commercialised sports'. The importation of luxuries would only be allowed in return for the exchange exportation of Irish food.[43]

The social Catholic lobby continued to gather momentum on the periphery of mainstream Irish politics during the 1930s. Perturbed by Mussolini's adoption of the term 'corporatism' to describe the new Italian economic model, Irish social Catholics coined their own phrase 'vocationalism'. However, the pursuit of a vocational order was in stark contrast to the conservative stance of the Irish hierarchy. The bishops concentrated more on the protection of the Catholic population against the perceived evils of the decadent modern world. The Free State was a Catholic state where the church had fought to secure a privileged position during the first decade of its existence. The development of popular political Catholicism could only serve to undermine the power of the bishops.[44]

The publication of *Quadragesimo Anno* in 1931 gave new impetus to the international Catholic social movement. The following decade witnessed a vigorous growth of clerical and lay interest in various Irish adaptations of Catholic Action. Journals such as *Catholic Bulletin, Catholic Mind,* and *Irish Monthly* redirected their editorial emphasis and disseminated the ideas of Catholic social teaching. The emergence of new magazines in the first half of the 1930s further reflected the growing importance of that movement; the magazine *Outlook* was founded in 1932, *Up and Doing* in 1934, and *Prosperity* in 1935. *Hibernia* was taken over by the Knights of Columbanus in 1936 and converted into a mouthpiece for Catholic Action. There also grew a proliferation of Catholic Action organisations such as Frank Duff's Legion of Mary and the rural-based Muintir na Tíre. It was also a time of short-lived anti-communist groups such as the League of St Patrick (1934) and the Irish Christian Front's (1936) flirtation with corporatist ideals.

The advocates of a vocational order saw the election of Fianna Fáil to government in 1932 as a step towards the creation of a new social order. When de Valera entered office, one Catholic weekly commented that 'this is the day of Catholic Action and it is up to the government of a Catholic country to be a Catholic Actionist Government in every sense of the word.'[45] This neo-Catholic ideology, coupled with a militant nationalism gave the impression to many that Fianna Fáil would attempt a social reconstruction along papal social lines. De Valera's Fianna Fáil party were given a further opportunity to claim to be the real and true Catholic political party with the International Eucharistic Congress held in Dublin in 1932. The preparations for the event covered the whole month of June and a wave of popular piety spread throughout the country. There were special candlelit masses in the Phoenix Park and general communion services for men and women throughout the country. Four thousand people were received at a State Reception in St Patrick's Hall in Dublin Castle, and 20000 people attended a garden party in the grounds of Blackrock College at the invitation of the Irish hierarchy.[46] The events of the week culminated in the celebration of mass in the Phoenix Park with an estimated one million of the faithful in attendance. In short the event transcended the religious celebration to become a manifestation of triumphant Irish catholic nationalism.

Following this wave of active Catholic sentiment, Fianna Fáil proceeded to utilise the power of the state in safeguarding moral standards in accordance with the standards set by Catholic Action pressure groups. In the budget of 1933, a tax was placed on imported daily, in effect British, newspapers. In 1935, the government introduced the Criminal Law Amendment Act, section 17, which prohibited the importation or sale of contraceptives.[47] Furthermore, de Valera asked a prominent civil servant, Thomas J. Kiernan, to furnish him with a study of how corporatism could be applied to Ireland. Kiernan reported on 29 March 1933 to Séan Moynihan, Secretary to the Executive Council.[48] Kiernan's memorandum argued that the aim of the corporatist system was 'to prevent exploitation, to give an incentive to initiative and to create an organism in which all working citizens find their place in the economic organisation of the nation'. The Kiernan model was not taken up. De Valera's 1937 Constitution made much reference to Catholic teaching but not to catholic social teaching *per se*. Article 43 reiterated catholic social teaching on the rights to private property, while articles 40 to 44 on fundamental rights drew heavily on Catholic social teaching in relation to the rights of the family and women. However, overall there was very little which could be claimed to be vocationalist in outlook – with the exception of the election process for the senate – and the Constitution did not set out any attempts to reconstruct the Irish state in a radical manner. De Valera had inherited a constitutional situation which he regarded as wholly unsatisfactory. His main concern was to attempt to weaken the constitutional link with Britain and not with restructuring Irish society according to the thinking of Edward Cahill and the Catholic Activists.

A number of government commissions were appointed during the 1930s to examine Irish financial and administrative policy, and to investigate a wide range of areas such as tillage, emigration unemployment, and vocational organisation. Each commission received evidence submitted by Catholic social commentators and other lobbies. However, the final reports of the Commission on Banking, Currency and Credit witnessed the most serious attempt made by a radical vocationalist lobby, headed once again by Edward Cahill, to see Catholic social principles implemented at the very heart of the nation's financial system. Fianna Fáil's main economic policy objective, rhetorically at least, was to make the Free State self-sufficient. Seán MacEntee, the Minister for Finance, had mentioned in March 1932 in a conversation with Joseph Brennan, a Department of Finance civil servant and chairman of the Currency Commission, that the government was interested in establishing a commission to enquire into the existing currency and banking situation in the Free State. There were several reasons why Fianna Fáil intended to establish such a commission. First, the Banking Commission in 1927 had stated that its findings should be reviewed within ten years, and, furthermore, it corresponded to Fianna Fáil's economic policy of striving for increased financial and economic self-sufficiency. Besides, the idea of establishing a central bank was very much on the international economic agenda during the 1930s, especially among many of the Commonwealth countries such as Canada and New Zealand.[49]

The Commission on Banking, Currency and Credit was appointed by McEntee on 20 November 1934 to 'examine and report on the system in Saorstát Éireann of currency, banking, credit, public borrowing and lending' and 'to consider and report what changes, if any, are necessary or desirable to promote the social and economic welfare of the community and the interests of agriculture and industry.'[50] De Valera had worked closely with MacEntee in the selection of the other members. He wanted a commission that would incorporate a wide cross-section of Irish society. Four university professors were appointed: John Busteed, Professor of Economics and Commerce at University College Cork; Alfred O'Rahilly, Professor of Mathematical Physics, University College Cork; George A. Duncan, Professor of Political Economy at Trinity College Dublin; and George O'Brien, Professor of Economics at University College Dublin. William O'Brien, General Secretary of the Irish Transport and General Workers' Union, and Séan P. Campbell, Honorary Treasurer of the Irish Trade Union Congress represented the trade unions. John C.M. Eason, Director of the famous Dublin shop, and John O'Neill, director of O'Neill Motors and long-time campaigner for protection, represented the 'industrialist lobby'. Peadar O'Loghlen, a Fianna Fáil local politician from Ballyvaughan, Co. Clare was appointed to represent the rural community. He had the highest record of attendance, excluding the chairman, but despite this remained a passive member throughout all the meetings of the Commission. However, it was to transpire that his role was to hold a watching brief for de Valera.

The Economist admired the selection of such a diverse range of commissioners.[51] Apart from the commercial and financial groups that gave evidence, there were numerous fringe groups and individuals who made submissions. The economic theories of the Italian economist Silvio Gesell were also represented in the evidence.[52] There were two submissions calling for the immediate implementation of Catholic-inspired economic reforms. This was a feature of the commission that was noted by Per Jacobsson, one of the outside members of the Commission and head of the International Bank for Resettlements, who commented at their inclusion in his diaries with some surprise.[53] Though no actual group were named on the submissions, Fr. Edward Cahill and the Ard-Comhairle [Executive Council] of An Ríoghacht were clearly involved in drawing up some of these memoranda. Cahill himself did not appear before the commission since his Provincial had forbade him.[54] Instead the task was taken up by Mrs B. Berthon Waters, an economics graduate and member of An Ríoghacht, Brian J. McCaffery and James O'Rourke, both members of An Ríoghacht's Ard-Comhairle, and a non-executive member Mr Cox Gordon. They presented evidence on three different occasions in 1935. In essence, all three memoranda were condensed denunciations of the existing economic system in the Saorstát.[55] They urged instead the establishment of 'a Department comparable in integrity and detachment to the Judiciary'[56] that would have the right to issue credit to private and public ventures. All attacked the interest-rate system used by the banks as 'usury' as being harmful to agricultural activity. They also called for the promotion of 'rural reconstruction on a national scale through afforestation, draining and reclamation of land and the multiplication of rural homes.'[57] They argued that 'a new orientation of the whole social and economic structure of the country is needed if it is to be brought into harmony with the people's needs and ideals. Such a re-orientation is synonymous with an open application of Catholic principles not merely in the political sphere but also in the sphere of economics.'[58] These memoranda were dismissed by most members of the Commission as simplifications of Catholic social teaching. They earned the particular criticism from George O'Brien and Bishop McNeely, who singled out the term 'from a Catholic standpoint' used in Water's memorandum. McNeely stated that he would 'not like the commission to get the impression that all this scheme of yours is based on Catholic social teaching.'[59]

Members of An Ríoghacht felt that public opinion needed to be informed on the Commission and this could, it was hoped, in turn lead to their proposals being considered seriously. The move to sway public opinion in favour of social Catholic teaching came in the winter of 1935 when a new journal appeared in Dublin entitled *Prosperity* published under the auspices of a new society, the League Against Poverty. The aims of the new organisation were to unite in the league people of all parties, or of none, who wished to see the standards of economic life raised in Saorstát Éireann,[60] with its main object being to see the potential for economic development in Ireland used to the full. It also called for the shedding of the old economic theories handed down by the British administration and the introduction of new more versatile ones. Funding for the journal came from Lord Monteagle Foynes, Frank Hugh O'Donnell, and Pat MacCartan, the ubiquitous Republican who alternated between New York and Ireland. The journal was managed by Fred Johnson, son of the former leader of the Labour party in the Dáil, Tom Johnson and edited by Bulmer Hobson. It managed, according to a Garda special branch report, to sustain a monthly circulation of 300 with a number of copies strategically sent free to the hierarchy and prominent members of the clergy.[61]

Prosperity interpreted the social encyclicals and also proposed policies in the area of financing economic reconstruction. Under the heading

'A Practical Policy' it called for the establishment of an Economic Development Commission with the objective of 'the progressive raising of the standards of economic life in Saorstát Éireann'. Its functions would be flexible and activity would increase and decrease with the rise and fall of unemployment. The Currency Commission would be 'invested with the power to issue legal tender notes to the Economic Development Commission' which in turn would be permitted to use this available credit for 'payment of the expenses of the Economic Development commission, and the financing of schemes of works of national advantage, to be carried out by or for the commission'.[62] The practical policy, which appeared on the face of it to ignore or not understand the risk of hyper-inflation, also envisaged that the fixed exchange rate link with sterling would be broken.[63]

MacEntee was perturbed by the criticisms that were being levelled against his party's financial policy by the League Against Poverty and he requested that the Department of Justice identify the group behind it.[64] The special branch made a number of enquiries and reported on 23 April 1936 with a full dossier on the group. The Department of Justice file remained open until 1938. In early 1936, Hobson, Cahill and Waters came together to establish a group to put the Banking Commission on the public agenda. Hobson was of the view that the Commission 'was heavily loaded with partisans of the existing order'.[65] Thus, between July 1936 and October 1938 the three set about changing the direction of the Banking Commission. In August 1936, the League Against Poverty became known as the League for Social Justice and effectively pursued the same policy as its predecessor in its own journal of the same name.[66]

Meanwhile, in December 1936 Hobson, Cahill and Waters were occupied with writing a memorandum which they intended to submit to the Commission. It was completed by the New Year and submitted on 14 January 1937. However, the Commission had already concluded hearing oral evidence and the League submission was delivered too late for consideration. The memorandum itself ran to 16 pages and was a more detailed exposition of the ideas already aired in its publication *Social Justice*. In order to correct any deficiencies in the memorandum, Hobson sent it to two economists in England,[67] the Dublin-educated John G. Smith, Professor of Finance and Dean of the Faculty of Commerce at the University of Birmingham,[68] and James E. Meade, a Fellow and Lecturer in Economics at Hertford College, Oxford and a future Nobel Prize Winner.[69] Both were critical of certain aspects of the memorandum but were positive overall. De Valera received copies of these criticisms from Cahill, and in September 1937 he received the draft heads of the 'report' that Cahill, Hobson and Waters had written. In a covering note they stated that it was a '… first and tentative draft of the form which a minority report might possibly take. It was written some weeks ago; the writers had access to such parts of the Majority Report as were then completed in typescript, but the Majority Report was not finished, nor was it in its final form.'[70] The draft heads corresponded to the proposals given in the original League for Social Justice memorandum. Cahill, who had already been in contact with de Valera concerning the drafting of the Constitution, stated that the submitted 'report' 'will enable the Government to give effect to the social aims announced in the Constitution.'[71]

In effect Cahill, Hobson and Waters were attempting to persuade de Valera that there was room for a minority report that would differ substantially from the majority recommendations of the Banking Commission. Eoin O'Keeffe, a personal friend of de Valera, had had an informal discussion with the Fianna Fáil leader in which he 'expressed misgivings that the report of the Commission would merely endorse the existing fiscal theory'. O'Keeffe was told by de Valera that those members of the Commission who favoured an alternative approach to financial policy should produce such an alternative report.[72] De Valera was attempting to ensure that the more radical element within Fianna Fáil could find solace in one of the minority reports and that those elements could not accuse him of losing the ideology of self-sufficiency that had brought Fianna Fáil to power. It was after the O'Keefe meeting that the race to produce a minority report picked up speed.[73] The final reports of the Banking Commission were signed on 23 March 1938. The majority report was signed by the chairman and 15 other members, and consisted of two volumes, four addendum, one note and two notes of reservations. In addition there were a total of 32 appendices covering a wide range of areas. The essential feature of the majority report, as James Meenan has stated, 'may be summarised as a recommendation to leave things as they were.'[74]

The Cahill, Hobson and Waters report was presented as a Third Minority Report and signed by member of the commission Peader O'Louglen. It began with an examination of the social and economic principles that governed the main text.[75] The report continued with an elucidation of the Social Encyclicals and took selected quotes from *Rerum Novarum*, *Divini Redemptoris* and *Quadragesimo Anno*. It argued that the essential duty of the state was to provide for social justice and safeguard the common good. The report cited the duties in Article 45 of the 1937 Constitution which stated the right to private property but reminded the reader that the same Article mede provision for state intervention where there was '...concentration of ownership...'.[76] The Report concluded that this combination of Papal teaching and Constitutional duties required the Irish government to endeavour to ensure those principles.[77] The report believed that in Ireland state intervention in the economic system and the attainment of full employment were possible if the government invested in reproductive works of 'a soundly economic character' such as afforestation. This would 'lay the foundations for the future growth of new industries and lead to the rapid development of secondary industry'.[78] The implementation of these proposals would be seen through by a proposed Economic Development Commission. As was stated in previous League Against Poverty publications, the activities of the proposed commission would increase or decrease with any rise or fall in the numbers of unemployed. The Economic Development Commission would receive all the credit it required for these public schemes from the Currency Commission, and this money would be repaid to the Currency Commission through two methods. First 'by the use of all funds resulting from the works undertaken'; and, second, these repayments could 'be supplemented, to whatever extent is necessary, out of the Exchequer'.[79] Finally, the report recommended that the exchange rate parity with sterling should be relieved, and that '...the external value of the Irish currency should not be held arbitrarily at any level which may be determined by circumstances in another country'.[80] It recommended that a Foreign Exchange Committee be established which would 'periodically fix the rates of foreign exchange in such a manner as to even out fluctuations, so that changes of rates should occur as seldom, and when necessary, be as gradual as possible.'[81]

The reaction of the chairman of the Banking Commission, Joseph Brennan, to the Third Minority Report was one of incredulity and undisguised hostility. Brennan and the Department of Finance immediately set about attempting to discredit the intellectual origins of the report.[82] The reaction was to grow even more hostile in the following months. One month after the reports were presented to the Minister for Finance, interest in them began to be raised within Catholic circles. A short article in the *Irish Ecclesiastical Record*, written by Eoin O'Keefe, raised the question of how the Commission responded to the promotion of '...the social and economic welfare of the community and the interests of agriculture and industry',[83] and it hoped that 'all the Reports will be in harmony with Catholic social philosophy'.[84]

On 8 August 1938, the Banking Commission reports were published
in full provoking a reaction from a number of Catholic commentators.
The September issue of *Hibernia* lauded the First and Third Minority
Reports for being 'of paramount interest to Catholics in Ireland and
abroad, who are genuinely interested in establishing a Christian social
order.'[85] The Majority Report was censured for its extreme conser-
vatism. The vocationalist, Edward Coyne, S.J., criticised the Majority
Report for ignoring the work of 'an economist such as John Maynard
Keynes',[86] and Cahill also became involved in the post-publication
debate when he denounced the report for failing to address the area
of social justice.[87] Instead, unsurprisingly, he applauded the Third
Minority Report. For his trouble Cahill was again silenced by the
Provincial on the 25 October stating that Cahill's views on the
Banking Commission 'will injure our work as Jesuits if allowed to
continue'.[88]

Some 2000 copies of the Third Minority Report were published
by the Three Candles Press in September 1938 on the suggestion of
Eoin O'Keefe.[89] Copies were sent to various ecclesiastical and political
figures with a covering letter from O'Loghlen that stated 'his views
were those of the rural population'. Authorities in the Department of
Finance became more alarmed at the growing public interest in the
Banking Commission Report, and some officials within the Department
acted in a questionable manner when an unsuccessful attempt was
made to gain an injunction against the printing company through the
Chief Solicitor's Office. The Secretary of the Department of Finance
J.J. McElligott, informed MacEntee that O'Loghlen submitted his report
on 'the day of the last meeting of that body [Banking Commission] ...
and that even then he would not allow any discussion to take place on
it.' In the covering letter McElligott stated that:[90]

> it is remarkable that Mr. O'Loghlen who was strangely silent for
> three and a half years has been since the report appeared one of the
> most vocal of our public men. Doubts have been raised as to the
> authorship of the document but no proof of one way or another
> have been forthcoming.[91]

Later, in December, McEntee sought further reassurance from his
staff. McElligott wrote to his minister that he was of the opinion that
'public opinion in regard to the Reports has been founded not on careful reading and study of the Reports themselves'. McElligott laid the
blame firmly at the door of what he considered 'partisans with a strong

bias in favour of the Minority Reports'.[92] Despite these assurances to their minister, the department continued to develop an extended tabular comparison on the Third Minority Report. This time, it purported to show the similarity of the two reports to the Labour Party Programme and the proposals of the IRA.[93]

In February 1939 in the *Irish Monthly*, Coyne wrote once again on the papal encyclicals and their relation to the Banking Commission's reports.[94] He accepted the good intentions of the Third Minority Report but warned that this 'certain type of earnest, zealous Catholic'[95] only led to 'an injury to the Church and a serious danger to the whole cause of Catholic social reform'.[96] Coyne denounced all the recommendations of the Third Report and concluded that such a move would in effect give the Economic Development Commission 'dictatorial powers (i) to make new offences, (ii) to judge about these offences, and (iii) to punish these offences. These sweeping powers were never endorsed by any of the teaching of the social encyclicals'.[97] The significance of Coyne's demolition of the Third Minority Report only served to highlight the fact that Irish social Catholicism was not the homogenous force it had appeared to be.

The Catholic social movement had by now effectively run out of the momentum that had been created at the start of the decade. To many the appeal of economic experimentation had worn off after the failure of the Fianna Fáil economic 'miracle'. Vocationalism, too, had lost support with its association with the authoritarian regimes of Salazar in Portugal, Franco in Spain and Mussolini in Italy. The vast majority of Irish people maintained their support for the major political parties which reflected the dominant Catholic values and culture of the time, and the Irish Catholic social movement was more developed than has been previously understood. The concentration on credit, currency and fiscal reform by Irish commentators was unique among their European counterparts. Contemporary British social Catholics, in particular the Distributists, had not gone so far as to draw up a detailed programme on monetary reform. There is no evidence, apart from the British case, to suggest that other European Catholic social movements believed that currency reform was basic key to reconstructing society along Catholic lines. The pressing need behind the Catholic social movement was a desire to create the opportunity for the social question to be properly addressed. Apart from the Irish labour movement, which had effectively been politically marginalised in the aftermath of the 1913 lock-out, the only other movement that constantly addressed the social question in post-independence Ireland was the Catholic social movement.

It must be admitted that the Irish Catholic social movement made its own positive contribution to the debate on the social question during the first two decades of the independence. It challenged existing views on how best to solve the social question and took away the emphasis on individual self-help and placed more emphasis on the collective role of the community. The movement also managed to apply its principles to Irish economic and social conditions and to make its proposals part of the public discourse on the social question. Despite this, the Catholic social movement failed in its aim to construct the Catholic state in Ireland that they envisaged. J.H. Whyte argued that 'one might have thought that a movement appealing to Catholic principles would have been kicking at an open door'.[98] Yet the door appeared firmly shut. The state, government and civil service, and for that matter the hierarchy, did not want to embrace the radical transformations that were proposed by the Catholic social movement. The main political parties were by their very nature confessional. The civil service was intellectually conservative and more concerned with what it deemed proper administration. The Catholic Church itself had arrived by 1937 at a satisfactory relationship with the state and complimented this by firmly ensuring that internal radicalism – political and economic – did not disrupt the new consensus.

Notes

1 D. Keogh, *The Vatican, the Bishops and Irish Politics, 1919–1939* (Cambridge, 1986); E. Larkin, *The Roman Catholic Church and the Home Rule Movement in Ireland, 1870–1874* (Dublin, 1990); D. Miller, *Church, State and Nation in Ireland, 1898–1921* (Dublin, 1973).
2 See for example, Minority Report to Royal Commission on the Poor Laws. Report on Ireland [cd. 4630], 1909.
3 L.M. Cullen, *An Economic History of Ireland since 1660* (London, 1987 edn.), pp. 134–71.
4 J.H. Whyte, *Church and State in Modern Ireland, 1923–1979* (Dublin, 1980), pp. 62–4.
5 E. Larkin, 'Socialism and Catholicism in Ireland', *Studies*, vol. 73 (Spring 1985), pp. 87–8.
6 C. Lucey, *Catholic Truth Society of Ireland: The First Fifty years* (Dublin, 1949), p. 76.
7 *Irish Catholic*, 28 February 1914.
8 *Ibid.*
9 E. Coyne, 'The Necessity for Social Education for Irishmen', *The Clongowes Annual*, 1914.

10 *Ibid.*, p. 26.
11 M. Ronan, 'Catholic Action in France, Germany, Switzerland, Italy (and Ireland?)', *Irish Ecclesiastical Record*, vol. 13 (April 1919), pp. 276–89.
12 *Ibid.*, pp. 289–90.
13 P. Coffey, *Between Capitalism and Socialism* (Dublin, 1920), pp. 5–6.
14 *Ibid.* pp. 14–15.
15 *Ibid.*
16 W. Moran, 'Social Reconstruction in an Irish State – I', *Irish Theological Quarterly*, vol. 15 (January 1920), pp. 3–5.
17 *Ibid.*, p. 108–9.
18 *Ibid.*, p. 260.
19 P. Coffey, 'An Injustice of the Capitalist System: Its Monopoly of Financial Credit', *Irish Theological Quarterly*, vol. 16 (January 1921), pp. 38–40.
20 I have been unable to find an existing copy of this work. It is referred to in D/Fin, 519, Department of Finance, NAI.
21 *Irish Times*, 23 September 1922.
22 *Ibid.*, 30 September 1922.
23 Peter Coffey to W.T. Cosgrave, 1922, D/Fin, 519, Department of Finance, NAI.
24 *Ibid.*
25 Peter Coffey to W.T. Cosgrave, 25 October 1922, D/Fin, 519, Department of Finance, NAI.
26 *Ibid.*
27 W.T. Cosgrave to Peter Coffey, 27 October 1922, D/Fin, 519, Department of Finance, NAI.
28 Peter Coffey to W.T. Cosgrave, 31 October 1922, D/Fin, 519, Department of Finance, NAI.
29 P. Hyland to W.T Cosgrave, 5 December 1922, D/Fin, 519, Department of Finance, NAI.
30 Quas Primas, quoted from *The Irish Ecclesiastical Record*, vol. 28 (October 1925).
31 Cahill was the most important and prolific member of the Irish Catholic social movement. Born in Callow, Co. Limerick, 1868, he received his secondary education at Mungret College, Co. Limerick and three years of theological training at Maynooth. He entered the Society of Jesus on 8 June 1891 and was ordained to the priesthood six years later. His career in teaching took him first back to his *alma mater* at Mungret, but he moved to Milltown Park in Dublin in 1924, as Professor of Church History, Lecturer in Sociology and later as spiritual director.
32 Notes on the Formation of An Ríoghacht, Cahill Papers, Jesuit Archives, Dublin.
33 *Ibid.*
34 *Ibid.*
35 D. Keogh, 'Church, State and Society', in B. Farrell (ed.), *De Valera's Constitution and Ours* (Dublin, 1988), p. 106; see also *idem, The Vatican*, pp. 208–9.
36 D. Keogh, 'Church, State and Society', p. 108.
37 J. Waldron, 'An Ríoghacht', p. 275.
38 An Ríoghacht Constitution, Cahill Papers, Jesuit Archives, Dublin.
39 Notes on the Projected National Programme, Cahill Papers, Jesuit Archives, Dublin.

40 *Ibid.*
41 *Ibid.*
42 *Ibid.*
43 *Ibid.*
44 D. Keogh, *The Vatican*, chs 6 & 7.
45 *The Assisi Irish Franciscan Monthly*, May 1932.
46 D. Keogh, *The Vatican*, pp. 188–96.
47 *Ibid.*, pp. 49–52; M. Nolan, 'The Influence of Catholic Nationalism on the Legislature of the Irish Free State', *The Irish Jurist*, vol. 10, 1975, pp. 128–67.
48 Department of the Taoiseach, S10183, NAI.
49 *Ibid.*
50 Commission of Inquiry into Banking, Currency and Credit – Reports and Minutes of Evidence (Dublin, 1938).
51 *The Economist*, 13 August 1938.
52 *Ibid.*, pp. 497–501.
53 Per Jacobsson Diaries, (7.12.34), quoted in Erin Elver Jucker-Fleetwood, *A Life for Sound Money: Per Jacobsson – his Biography* (Oxford, 1979), p. 73.
54 Provincial to Edward Cahill, 6 April 1935, Edward Cahill Papers, Jesuit Archives, Dublin.
55 Commission of Inquiry into Banking, Currency and Credit – Memoranda and Evidence (Dublin, 1938), pp. 310–11.
56 *Ibid.*, p. 560.
57 *Ibid.*, pp. 565–6.
58 *Ibid.*, p. 918.
59 *Ibid.*, para. 4321.
60 *Prosperity*, no. 1 (November 1935), p. 1.
61 D 14/36, Department of Justice, NAI.
62 *Ibid.*, p. 6.
63 *Ibid.*
64 D 14/36, Department of Justice, NAI. The Special Branch kept files on a large number of societies and organisations in the 1930s. The Unemployed Workers Movement, the Catholic Unemployed Workers Movement, the Irish Christian Front are examples of the extent to which the Special Branch maintained surveillance.
65 B. Hobson, *Ireland*, p. 171.
66 *Social Justice*, no. 11 (September 1936), p. 83.
67 Bulmer Hobson to Edward Cahill, 9 June 1937, Department of Taoiseach, S12293, NAI.
68 J.G. Smith to Bulmer Hobson, 4 May 1937, Department of Taoiseach, S12293, NAI.
69 J.E. Meade to Glynn, 27 May 1937, Department of Taoiseach, S12293, NAI.
70 Edward Cahill to Eamonn De Valera, 8 September 1937, Department of Taoiseach, S12293, NAI.
71 *Ibid.*
72 J.A. Gaughan, *Alfred O'Rahilly: Public Figure,* vol. 2 (Tralee, 1989), pp. 307–9.
73 Peadar O'Loghlen to Edward Cahill, 8 December 1937, Cahill Papers, Jesuit Archives, Dublin.
74 J. Meenan, *The Irish Economy since 1922* (Liverpool, 1970), p. 221.

75 Peadar O'Loghlen, Commission of Inquiry into Banking, Currency and Credit, 1938 – Minority Report No. III (Dublin, 1938), p. 4. This report was printed privately (see above) and all quotations come from this edition.
76 *Ibid.*, pp. 5–9.
77 *Ibid.*, p. 7.
78 *Ibid.*, pp. 39–43.
79 *Ibid.*, pp. 44–6.
80 *Ibid.*, pp. 46–7.
81 *Ibid.*
82 Department of Finance, D F 9/18/38, NAI.
83 E.O. Cáoimh, 'The Banking Commission', *The Irish Ecclesiastical Record*, vol. LL, no. 5 (May 1938), pp. 499–500.
84 *Ibid.*, p. 503.
85 *Hibernia*, September 1938.
86 E. Coyne, 'Report of the Banking Commission', *Studies*, vol. 26 (Septmeber 1938), p. 395.
87 *The Standard*, 21 October 1938.
88 Provincial to Cahill, 25 October 1938, Edward Cahill Papers, Jesuit Archives, Dublin.
89 *Ibid.*
90 *Ibid.*
91 Department of Finance, D F 9/18/38, NAI.
92 *Ibid.*
93 *Ibid.*
94 E. Coyne, 'The Papal Encyclicals and the Banking Commission', *The Irish Monthly*, vol. LXVII, no. 2 (February 1939), p. 76.
95 *Ibid.*, pp. 77–8.
96 *Ibid.*, p. 79.
97 *Ibid.*
98 J.H. Whyte, *Church and State*, pp. 158–9.

8
Golden Dreams, Harsh Realities: Economics and Informal Empire in the Irish Free State

Mike Cronin

In the post-treaty years the politicians of the Free State, both in government and in opposition, sought to advance their vision for the independent state. Their ideas of how Ireland should be run had to attempt
to assimilate, superficially at least, the ideologies of the revolutionary
era, yet were also tempered by the experience of a divisive civil war and
the reality that, whatever the nationalist dreams may be for the new
nation, Ireland was a small country in an increasingly competitive and
globalised market. It was in the sphere of economics that the division
between dream and reality was thrown into its starkest relief. Foster
noted that 'the rigorous conservatism of the Irish Free State has become
a cliché; what matters most about the atmosphere and mentality of
twenty-six county Ireland in the 1920s is that the dominant preoccupation of the regime was self-definition against Britain – cultural
and political'.[1] For the government of Cumann na nGaedheal during
the 1920s and Fianna Fáil in the 1930s and 1940s, self-definition
against Britain in the economic sphere was difficult, if not impossible,
in the long term. For both governments the problems and demands
which had in part fired the revolutionary period up to 1922 remained
unmet in the post-treaty years. The ownership of land was a contentious issue, emigration was continuing at a high level, and while
the Free State failed to industrialise in any sustained manner there were
problems of unemployment and poverty. The dichotomy for both governments was that while these problems had their roots in the years of
Union and the one-sided trading relationship with Britain, independence could offer no quick fix. While the dreamers of revolutionary
republicanism may have wanted to sever all ties with Britain and
advance a new economic structure based on self-sufficiency and a policy of protectionism, the reality was different. Without firm links to

the British market, thereby enabling Ireland to function in the imperial and international economy, Ireland could never prosper as there was no viable alternative to an Anglo–Irish economic relationship.

The aim of this chapter is to assess the economic ideas which were present in independent Ireland and explore them within the context of the golden dream of national freedom, self-sufficiency and protection-ism, the main components of the dominant revolutionary agenda as opposed to the harsh reality that Ireland had little real freedom in the economic realm as a result of dependence on the British market and an overriding belief in the orthodoxy of British economic thinking. Writing in *Studies* in 1951, R.C. Greary stated his opinion that 'popular sentiment in Ireland has always been protectionist'.[2] This ideal, which had its roots in the ideas of Arthur Griffith is in stark contrast to the public statements of Ernest Blythe who argued in 1924 that 'the Government takes up no doctrinaire attitude on the question of free trade and protection. It regards the matter as one of expediency which may be variously decided in different circumstances'.[3] The expediency in economic matters produced a Cumann na nGaedheal policy which stressed orthodoxy over ideology. As T.K. Whitaker noted:

> It is true that a few moderate tariffs were introduced during the 'twenties but they were certainly not designed in scope or degree to promote the ideal of self-sufficiency. Perhaps this reluctance to embrace an outright protectionist policy can be explained by the first Irish government's desire to establish the standing of the state in the eyes of the world by observing a rather strict orthodoxy in this as well as in other economic and financial matters. Free trade was the accepted commercial philosophy of the day.[4]

Fianna Fáil rallied against this essentially free trade philosophy which resulted in practice in a continued overreliance on trade, pre-dominantly agricultural exports, to Britain. Fianna Fáil argued that Ireland should be moving towards self-sufficiency and increased indus-trial production to ensure future prosperity and that this could be achieved through the construction of a tariff wall as envisaged by Arthur Griffith in the pre-treaty years. In 1928 Sean Lemass informed the Dáil that there was only one way forward for the Irish state eco-nomically and that 'until we get a definite national policy decided on in favour of industrial and agricultural protection and an executive in office prepared to enforce that policy, it is useless to hope for results'.[5] Lemass and his colleagues were presenting the ideal of the golden dream in their opposition to Cumann na nGaedheal's policies during the 1920s, and although attempting to introduce an isolationist version of protectionism and self-sufficiency during the 1930s, by 1938 Lemass had shifted his opinions and returned to the overriding orthodoxy of the 1920s which placed the Irish economy once more alongside that of Britain. He stated 'it was never conceived as possible that the state could be made completely independent of foreign trade or locked in a water tight compartment cut off from the current of international life'.[6] From 1922 right through to the end of the Second World War, Irish economic ideas, with the exception of the economic war years, stressed continuity. Although the rhetoric of the two parties was superficially diametrically opposed, the substance of policy in the economic sphere was near identical. Economic ideas were not the ideas of revolutionary Sinn Féin, but were instead the ideas of post-treaty pragmatism. As Kennedy, Giblin and McHugh noted:

> the initial division between them [Fianna Fáil and Cumann na nGaedheal/Fine Gael] was primarily on nationalist issues. As these issues became blurred with the passage of time, both parties have competed more and more for the centre, following pragmatic economic policies that are often indistinguishable from each other. Irish politics has not provided a hospitable reception for strong economic ideologies, whether of the left or of the right.[7]

The aim of this chapter is not to advance new evidence relating to Ireland's experience of economic life in the post-treaty era as the available government records have been admirably plundered by historians such as Dierdre McMahon[8] and Paul Canning[9] and the statistical detail recently explored by Cormac Ó Gráda[10] amongst others. What is proposed here, instead, is a reinterpretation which aims to place the dichotomy of the revolutionary golden dream and harsh reality in the context of Anglo–Irish relations.

Writing in 1953, Gallagher and Robinson advanced the concept of informal empire[11] where they argued that the nineteenth century spread of British imperialism was conducted on both an informal and formal basis. They stated that:

> It is only when the politics of these new regions fail to provide satisfactory conditions for commercial or strategic integration and when their relative weakness allows, that power is used imperialistically to adjust those conditions. Economic expansion, it is true, will tend

to flow into the regions of maximum opportunity, but maximum opportunity depends as much upon political considerations of security as upon questions of profit. Consequently, in any particular region, if economic opportunity seems large but political security small, then full absorption into the extending economy tends to be frustrated until power is exerted upon the state in question. Conversely, in proportion as satisfactory political frameworks are brought into being in this way, the frequency of imperialist intervention lessens and imperialist control is correspondingly relaxed. It may be suggested that this willingness to limit the use of paramount power to establishing security for trade is the distinctive feature of the British imperialism of free trade in the 19th century, in contrast to the mercantilist use of power to obtain commercial supremacy and monopoly through political possession.[12]

Although pre-Independence Ireland was part of the Union rather than as a colonial nation, the nature of British rule in Ireland during the nineteenth century meant that, despite any trading relations which existed, Ireland was run as part of the formal empire. With the enactment of the Irish Free State Constitution in December 1922 Ireland attained the substance of an independent sovereign nation; however, in line with Gallagher and Robinson, it can be argued that Ireland, far from being independent in the economic sphere remained part of the informal empire:

> Historically, the relationship between these two factors (the economics and politics of informal empire) has been both subtle and complex. It has been by no means a simple case of the use of gunboats to demolish a recalcitrant state in the cause of British trade. The type of political line between the expanding economy and its formal and informal dependencies, as might be expected has been flexible. In practice it has tended to vary with the economic value of the territory, the strength of its political structure, the readiness of its rulers to collaborate with British commercial or strategic purposes, the ability of the native society to undergo economic change without external control, the extent to which domestic and foreign political situations permitted British intervention, and, finally, how far European rivals allowed British policy a free hand.[13]

Gallagher and Robinson argue that India has, in the last two hundred years, passed from informal to formal association, and after independence back to an informal association. Ireland, it can be argued, has gone through a similar progression. Prior to the Act of Union, Ireland's relationship with Britain can be viewed as informal, the years of Union as formal, and the post-independence years as a return to informal association. This post-independence return to a position of informal empire was a negation of the dreams of the revolutionary period which demanded outright separation and an acceptance by the politicians of both Cumann na nGaedheal and Fianna Fáil that an economic relationship with Britain was central to the economic well-being of the Free State.

A problem for the pre-independence revolutionary movement was that national independence, especially after the divisions caused in 1916 between physical force and constitutional Home Rulers, had to be the primary driving force to provide unity amongst the nationalist population. To delve too far below the surface of Sinn Féin post 1916 was to uncover an ideologically diverse movement; unsure of what detailed shape the future should take. In hiding potential schisms under the cover of the goal of independence as the first and foremost objective of the nationalist struggle, Sinn Féin was able to convey an image of unity which would eventually be translated into political success with the achievement of independence. Pre-independence views of the economic future were part of this hidden schism. For most nationalists the line of least resistance meant that the relative weakness of the Irish economy could be explained in terms of Britain's abusive rule and the unfair distribution of wealth to the northeastern corner of the island. Garvin summed this past vision up by stating the commonly held nationalist view in talking of the 'historically often expressed English wish to convert Ireland into a monocrop cattle ranch for metropolitan Britain',[14] or what can be seen in the context of this chapter as the successful product of a policy of formal empire during the nineteenth century. For nationalists the economic future of Ireland once she was an independent nation would be like all else brighter but the actual substance of the planning behind the future was weak. The weakness of the future image is demonstrated by the manner in which the views of Arthur Griffith came to dominate pre-independence Sinn Féin, or as Richard Davis commented, 'Griffith was a propagandist not an objective student of economic theory; like other nationalist politicians he was compelled to account in psychologically satisfying terms, for his country's subjection.'[15]

Griffith's inspiration for his an Irish autarky came from those of the German economist Friedrich List which he attempted to apply, albeit in a very haphazard fashion, to the Irish situation. These ideas were presented to the 1905 Sinn Féin convention and remained at the heart of the economic policy of the independence movement until the reality of self-government dawned in 1922. In brief, Griffith was arguing that Ireland should develop a sound industrial base and not continue to be over reliant on agriculture. To encourage industry the economy would function behind a protectionist wall and not as a free trading nation. The whole policy would be underpinned by the active participation in economic life by the individual, local government and a national assembly. With the onset of independence the banking system and the stock exchange would come to serve the interests of the Irish economy and would sever their links with British capital. Providing for the new industrial base would be Ireland's wealth of natural resources as outlined decades earlier by Thomas Davis who absurdly suggested that Ireland had 400 million tons of coal at her disposal. That Griffith could support the ideas of Davis at the beginning of the twentieth century demonstrates the lack of credible thought which had gone into Sinn Féin's economic policy. The revolutionary dream of a protected, affluent agricultural and industrial mixed-base economy owed more to a rejection of the English stereotype of Ireland as backward than it did to a stringent intellectual assessment of what Ireland could potentially achieve once independent. As Davis concludes, 'Racial pride was thus the motivating power behind Griffith's ambitious programme for economic development... Griffith required proof of his conviction that the Celtic races were inherently superior to the Saxon English. National power through rapid industrial advance appeared the unavoidable acid test of such Celtic preeminence.'[16]

There is a commonly held view that Griffith's economic ideas were poorly conceived and presented a confusing series of images. As Garvin has stated, Griffith 'wanted an industrial Ireland, built up behind tariff barriers; he even contemplated Ireland getting her place in the sun, in the form of African colonies. A common and perhaps accurate criticism of Griffith was that what he really wanted was not a resurgent Gaelic Ireland but Sasca nua darab' ainm Eire (a new England called Ireland) or a Gaelic Manchester'.[17] Equally critically is Brian Girvin's assessment that 'the 1918 election manifesto advocated the protection of Irish industry and other economic changes. The main objective, however, remained the maintenance of a united front against Britain; consequently little thought appears to have been given to economic policy'.[18] Once independence had been won however hard decisions had to be made and a genuine and pragmatic economic policy had to be fashioned. With his death in August 1922, Arthur Griffith was unable to test his ideas against the reality of independence.

Once in power Cumann na nGaedheal had to deal with the reality of an independent Ireland which excluded the industrial wealth of Ulster and, in the economic sphere had to balance the books on the back of a costly civil war. Cumann na nGaedheal rejected many of the ideals of revolutionarw Sinn Féin and their attitude towards the economy is foremost amongst these. A problem for Cumann na nGaedheal was that the Griffith's economic policies of pre-independence did not have the substance to stand the test of transition from Union to Independence. The Cumann na nGaedheal government ran its affairs on the principle that state building must not be antagonistic towards British interests. In the economic sphere this meant a balanced budget and the advancement of economic and social orthodoxy as defined by English pundits. Such a path, as J. J. Lee has pointed out, would 'reassure sceptical English and Anglo–Irish observers of the adult attitude of the infant government'.[19] The need to convince Ireland's old masters that they were responsible demonstrates a school boyish desire to impress, while also illustrating the lack of a plausible economic policy which had a revolutionary pedigree. Garvin noted that 'the Irish rebels were good at agitational politics and conspiracy, but knew nothing about real government. They fondly imagined that the independent Irish state that was to be born would solve problems of culture, and even problems of human nature; economic problems would be easy'.[20] Economic problems were not easy. Cumann na nGaedheal no longer had recourse to the wealth and influence which being an integral part of the Union had afforded and thus had to attempt to realign their new position in the world with their continued economic well being. As Daly noted:

> the achievement of political independence meant for the first time since 1800 an Irish government had full control over economic policy … In theory, at least, the Irish Free State was free to adopt any tariff protection or taxation policy that she might wish. In practice of course, dependence on the British market as the main consumer of Irish imports was not lessened while the relationship between the Irish and British banking systems remained very close. However, given the popular belief held by Arthur Griffith and many others that economic decline in the nineteenth century had been the result of lack of power to impose tariffs, political independence should have meant a new economic era.[21]

Despite the upheavals of the revolutionary period and Sinn Féin dialogue which had championed separatism in all spheres of life, the Irish Free State became during the 1920s part of Britain's informal empire. Relationships between Dublin and London were healthy from the British perspective, with the Irish market providing a profitable export–import balance. In 1929, 92 per cent of all Ireland's exports went to Britain, and 78 per cent of her imports came from Britain.[22] The Free State provided much needed agricultural produce and in turn imported a glut of British industrial goods and raw materials. With the ending of the post-First World War boom, Ireland became a dumping ground for British goods which could not find a market at a time of contracting worldwide business.

In 1923, Cumann na nGaedheal brought together a Fiscal Inquiry Committee to investigate the issue of tariffs. The final report concluded that tariffs would damage Ireland's primary business, that of agriculture. Patrick Hogan stated that 'from the assumption that agriculture was and would remain by far the most important industry in the Free State and that the touchstone by which every economic measure must be judged was its effect on the prosperity of farmers'.[23] The simple conclusion from Hogan's statement is that Cumann na nGaedheal were prepared to let the farming interest and thereby the sanctity of the British market, dictate economic policy. If the introduction of tariffs would in any way disrupt trade between Ireland and Britain, as it appeared they would in 1923, then Ireland would remain a free trader in line with the British economic orthodoxy of the time.

Problems continued throughout the 1920s for the newly-independent Irish state. The lack of a separatist fiscal direction from 1922 had also left the Irish pound on a rate set by the pound sterling, and a decision to retain parity with sterling had been recommended in 1926 by the Banking Commission. The decision was based on the 'assumption that Ireland would remain part of the UK economic unit'[24] or, more challengingly here, that Ireland would remain part of the informal empire. As such the relative overvaluing of sterling throughout the 1920s meant that the Irish pound was also too strong which allowed many continental producers to enter the Irish market and undercut the fledgling Irish firms. Cumann na nGaedheal reacted in 1924 by applying duties to, a limited range of products, but this was in part politically motivated and such a small-scale measure that it had little impact. The tariff issue was again brought to the fore with the 1926 Tariff Commission that was closely based on the British Safeguarding of Industry Act. However, there was a widespread contemporary feeling that the Commission, was stacked in favour of free traders and no wholesale tariff policy emerged. On the back of the Tariff Commission, Gordon Campbell, secretary at the Department of Industry and Commerce, told his minister Patrick McGilligan that 'it was pointless… for officials to devise proposals unless the political will existed to depart from British economic orthodoxy. That will did not exist'.[25] Campbell's argument and both the Fiscal Inquiry Committee and the Tariff Commission demonstrate how clearly the Cumann na nGaedheal administration failed to act independently of Britain. In rejecting the economic philosophy of Griffith, no matter how muddled this may have been, the Free State was left with no option but the acceptance of the British norm. It was as if economic policy was still governed in London rather than Dublin. As Daly has concluded:

> by 1927 Cumann na Gaedheal's economic policy was committed towards continuing the post-famine pattern of close trading connections with Britain with consequent emphasis on agriculture and food based export industries – a beer, biscuits, cars and cattle coalition – and a continuing sterling link. Tariff protection had been depoliticised and was no longer on the agenda.[26]

A prime example of the Irish lack of independent direction and its over-dependence on the British for a lead came in 1931. On the back of the Wall Street crash, the national government in Britain adopted a wholesale policy of protection. As Daly noted, this left 'Ireland as virtually the only free trade economy in Western Europe'.[27] If Cumann na nGaedheal had rejected the revolutionary principles of tariff protection for ideological reasons, this was the time that it could have shown evidence of a truly independent economic policy. Instead, the Free State followed the British lead and in November 1931 the government introduced widespread emergency duties and fell once more in line with Britain. Even those tariffs which were passed contained clauses which were favourable to the continuation of mutually advantageous trade between Ireland and Britain.

In 1932, Cumann na nGaedheal lost a general election and Fianna Fáil entered power for the first time, a position they would retain for 16 years. During their term of office, Cumann na nGaedheal had rejected the golden dream of self-sufficiency and protection as envisaged by Griffith and had done little to advance the cause of Irish industry. The economy was near dependant on the British market with more than 95 per cent of exports crossing the Irish Sea. The party had allowed British economic orthodoxy and British government actions to guide them throughout their term in office. While achieving independent status for the nation Cumann na nGaedheal had, for better or worse, allowed Ireland to become economically part of Britain's informal empire.

In fighting the 1932 election, Fianna Fáil 'explicitly appropriated Griffith's economic policy, spiced with de Valera's own social policy which he presented as the essence of 1916 social doctrine'.[28] In embracing the beliefs of Griffith, Fianna Fáil was turning its back on a decade of harsh reality in the economic sphere and would instead attempt to reinvigorate the golden dream of the revolutionary era. Fianna Fáil motivation for such a path appears multi-faceted. There is the straightforward argument that they were the true representatives of the revolutionary spirit and as such they had to reinvoke all the old ideals and philosophies. This idealism was, however, tempered by an assessment that Cumann na nGaedheal's economic policies had been damaging to the Free State. Whereas the ideological ethos of Fianna Fáil and Cumann na nGaedheal/Fine Gael can be seen to mirror each other in the period following the Second World War, they were still ideologically distinct during the 1930s. Fianna Fáil believed that the continued acceptance of the primacy of the British market and the failure to develop an indigenous industrial base were the ultimate errors of the Cosgrave administration. The Free State should have sought separation from Britain, promoted domestic industry and moved towards a more stridently self-sufficient economy. These ideals were both an embrace of Griffith's thinking as well as an acceptance that the changing worldwide economic system, dominated as it was by depression, trade barriers and mass unemployment, gave credence to the ethos of self-sufficiency and economic isolationism. Also apparent in Fianna Fáil's proposed direction was a rejection of the link between Ireland and the informal empire. As Girvin has noted:

> Fianna Fáil's charge against Cumann na nGaedheal was that their economic policies, however well intentioned allowed economic policy to be formulated outside the state. Fianna Fáil's strategy called for the nationalisation of economic policy. This necessitated breaking trading links with Britain and integrating economic policy firmly within the state apparatus. Policy formation would therefore be determined internally: the state would not just administer the existing system, it would define the context within which all economic activity would take place.[29]

The real difficulty for Fianna Fáil was to define the context within which economic activity would take place while ensuring the material well-being of the nation and finding some kind of alternative to the British market. Separation from Britain, if it was to be genuine, would also necessitate separation from the influence of British capital and a rethinking of the banking, currency and stock exchange issues. Ideologically the continuation of the links with British capital were an anathema of Fianna Fáil while in opposition. Sean MacEntee had stated shortly after Fianna Fáil's entry to the Dáil:

> The banks, which have been leading the Irish farmer, crushing Irish industry, investing Irish money abroad, jeopardising it in British securities, want to retain the present government in office for their purposes... A Fianna Fáil government would not be tied up with the old Unionist Party and the banks.[30]

In this context, the statement that 'the long-standing connections between the two countries could not be dismantled without pain'[31] has as much relevance for 1932 as it had in 1922. The question for Fianna Fáil as it embarked on its economic programme was whether it could deal with the pain which their stated policy aims would induce. To destroy the links with Britain, to develop an indigenous industrial base and to challenge the power of the banking system would require a genuine and resolute sense of purpose.

Sean Lemass, as Minister for Industry and Commerce, had a clear set of objectives for his time in office. As Girvin noted, 'he came to office armed with a coherent ideology and a specific set of policies... Indeed there is a close correlation between 1932 and 1938 and the various statements of policy attributed to Lemass and Fianna Fáil between 1926 and 1932'.[32] The basic tenet of Fianna Fáil's economic policy was self-sufficiency. This ideal would apply to both the agricultural and industrial sphere and would, it was believed, produce a reasonable level of prosperity, secure jobs for the future and separate Ireland from its dependence on the British market. To secure such self-sufficiency the Irish economy would be protected by a high level of tariffs and quotas. All the benefits of such a policy would filter down to Irish concerns, thus a direct contradiction of the Cumann na nGaedheal experience where any benefits found their way into British hands. The ultimate symbol of Fianna Fáil's economic policy was the economic war that began in June 1932.

De Valera and his party had long held that the land annuities payments due to the British government under the terms of the treaty were founded on dubious legalities. This weakness was reinforced by the financial agreements of 1923 and 1926 between Cumann na nGaedheal and the British government, the first of that was secret, the latter that had not been ratified by the Dáil.[33] De Valera was using the issue of land annuities to pursue his dream of a full sovereignty as distinct to the Free State's dominion status which had emerged from the treaty and his behaviour in early negotiations with the British fit in with the general pattern of treaty dismantlement which he pursued in office. In June 1932, at a meeting with the representatives of the British government in Dublin, Dominions Secretary J.H. Thomas and Secretary for War Lord Hailsham, to deal with the annuities issue, de Valera brought national, not economic issues to the fore by haranguing the British once more with his Document number two.[34] The British perceived this as 'a long interned relic of the Treaty negotiations' and they 'could hardly believe that de Valera meant them to take it seriously'.[35] At the meeting de Valera informed the British that the next £3 million instalment of land annuities would not be paid. The British responded with the Special Duties Act on 14 July 1932 that put a 20 per cent duty on most Irish agricultural imports. The Irish responded in turn with the Emergency Duties Bill which put a reciprocal 20 per cent duty on a host of British industrial exports such as coal, cement and electrical machinery. Considering that 96 per cent of all Irish exports were bound for the British market such a policy was high risk and cost Ireland some £18 million per year during the duration of the war. The cost for Britain at a time of economic depression was also damaging, but the effects not as extreme as Ireland was a much smaller source of income as a percentage of GDP for Britain, than Britain was for Ireland.

Within the context of this chapter the economic war has to be viewed as the ultimate symbol of the pursuit of the golden dream of untrammelled sovereignty. The problem however is to fathom why such a policy was pursued. Lemass, as previously stated, had a clear set of economic objectives planned for his time in government, which, with the addition of his greater understanding and analysis of the economy, would essentially invoke the ideals of Griffith. Such ideals would have challenged the supremacy of the British market yet was the economic war necessary as part of this plan? There is widespread agreement that the economic war had more to do with de Valera's pursuit of a political settlement for the Free State rather than the requirements of economic strategy. As Daly noted:

> The dispute over financial payments was part of a broader constitutional disagreement, and the deterioration in Anglo-Irish relations

owed more to de Valera's wish to dismantle the 1921 Treaty than a failure to repay monies owed.[36]

If the economic war can thus be viewed as an essentially political crusade, but one that had huge economic ramifications, where did this leave Lemass in his pursuit of economic policy? It appears that any ideals he may have had prior to 1932 were to be completely overshadowed by the financial cost and dislocation caused by the economic war. By breaking so clearly with Britain in the pursuit of economic war and destroying the mutual trading relationship Ireland had attempted to break the link to informal empire. Such attempted destruction of a profitable relationship was completely unwelcome to Britain and was a relationship that the British were keen to restore. As the economic war progressed, many Fianna Fáil politicians would also seek a restoration to favoured-nation status – mutual antagonism was too costly. By pursuing the economic war policy the Free State had failed to reach a preferential agreement with Britain at the Ottawa conference, as had been the case for most empire nations. Whereas Britain and her dominions, and some other nations such as Argentina had achieved a mutually beneficial system of preferential tariffs to cope with the post-depression world that had signalled the end of free trade, the Free State was excluded. Accompanied by the cost of the economic war such exclusion was damaging. While Britain and her fellow Commonwealth nations benefited Ireland was left out in the cold. This is the wider context against which Fianna Fáil policies and general Anglo–Irish relations must be judged. While the empire moved in the direction of mutual accommodation and profitability, the Free State languished in the poverty of exclusion for the sake of a political crusade.[37]

Lemass attempted to invigorate industry through his Trade Loans Acts which encouraged investment in native industry and the Board of External Trade that he proposed would regulate the Irish market. The creation of the Industrial Credit Organisation (ICO) in 1933 was a direct boost to industry as credit was more freely available than had been the case. Although the ICO was not a direct challenge to the power of British banks and the comparative weakness of the Irish stock exchange it did make funds available which had previously been difficult for Irish firms to access. By 1935 some £3.5 million had been made available. All this legislation was underpinned by a firm belief in the policy of protection. It has been argued that such a protectionist stance generated some 51 000 jobs by 1939 with 50 per cent of industrial concerns protected.[38] Despite the wealth and imagination of his legislation how should Lemass' policies in the period up to 1938 be perceived? He undoubtedly applied many of the basic ideals which had belonged to revolutionary Sinn Féin although this was done on an informed basis and not in the muddled fashion which had been apparent in the work of Griffith. Girvin stated that

> Between 1932 and 1938 some major blockages to industrial develop-ment had been removed. The political commitment to industrial protection and tillage, the economic war with Britain, and the gen-eral international situation in 1932 permitted a greater flexibility than heretofore in policy making. The changed nature of state inter-vention was crucial to the success of the policy initiatives during the 1930s.[39]

Lemass then had brought a new vigour to the state's role in the eco-nomic sphere. Self-sufficiency, protectionism and industrial growth had become the combined mantra of Fianna Fáil during their first half decade in office. By pursuing such a course, Fianna Fáil had seemingly jetti-soned the overriding economic orthodoxy which had been present during the years of the Cumann na nGaedheal administration and had broken with Britain. The link to empire, informal or otherwise, had been challenged – or so it seemed. The pursuit of economic war as part of the nationalist crusade by de Valera had enforced a set of rules and decisions on Lemass and other economic planners which essentially strait-jacketed them. An independent economic policy, although put into practice and having a revolutionary pedigree, was subservient to the nationalist dream in the same way that the economic ideas of Griffith had been sidelined in the quest for national independence. By survey-ing the non-legislative actions of Lemass and the events of 1938 it is possible to see that, despite the veneer of breaking with Britain, eco-nomic reality demanded that the status of informal empire nation had to be maintained if Ireland was to prosper. Despite the liberation which the economic war afforded to generate self-centred economic policy, such a non-viable policy could not be continued in the long term. Ideological commitments and golden dreams were one thing, economic reality was another.

Despite the positive legislation enacted by Lemass up to 1938, which allowed the Free State to pursue self-sufficiency and protection, he had misgivings throughout over the pursuit of the economic war. Despite his own economic ideals all the plans were being thrown out of line by such a costly campaign and this cost was showing itself in growing unemployment and a failure to increase domestic consumption. In November 1932 Lemass stated that

> It is, to say the least doubtful if we are in a position to maintain the economic war. It is equally doubtful if the termination of the economic war will alone greatly improve our position. We have reached the point where a collapse of our economic system is in sight.[40]

The strength of Lemass' forecast of impending doom was undoubtedly exaggerated to mobilise his colleagues yet an essential fact remains: Lemass did not believe in the long-term viability of an Irish economy cut off from Britain. This ideal is reinforced by Fianna Fáil's lack of activity in other policy areas, particularly banking. The ideology of the revolution had stressed that a reform of the banking system and the control of capital as centrally important. Without reform of these dated structures which allowed for an over bearing influence of British banks and money, then Ireland, despite any other independent developments could never truly be free. Sean MacEntee appointed a Banking Commission in 1934 which did not finally report until 1938. Admittedly the make up of the Commission was essentially conservative in outlook, but the contents of its report, in the context of a Fianna Fáil government are quite revealing. The Commission 'reaffirmed the correctness of Cosgrave's economic and social policy'. It criticised 'the increase in national debt … and found that the commercial banking system adequately served the needs of the country'.[41] That MacEntee, Lemass and Fianna Fáil could bring together a Commission with such a conservative outlook and unblinkingly accept their findings shows a lack of gusto for the pain of separation. The same is true of the sterling link. With the departure from the gold standard in 1931 Cumann na nGaedheal had followed Britain. Once in office Fianna Fáil did nothing to try and break the links between the two currencies and continued to allow the Bank of England to set the value of the Irish pound on international markets. Despite any wishes to the contrary Fianna Fáil could not have broken the link with sterling. In the wake of the depression the realignment of international finance around the sterling area, of which Ireland was part, freedom from British money markets would not only be highly damaging to the domestic economy but would be difficult to achieve. As Cain and Hopkins have noted, 'apart from the dependant parts of the empire, which had no option, the rest of the countries which followed sterling after September 1931 were theoretically free to resist incorporation but, in practice, were forced into it because of a heavy dependence on British trade, or British credit, or both'.[42] As a small nation, and one with an over-reliance on the British market, the Free State had to become part of the sterling area and thus had no opportunity for genuine fiscal independence. By being so clearly locked into Britain's sphere of economic influence, Fianna Fáil, despite pursuing the policy of economic war, could have no freedom from the power of informal empire. In this Ireland was no different from Australia who only did 50 per cent of her business with Britain, or South Africa who did not want to join the sterling area but because of the depression in gold prices had no choice and joined in 1933. The sterling area was the ultimate symbol of informal empire throughout the 1930s and Ireland was a constituent part of this.

The final judgement on Fianna Fáil's economic policies and the links with informal empire have to be judged in the context of the 1938 Anglo–Irish Trade Agreement. The 1938 agreements signalled the end of the economic war and settled other constitutional issues which had long troubled relations between Ireland and Britain. The 1935 Coal–Cattle pact had allowed for the import of Irish cattle to Britain and the export of British industrial goods to Ireland on a mutual pound to pound basis. While this had steadied trade between the two nations, further agreement was required. The 1938 agreement settled the land annuities issue with a one-off payment of £10 million by the Irish, it returned the treaty ports to Irish hands and set up an open trading relationship once more between the two nations. Ireland was given free access to the British market in line with other dominion states while Britain could enter the Irish market without paying excessive tariffs. There are two main issues which need exploring in the light of these agreements. First the reasoning behind the settlement for both nations, and second where the agreements left the relationship between Ireland and Britain.

Britain's stance throughout the economic war had been one of opposition to the Irish position. This opposition was due to the cost of such a policy to Britain; the Free State was after all one of her most important markets. At the outset of the economic war a Board of Trade note which was circulated to the British Cabinet showed that Ireland had surpassed Australia, Germany and the USA to become Britain's most important trading partner.[43] The Free State's policy of economic war was thus endangering British profits, especially in the coal market, and was a direct challenge to the ethos of informal empire. There were also concerns raised that the Irish policy would spread unease through the empire and could possibly lead other nations to challenge the British position. As a result of the potentially high cost of the economic war there were certain figures in the British government who demanded a settlement. While they understood that the wider policies of Fianna Fáil in dismantling the treaty were damaging, there was also a realisation that a profitable trading relationship with the Free State was more important and that informal empire had to be restored. As the 1930s progressed and the threat from Hitler and his allies increased so the need for British settlement with Ireland grew. A factor not missed by the Irish. In late 1937 McElligott was

> stressing the absolute necessity, from our point of view, of finally set-
> tling all our outstanding economic and finical differences with Great
> Britain … The international outlook is at present obscure and the
> government as well as public opinion in Great Britain are so alive to
> the imperative need of strengthening their defences that we should
> take advantage of this situation. Great Britain can provide most of
> her war requirements, except food, and she undoubtedly wishes to
> draw her imported food supplies from the nearest possible source.[44]

If the changing worldwide situation and the cost of the economic war to Britain was altering her approach to the situation, then the long-term sustainability of such a policy was also directing the Irish towards compromise. As stated, Lemass was lukewarm on the policy through-out the course of the economic war, but as the 1930s progressed it became clear that Ireland was not only paying dear for such a policy, but the supposedly positive aspects of Fianna Fáil's general economic policy were failing to emerge. Ireland had failed to develop alternative markets to those of Britain, domestic industry was not developing as quickly as it should, and the cost to the state in unemployment and emigration were too high. 'From the Irish viewpoint the policy of self-sufficiency had been implemented as far as it could sensibly go, if not further, and once this had been accomplished there was no good rea-son to prolong a conflict that was now needlessly damaging. Moreover the failure to achieve any substantial redirection of trade had under-lined the essential dependence on the British market'.[45]

It is apparent that by 1937 both nations required an ending to eco-nomic conflict. The challenge of the Free State which questioned infor-mal empire since 1932 was damaging to Britain and the impending international upheavals did nothing to calm concerns. For the Irish it was becoming clear that the golden dream, despite its merits and its links to the revolutionary ethos of Fianna Fáil, was unworkable. While

Fianna Fáil had constitutionally deconstructed the Treaty, economic separation was unsustainable. As Daly noted in relation to 1938, 'much of the gloss was fading off the Fianna Fáil economic program … a return to more traditional policies was gaining favour'.[46] Girvin is equally clear stating, 'the failure of agriculture to respond to state policy, particularly tillage, reduced government flexibility in economic matters. Without a radical re-orientation of agricultural production and a dynamic industrial sector the pressure to renegotiate trading relations with the United Kingdom remained strong'.[47] McMahon makes the most damning conclusion on the whole Fianna Fáil policy by stating, 'the dispute showed just how vital the British market was, whatever high-flown ideals were being touted to the contrary in 1932'.[48]

That Fianna Fáil's pursuit of the golden dream failed is clear, although this is not to condemn the policies of Lemass outright as definite improvements were made in the economic sphere. These improvements were not enough however and could not be sustained by an economic policy which attempted to exclude Britain. It is through the British attitude to the 1938 agreements that the move back to informal empire status can best be understood. In 1935 Sir Horace Wilson informed J.H. Thomas, the Dominions Secretary, that progress had to be made in the trade dispute with the Free State, ideally with a return to the 1932 position, otherwise Lemass' policy of promoting Irish industry would weaken the demand for British goods on the Irish market.[49] Wilson's argument is enlightening, as it demonstrates a British desire not only return to the Irish market, but to do so in a position of supremacy. Equally illuminating was J.W. Dulanty at the Treasury who warned the Cabinet in 1938 that a German trade delegation was visiting Dublin to further economic links between the two nations. Dulanty argued that Britain should settle its dispute with Ireland even if sacrifices were needed so as to secure the Irish market and thereby deflect the economic threat of Germany.[50] Dulanty, as with Wilson earlier, was showing the classic symptoms of a desire to return to informal empire. Britain should be in a situation of primacy with her dominions and that primacy should not be challenged by outsiders.

With the conclusion of the 1938 agreements Ireland returned to the informal empire. Not only that, but Fianna Fáil had accepted the harsh reality that separation from Britain could not be achieved economically no matter what the dream of revolution had demanded. The economic war had demonstrated that Ireland needed Britain and vice versa. Although Britain could exclude her dominions from a favourable status, as had happened with the Australians and their cattle during the 1930s, she was far more interested in having a profitable relation-ship as was the case with Ireland after 1938. In 1937 Ireland was still exporting 91 per cent of her total output to, and 50 per cent of her imports from Britain.[51] The power of the sterling area, of which Ireland was part, cemented the overriding importance of the shared market between the two nations. Fianna Fáil's period of office from 1932 allowed for the resolution of many issues surrounding the treaty and in this they were more nationally and radically-minded than Cumann na nGaedheal. In economics however there was no escape and the whole tenor of the 1938 agreement and Anglo–Irish trading relationships dur-ing the Second World War demonstrate that pragmatic profit, even if that meant a deal with the devil, was more important to Ireland than the revolutionary dream.

Notes

1   R.F. Foster, *Modern Ireland, 1600–1972* (London, 1989), p. 516.
2   R.C. Greary, 'Irish Economic Development since the Treaty', in *Studies*, vol. 50, 1951, p. 403.
3   *Ibid.*, p. 405.
4   T.K. Whitaker, 'From Protection to Free Trade – The Irish Experience', in *Administration*, vol. 40, 1973, p. 407.
5   *Parliamentary Debates*, Dáil Eireann, 22, cols. 213/4, 22 February 1928.
6   See J.J. Lee, *Ireland 1912–85, Politics and Society* (Cambridge, 1989), p. 217.
7   K.A. Kennedy, T. Giblin. and D. McHugh, *The Economic Development of Ireland in the Twentieth Century* (London, 1988), p. 34.
8   D. McMahon, *Republicans and Imperialists. Anglo–Irish Relations in the 1930s* (New Haven, 1984).
9   P. Canning, *British Policy Towards Ireland, 1921–41* (Oxford, 1985).
10   C. ÓGráda, *Ireland, A New Economic History, 1780–1939* (Oxford, 1994).
11   J. Gallagher and R. Robinson, 'The Imperialism of Free Trade', in *Economic History Review*, vol. 6, no. 1, 1953.
12   *Ibid.*, p. 6.
13   *Ibid.*, p. 7.
14   T. Garvin, *Nationalist Revolutionaries in Ireland* (Oxford, 1987), p. 130.
15   R.P. Davis, *Arthur Griffith and Non-Violent Sinn Fein* (Dublin, 1974), p. 127.
16   *Ibid.*, p. 144.
17   T. Garvin, *Nationalist Revolutionaries*, p. 113.
18   B. Girvin, *Between Two Worlds. Politics and Economy in Independent Ireland* (Dublin, 1989), p. 11.
19   J.J. Lee, *Ireland*, p. 109.
20   T. Garvin, *Nationalist Revolutionaries*, p. 131.
21   M.E. Daly, *Social and Economic History of Ireland since 1800* (Dublin, 1981), p. 136.

22 See P. Cain, and A.G. Hopkins, *British Imperialism: Crisis and Deconstruction 1914–1990* (London, 1993), p. 81.
23 Statement by Patrick Hogan, Minister for Agriculture in M.E. Daly, *Social and Economic History*, p. 140.
24 M.E. Daly, *Industrial Development and Irish National Identity, 1922–39* (Dublin, 1992), p. 17.
25 J.J. Lee, *Ireland*, pp. 123–4.
26 M.E. Daly, *Industrial Development*, p. 32.
27 M.E. Daly, *Social and Economic History*, p. 144.
28 J.J. Lee, *Ireland*, p. 170.
29 B. Girvin, *Between Two Worlds*, p. 89.
30 See K. Allen, *Fianna Fail and Irish Labour, 1926 to the Present* (London, 1997), p. 21.
31 M.E. Daly, *Industrial Development*, p. 7.
32 B. Girvin, *Between Two Worlds*, p. 90.
33 Ronan Fanning, *Independent Ireland* (Dublin, 1983), p. 112.
34 Document number two was de Valera's alternative to the Treaty which he had released to the press during the Treaty debates in the Dáil during January 1922. The main differences between the Treaty and Document number two was the legal status of Ireland, the new state's relationship with the Commonwealth and the wording of the oath of allegiance. For details see, F.S.L. Lyons, *Ireland Since the Famine* (London, 1971), pp. 441–50.
35 D. McMahon, *Republicans and Imperialists*, p. 56.
36 M.E. Daly, *Industrial Development*, p. 155.
37 For details on the Ottawa conference and its benefits to empire see P. Cain and A.G. Hopkins, *British Imperialism*, pp. 84–93, and for Irish participation at the conference see D. McMahon, *Republicans and Imperialists*, pp. 74–9.
38 B. Girvin, *Between Two Worlds*, p. 106.
39 *Ibid.*, p. 113.
40 *Ibid.*, p. 92.
41 J.J. Lee, *Ireland*, p. 199.
42 P. Cain and A.G. Hopkins, *British Imperialism*, p. 79.
43 See P. Canning, *British Policy*, p. 136.
44 See R. Fanning, *The Irish Department of Finance* (Dublin, 1978), p. 295.
45 K.A. Kennedy, T. Giblin and D. McHugh, *Economic Development of Ireland*, p. 48.
46 M.E. Daly, *Industrial Development*, p. 159.
47 B. Girvin, *Between Two Worlds*, p. 127.
48 D. McMahon, *Republicans and Imperialists*, p. 288.
49 See P. Canning, *British Policy*, p. 161.
50 *Ibid.*, p. 163.
51 P. Cain and A.G. Hopkins, *British Imperialism*, p. 81.

9

New Ireland, Old Empire and the Outside World, 1922–49: The Strange Evolution of a 'Dictionary Republic'

Donal Lowry

The right to pursue a policy of neutrality in wartime has generally come to be considered in the twentieth century as the ultimate yardstick of national sovereignty. Yet within a year of the end of the Second World War, in which Irish neutrality had been so successfully asserted, and almost a decade after all monarchical forms had been expunged from the internal institutions of the Irish state, there took place in the Dáil what must surely rank as one of the most extraordinary parliamentary exchanges in the history of national autonomy. In the summer of 1946, James Dillon, one of the few parliamentary critics of neutrality, read – to the embarrassment of the Taoiseach, Eamon de Valera – the letter of credence recently presented by the Irish Minister Plenipotentiary to the King of Sweden. The Irish Minister's credentials opened with the words, 'My Brother', and concluded, 'Given at my Court at Buckingham Palace, 20th day of June, 1946. I am, Sir, my Brother, Your Majesty's good Brother George, Rex Imperator. Countersigned – Eamon de Valera'.[1] Dillon alleged, moreover, that Dáil deputies felt a greater sense of indignity when Joseph Walshe, the first Irish diplomat to hold the formal rank of Ambassador, was appointed as envoy to the Holy See with letters of credence signed by the British sovereign, who was also titled, of course, 'Defender of the [Protestant Reformed] Faith' (even if on this occassion the King did not include this title, in deference to Irish sensitivities).[2] De Valera sought to counter such disclosures by referring – in the face of this satirised account of his 'dictionary republic' – to several reputable dictionaries and encyclopaedias in order to demonstrate that Ireland was effectively a republic 'externally associated' with, but not a member of, the British

Commonwealth of Nations:

> We are an independent republic, associated as a matter of our exter-
> nal policy with the States of the British Commonwealth. To mark
> this association, we avail ourselves of the procedure of the External
> Relations Act [of 1936]…the King recognized by the States of the
> British Commonwealth therein named acts for us, under advice, in
> certain specified matters in the field of our external relations…The
> British Commonwealth claims to be an elastic, growing, developing
> organism, and the statesmen of the Commonwealth have, I think,
> adopted the view of Joseph de Maistre that 'In all political systems
> there are relationships which it is wiser to leave undefined.'[3]

John A. Costello, however, de Valera's successor as Taoiseach, who
put an end to this ambivalence by taking Ireland formally out of
the Commonwealth in 1949, mocked the idea of external association
which had motivated de Valera for a generation as 'pirouetting on the
head of a pin'.[4]

Since the Second World War, the advance to independence of several
other former British imperial territories may be regarded as peculiar,
but none was as irregular as Ireland's progress. The symbolic ambigui-
ties of post-war Irish diplomatic appointments to Sweden and the Holy
See, at a time when Irish sovereignty had been thoroughly established
in international law, serve to remind us that it is difficult either to fit
Ireland simply into the grouping of those small independent states
which emerged from the defeat and collapse of European dynastic
empires at the end of the First World War, or into that category of the
British dominions, whose status within the British Commonwealth of
Nations Ireland shared fully from 1922 to 1936, and somewhat equivo-
cally, in the field of external relations, from 1937 until the declaration
of a republic in 1949.[5] Unlike Ireland, the new European states which
emerged in 1918–19 immediately attained full sovereignty in both
internal and external affairs. The British Empire, Ireland's former 'colonial
master', was, in contrast to the defeated multi-ethnic European
empires, a victorious power at the fullest of its territorial extent, overshadowed but by no means yet wholly eclipsed by the United States.[6]

The creation of an Irish foreign policy and diplomatic service coincided with a transitional moment in the evolution of international
relations, and this generational impression stamped the character of
Irish foreign policy until the 1950s. The revolutionary leadership
which emerged after the 1916 Insurrection was acutely aware of the

importance of world opinion in the campaign for independence, not least because global recognition of Irish sovereignty remained the goal by which true independence would be measured. After all, Ireland's 'exaltation among the nations' was a principal objective of the 1916 Proclamation, and this international awareness, latently imbued with the fashionable Wilsonian vocabulary of self-determination, continued to infuse nationalist rhetoric in the revolutionary years. One of the first documents to be ratified by the First Dáil on 21 January 1919 was a 'Message to the Free Nations of the World', which called on friendly countries to support the right of the Irish Republic to recognition at the Paris Peace Conference.[7] Between 1919 and 1921 Dáil Eireann established a Publicity Department and a Department of Foreign Affairs, both of which were primarily concerned with neutralising and countering British propaganda about political unrest in Ireland. There was considerable overlap in function between both departments, which were served by an international network of propagandists and envoys. In their campaign to bring the British before the bar of world opinion, these often relied on the assistance of elements of the Irish diaspora in Europe, the Americas and the dominions, and not least on the extensive facilities offered by Irish Catholic clergy. 'Permanent', if unaccredited, Dáil envoys were appointed in a number of countries, including Italy, Germany, Spain, the USA, Argentina and Chile, while other representatives visited South Africa, Canada, Australia and the rest of Latin America.

Arms supplies were promised by the fascist journalist and future dictator, Benito Mussolini, and contact was established with the Italian nationalist, Gabriele d'Annunzio, who wished to form a 'League of [the] Oppressed' nations, including the Irish and other 'victimised peoples'.[8] Sean T. O'Kelly, Sinn Féin envoy in Paris, also attempted to form an anti-imperialist alliance of Egyptian, Indian, Afrikaner and other subjugated nationalities 'to alarm the English', and Eamon de Valera during his tour of the United States in 1920 enjoyed strong support from the 'Friends of the Freedom of India'.[9] A draft treaty negotiated with Russian representatives in Washington in 1920, provided that the Irish Republic would assume responsibility for the interests of Catholic citizens within Russia. This somewhat implausible arrangement, conducted more with an eye to the Vatican than to Moscow, reflected the somewhat unreal world of Irish diplomacy in this period. In spite of notable successes in fundraising and establishing advantageous contacts with foreign journalists to counter British propaganda, however, Sinn Féin foreign policy failed in its major objective of gaining official recognition from either the Paris Peace Conference or the American government.

However sympathetic public opinion may have been in other countries, foreign governments were not willing to alienate the British. Sinn Féin's cause was not helped by being associated in French minds with the 'pro-German' insurrection of 1916, and not a single foreign government, with the transitory exception of the Soviet Union, recognised the international legality of Dáil Eireann. As Sinn Féin would find, in common with other stateless nationalists then seeking recognition in Paris, the world of diplomacy, for all its latent idealism, was still traditional, legalistic and obsessed with matters of protocol and precedence.[10] One significant success for Irish foreign policy at this time, however, was the mission in April 1921 of Sinn Fein envoy Colonel Maurice Moore to South Africa, where he gained access to the Prime Minister, General Jan Christaan Smuts, one of the founders of the League of Nations, who at that time was regarded as the most influential statesman in the Empire. Moore's mission further contributed to Smuts's intermediary role in bringing about the Truce, as well as providing the basis for a memorandum on the working of dominion status for the delegates to the Treaty negotiations in London later that year.[11]

Irish self-government also occurred critically at a time when Britain's relationship with the dominions – those 'senior' self-governing states of the Empire which were increasingly being described collectively as the 'British Commonwealth of Nations' – was being redefined. Irish self-government came in the form of dominion status enshrined in a treaty, rather than that unfettered international sovereignty enjoyed by the other emerging states of Europe. The Treaty demanded an oath of allegiance to the British King, and the retention of military bases locked Ireland into Britain's defence network, thus making neutrality in any future war seemingly impossible. Although Irish dominion status had been linked to that of Canada, the 'senior dominion', the precise extent of that status for both dominions was still unclear. Optimists could point to the enhanced postwar international prestige of Canada, Australia, New Zealand and South Africa, as well as Canadian and South African assertions of national rights. Sceptics argued, however, that these countries were still, at best, 'junior' partners, enjoying only such influence as had been devolved to them by Westminster. True, Arthur Berriedale Keith, generally acknowledged as the Empire's greatest legal authority, publicly reminded the British Government that, in 1920, Andrew Bonar Law, Leader of the House of Commons, had declared that membership of the Commonwealth was based on free association and that the dominions could therefore not be coerced. Such statements, however, were designed to diffuse dominion nationalism rather than encourage secession. In practical terms, Canada and Australia would have found it virtually impossible to secede due to the confederal or federal structures of their respective constitutions, as well as in the case of Canada – Ireland's constitutional template – internal ethnic divisions.

Of the remaining unitary dominions, Newfoundland and New Zealand were if anything keen on closer imperial ties, while the Union of South Africa was the only dominion with serious 'non-British' republican elements, and it was these that Bonar Law's declaration was primarily designed to disarm. His statement, then, was an empty gesture, since both he and the Cabinet were determined to keep the other dominions in line by a combination of diplomacy and defence and economic interest. In keeping with this policy, nothing was left to chance in the case of Ireland; its membership of the Commonwealth was made fundamental to the Treaty. Historians might later debate what additional concessions might have been won by a firmer Irish diplomacy over the Treaty, including revisions of its financial clauses and on the border issue, but British governments in the 1920s would never have conceded a *republic* associated with the Commonwealth; it simply did not form part of their mental framework or constitutional furniture. Berriedale Keith was asking for a bold political initiative which, in his view, would lead to less damage of Crown and Commonwealth prestige by not forcing Irish allegiance, but the British Cabinet regarded such views as eccentric and unrealistic.

For perhaps a majority of the war-weary British electorate, the prospect of a continuing conflict in Ireland was not popular, except in the case of a perceived vital interest such as the titles and constitutional recognition of the Crown in its 'oldest overseas possession', at a time when 'Bolshevikism' was believed to be threatening the established order of society. The British had at great human and material cost recently expanded their Empire to what was to be its greatest extent, and in the years coinciding with the Irish Revolution were planning the creation of a vast new empire in the Near and Middle East; these gains would not be yielded easily. Besides, members of the British Cabinet had themselves participated in imperial wars, and in several cases they had lost sons in the Great War, in which they had become accustomed to committing enormous numbers of soldiers to massive offensives, which dwarfed the Anglo–Irish conflict. Such men did not tend to regard war lightly, but neither did they believe, after such losses, that there were not fundamental interests worth upholding at almost any cost. Moreover, there were wider imperial issues at stake in Ireland in this period, and the British always had an eye to the potential impact of Irish politics on vulnerable regions of their Empire, including South Africa, India and Egypt. As Michael Collins correctly anticipated, once the British had withdrawn in good order without significant loss of prestige, dominion attitudes would prove crucial in restraining British responses to Irish assertiveness:

> [The British] had reached their high-water mark. They had the power, the force, the armament, to reconquer us, but they hesitated to exercise that power without getting a world mandate...They could not acquiese in the establishment of a Republican government so close to their own shores. This would be regarded by them as a challenge – a defiance which would be a danger to the very safety of the British Empire and would form a headline for other places. South Africa would be the first to follow and Britain's security and prestige would be gone. The British...believed they dare not agree to such a forcible breaking away. It would show not only their Empire to be intolerable, but themselves feeble and futile...Separation by peaceful stages of evolution does not expose her and does not endanger her...Our [dominion] immunity can never be challenged without challenging the immunity of Canada...a violation of our freedom would be a challenge to the freedom of Canada.[13]

Whatever its possible advantages, dominion status remained at the heart of the theoretical dispute among nationalists over the Treaty which erupted into civil war in 1922. Even Kevin O'Higgins, champion of the agreement, did not believe that dominion status as defined by the British could form the basis of a lasting settlement, since Ireland was coerced into a supposedly 'free' association of the British Commonwealth, and could not therefore be considered to be truly equal with Britain and the dominions.[13] Irish advocates of the Treaty were not helped by David Lloyd George, the British Prime Minister who had led the British Treaty negotiations, who preferred not to define dominion status. 'That is not the way of the British Constitution', he told the House of Commons: 'We realise the danger of rigidity and the danger of limiting our constitution by too many finalities'.[14]

He was extremely rigid himself, however, when it came to defining what could not be accommodated within dominion status. Besides, the northern border of the new state had yet to be agreed. Moreover, the

Irish Free State was radically different in several key respects to any other dominion. The latter had evolved from colonies of settlement and to varying degrees accepted their roles within the Empire, but Irish nationalists considered Ireland to be a European motherland in its own right. Even Lionel Curtis, imperialist ideologue and adviser to the British Government during the Treaty negotiations, conceded that Ireland possessed one of the most ancient civilizations in Europe. It could not be called one of the 'daughter nations' but was, in fact, one of 'the most prolific of all the mothers'.[15] Nevertheless, dominion status was imposed on the Irish plenipotentiaries after the conclusion of a bitter guerrilla war, while the six counties of Northern Ireland, the only region which could be regarded as analogous to a colonial settlement, was excluded from the new state. Furthermore, the Irish Free State, unlike the other dominions, was on the doorstep of Britain, leading many to suspect that Irish self-government might not remain secure from the interference of its powerful and proximate neighbour.

The uniquely complex progress of Ireland to international sovereignty is reflected in the several emphases and approaches in the historiography of Irish foreign policy. Until the official opening of the Irish National Archives in 1991, scholars working in the field, including the pioneering T. Desmond Williams, were greatly hampered by the lack of official material and were thus largely forced to rely on personal contact with former members of the Department of External Affairs.[16] Not surprisingly, given the continuing irritant of partition, there has been a strong tradition of work, represented most prominently by such scholars as Nicholas Mansergh, Patrick Keatinge, John Bowman, George Boyce and Conor Cruise O'Brien, which focuses on Anglo–Irish relations.[17] Related to this is the dominion context which stresses the importance of the imperial and Commonwealth framework in the development of an independent Irish foreign policy, and this work has been complemented by the efforts of British and imperial scholars.[18] Nevertheless, Ireland's dominion career was generally regarded as too anomalous by Irish historians and too transitory by imperial historians to have had any lasting effect on imperial relations, until David Harkness's innovative work claimed a major part for the Irish in shaping the character of that decentralised, unmonarchical and un-British Commonwealth which emerged after the Second World War.[19]

This view has been significantly modified, however, by Ged Martin who has argued that, while the Irish made some notable contributions to the development of dominion sovereignty, dominion nationalism was already well-advanced and British aspirations to centralised control of the dominions had already been frustrated by Canada and South Africa when the Irish Free State was created.[20] More recent works by Deirdre MacMahon and Paul Canning on Anglo–Irish relations, however, have provided ample evidence of the continuing importance of the Commonwealth dimension.[21] This aspect is further emphasised in David Swinfen's study of the appellate role of the Privy Council in the Empire–Commonwealth, in which he concludes – contrary to Harkness – that, while Irish assertiveness benefited from the Commonwealth connection, there were 'no grounds for arguing, as regards the appeal, that the Irish Free State advanced either the concept or practice of dominion status one iota … [I]n the matter of the appeal if no other, that the Irish owed more to dominion status than dominion status owed to Ireland'.[22]

Although situated within the Commonwealth historiographical tradition, the work of John Darwin also offers significant insights for historians of Irish–Commonwealth relations. He has challenged the whig-dominated historiography of the dominions between the wars, which has emphasised the apparently irresistible pressure of Irish, French-Canadian, Afrikaner and Indian nationalisms in the evolution of Ireland, Canada, South Africa and India into nationhood. Darwin argues persuasively that these nationalist movements were not the sole determining factors in British–dominion relations in this period. Equally significant was the presence of vociferous loyalist populations in Northern Ireland, Ontario, Natal and Southern Rhodesia, as well as in the case of India the strength of religious minorities and the Princely States, which severely curtailed the freedom of action of dominion nationalist leaders. Moreover, contrary to the arguments of nationalist conspiracy theorists, these loyalists were, even in the case of Ulster, largely outside the effective control of British governments, and they thus presented potentially serious obstacles to British ambitions for a more quiescent evolution of Anglo–dominion relations.[23] Also relevant to Irish foreign policy is the work of Lorna Lloyd and Alan James, in the field of international relations. Their work on the dominions, including Ireland, has emphasised the central importance of protocol and legalism in understanding the progress of the dominions to international sovereignty.[24]

There have also been a number of analyses of Irish bilateral relations with the dominions of Canada, Australia and South Africa, although these have tended to concentrate on the wartime relationship and the impact of Ireland's republican secession on the Commonwealth in 1949 rather than on the interwar period.[25] Irish relations with the

United States have also figured prominently in the work of Donald Akenson, Carolle Carter, T. Ryle Dwyer, R.J. Raymond, Francis Carroll, Joseph Rosenberg, Sean Cronin and Joseph Carroll.[26] Other scholars, including Dermot Keogh and Paul Sharp, have explored Ireland's historical connections with Europe, an increasingly topical theme in an era of Ireland's growing integration in the European Community/Union. Keogh in particular has made extensive use of British, European and American archives, providing crucial insights into foreign perspectives about the workings of Irish international relations.[27] He has also explored that other central feature of Irish foreign policy: the intimate relationship between the Catholic Church and the Irish state and national identity which was manifested in such occasions as the Eucharistic Congress in Dublin in 1932 and Irish opposition at the League of Nations to a document supporting artificial birth control. At the same time he has been careful to stress de Valera's ability to withstand clerical and crypto-fascist pressure and maintain a strict policy of neutrality during the Spanish Civil War. Keogh also traces the role of the League of Nations' apparent impotence in de Valera's increasing interest in neutrality as the only viable option in the event of a European conflict.[28] The study of these relationships has been manifested in the scholarly concern with the campaign for the internal and external recognition of the 'Irishness' of Irish state symbols such as the governor-generalship and the national anthem, the character of both of which institutions profoundly differentiated the Free State from the more apprehensive figurative assertions of the other dominions.[29]

Another conspicuous feature of modern Irish controversy, the 'tradition' of neutrality, has been examined by several scholars, including Ronan Fanning, J.P. Duggan, T. Ryle Dwyer, Joseph Carroll, Robert Fisk, Trevor Salmon and Donal O'Drisceoil. These have provided ample evidence of the extent of Irish military and defence collaboration with the allies during the Second World War, which far exceeded the conventional bounds of neutrality.[30] Salmon in particular has argued that while there were neutralist sentiments which originated in the anti-conscription campaign of 1918, there was no significant aspiration to neutrality until the late 1930s, when the principle of collective security had broken down.[31] Other writers, including Conor Cruise O'Brien, Patrick Keatinge, Stephen Barcroft, Norman MacQueen, and, most recently, Michael Kennedy and Joseph Skelly, have been concerned with examining the origins of Ireland's aspiration to the role of international 'good citizen' through involvement in such international bodies as the League of Nations and United Nations, as well as its support for human rights, the peaceful settlement of international disputes and the rights of small nations. Kennedy in particular has sought to argue that the inter-war period witnessed the development and maturation of a coherent independent foreign policy which transcended Anglo–Irish fixations. This was manifested in the Free State's emergence as a influential voice among the small states on such questions as disarmament, the codification of international law and the ratification of League conventions. Also emphasised by Kennedy are the prominent roles taken by the Irish in crises over the Japanese invasion of Manchuria in 1931, the Bolivian–Paraguayan and Peruvian–Colombian border disputes in 1933, and the Italian invasion of Abyssinia in 1935, in which de Valera, sometime President of the the League's Council, was a respected voice. The admiration accorded to the Irish was also demonstrated by the appointment in 1933 of Sean Lester to the High Commissionership of the Free City of Danzig, following his distinguished role on various League committees.[32]

Related to the neutralist legacy is the significance attached by some scholars, including Brigid Laffan, Bernadette Whelan, Michael Holmes and Nicholas Rees, to Ireland's relationship to the colonised and 'developing' world. Although these writers acknowledge that 'people within Ireland have preferred to recall the country's anti-colonialism rather than its [imperial and colonial] collaboration with Britain', they have drawn on the idealism that has pervaded Irish foreign policy since its foundation in the revolutionary years.[33] This outlook was epitomized by George Gavan Duffy, Minister of Foreign Affairs, in a statement to the Dáil in April 1922:

> No country ever started its international career with better prospects, for our soldiers had won us warm friends everywhere, and we had no enemies to speak of throughout the Continent of Europe. Ireland had every reason rapidly to become recognised as the *First of the Small Nations*.[34]

Shortly afterwards, he outlined in a memorandum a future global role for what, emulating the practice of the former imperial power, he grandly termed the Irish 'Foreign Office':

> [We] are still beyond question, in high favour among influential people on the continent and our Envoys will be much sought after. The reasons are: first, that Ireland is a world-race with great possibilities; secondly, that we are supposed to have great influence upon

American politics and policy; thirdly, that we know England better than the continental peoples and that the friendship of an Ireland lying on England's flank may at any moment be very useful. Moreover, we have a reputation for frankness and fearlessness which stands us in good stead, and it has often been said that Ireland in the League of Nations will be invaluable, because she may be expected to say plainly the things that everyone is thinking and that other Powers are too cowardly to be the first to say.

Gavan Duffy believed that small nations would want close relations with Ireland because it stood for 'democratic principles, against Imperialism and upon the side of liberty throughout the world'. He went on to argue somewhat idealistically that Ireland's geographical position, combined with advances in air transport, would enable the country to provide a bridge between Europe and America, as well as a centre for the League of Nations should it ever relocate from Geneva.[35] Here, then, in Gavan Duffy's memorandum, we have the essence of the Irish nationalist self-image: a small nation with great international moral stature based on its historic struggle against colonialism; an exemplary symbol to oppressed peoples everywhere; a traditional friend, not least through its diaspora, to the great European nations and the United States; a Catholic nation with a continuing mission, inherited from the Dark Ages, to lead the Christianization of the world; a country far more fortunate in spiritual and cultural treasure than the British Empire of Mammon, which was built on transient materialist values. These were resilient mobilising myths within Irish nationalism, especially evident in the notion of Ireland as a peculiarly 'good' international citizen, even though involvement in the real – as opposed to idealised – world of diplomacy made large-scale compromise inevitable; so much so that, for all the rhetoric to the contrary, it is difficult to sustain belief in an essentialised anti-imperial Irish identity in the area of foreign policy.[36] It is always relatively easy, of course, for diplomats and politicians to hold principled opinions about issues which involve no vital national interest. Nevertheless scholarly regard for good citizenship as an innate feature of Irish foreign policy remains strong. In Joseph Skelly's pioneering study of the Irish pursuit of national and international interests at the United Nations, for example, we read that Ireland possessed 'an impartial approach to foreign affairs'; on the next page we read that the 'Irish delegation did endorse the principle of self-determination in Asia and Africa in its speeches, but not in the more essential manner of voting when the demands of western solidarity overruled it'.[37] In other words, Irish action – as opposed to rhetoric – was far from 'impartial' when Irish interests were threatened, which later became apparent in Irish approaches to such issues as French colonialism in Algeria and South African apartheid.[38]

One approach to foreign policy, that of economic dependence, can be largely dismissed from the outset with the possible exception of the Irish response to the Geneva Protocol in 1924–25 (see below). While it may be argued that economic dependence on the British and consider-ations of imperial defence had moderating effects on the assertiveness of the Australasian dominions and South Africa in the period of the Great Depression of the 1930s, it can scarcely be argued that it dictated Irish relations with the United Kingdom. The Irish Free State, more economically dependent on Britain than any other dominion even including loyalist New Zealand, was also the most outspoken domin-ion in the Commonwealth. In 1933, for example, 93.9 per cent of Irish exports and 86 per cent of New Zealand exports were destined for the United Kingdom, when the Free State was already engaged in a tariff war with Britain. Ireland, however, unlike New Zealand, was in a rela-tively strong creditor position, which cushioned it from the economic consequences of its political actions. At most economic dependence on the British might be said to have deterred an Irish secession rather than determined Irish relations with the Commonwealth.[39] In so far as Irish government policy was restrained by external factors, partition and the continuing cultural and religious connections to Britain and to loyalist sentiment within and without the state were more significant than economics, thus appearing to support Darwin's contention that the residual power of loyalism was as significant as that of nationalism in the functioning of dominion status in the interwar years. As Joseph Lee has argued, in the first decade of independence the Cosgrave adminis-tration was curtailed in making what little capital there was in foreign policy success by its need to woo the votes of ex-Unionists who would have been unimpressed by the weakening of Commonwealth bonds.[40] The loyalist factor was also evident in the delicate negotiations with the Holy See surrounding the rights to be accorded to religious minori-ties in Ireland under the 1937 Constitution, as de Valera's confidential memorandum to Walshe noted:

> The Protestant Churches in this country are closely associated with the corresponding Churches in Great Britain, in which there are more than 40,000,000 Protestants. With this strength so close to hand, and with the recollections of their past supremacy, the

Protestant members of our population find it hard to accept a second and subordinate place. If the attempt were made to embody in the new constitution the full Catholic ideal [of not giving exclusive recognition to the Catholic Church] there would be an immediate outcry from the Protestant section of the population, and a bitter religious controversy might easily ensue.[41]

Understandably, perhaps, Marxist historians have largely avoided the detail of Irish foreign policy in the post-independence decades, in spite of British official concern about the impact of Ireland on dominion relations, while economic historians of the interwar Empire have virtually ignored Ireland altogether.[42] Generally, the study of Irish foreign policy has differed from its British and American counterparts in that it has not generally been affected by the scholarly reaction against 'high politics' which accompanied the revolution in the historiography of social history in the 1960s.[43] Unlike the affairs of great powers, which possessed large and anonymous foreign office staffs and diplomatic corps and whose foreign relations were subject to some degree of parliamentary scrutiny, the world of Irish diplomacy was small indeed and – in the de Valera years particularly – deliberately conducted far from the public gaze. The exceptionally small size of the Department of External Affairs, together with the dominance of a few individuals over a protracted period, has made it extremely difficult to take a wholly impersonal, structural approach to Irish foreign relations. Although constituted formally under the Ministries and Secretaries Act in 1924, as late as 1930 the senior staff of the Department of External Affairs, after almost a decade of demanding diplomacy in Anglo–Irish relations, the Commonwealth and the League of Nations, consisted of a Secretary, an Assistant Secretary, a Principal Officer, two Junior Administrative Officers, a Legal Advisor and an Assistant Legal Advisor: a total of seven officials. The whole of the department at home and abroad amounted to a mere 50 people, out of some 20000 civil servants, making it extremely difficult to translate the rhetoric of an independent foreign policy into reality.[44] The formulation of foreign policy took place largely away from parliamentary and public scrutiny, since the Dáil lacked a foreign affairs committee, and members of this very small service generally enjoyed a peculiarly intimate and highly influential relationship with successive Ministers of External Affairs. As a result, even ostensibly institutional histories of the Department and its policies until the expansion that followed the Second World War have unavoidably paid considerable attention to some of its leading personalities.

The historiography of Irish foreign policy has inevitably included a number of studies of leading political and diplomatic *dramatis personae*, including Kevin O'Higgins, Patrick McGilligan, Eamon de Valera (who characteristically insisted on the retention of foreign affairs as a personal preserve far from potentially volatile public interference), John A. Costello, Joseph Walshe and Conor Cruise O'Brien.[45]

As this outline of the historiography suggests, the emphases of much of this literature have been determined by many of the concerns and crises of post-independent Irish identity, including Anglo–Irish relations, partition, the United States, church–state relations, Europe, neutrality, 'good citizenship' in international bodies, and sympathy for the developing world, as much as by the availability of material. The truism that historians, unlike historical participants, have the benefit of hindsight is particularly applicable to studies of foreign policy, and a careful balance needs to be retained between contemporary expectations and outcomes, as well as the role of contingency, in the Irish case not least in the areas of Commonwealth membership and neutrality. To take one example: after 1935 de Valera was determined to introduce a new constitution devoid of references to the Crown and Commonwealth. Once this had been achieved and Irish sovereignty fully asserted, he intended to bring in legislation retaining the King for the purposes of foreign relations. Such an overt breach in the monarchical connection might well have led to a damaging rift with the Commonwealth. Fortunately for de Valera, the timing of the abdication of Edward VIII in 1936 forced him to bring in his External Relations Bill in advance of the new constitution. Potential British opposition to the new constitution was thereby blunted by the fact that a measure of continuity was maintained in the preservation of the 'external' authority of the Crown throughout the constitutional transition.[46]

Chronology and wider imperial interests were also highly significant factors in the wartime policy of neutrality. Such a course would not have been tenable but for the return of the Treaty ports in 1938. This was an undoubted triumph for Irish diplomacy, but it was fortunate for de Valera that in British Cabinet discussions advocates of withdrawal from the ports won the day. There was nothing automatic about this. British willingness to negotiate resulted partly from the belated official admission in 1936 by the Committee of Imperial Defence that France would not be the likely enemy in the next war, making ill-equipped southern Irish ports seemingly superfluous, while the British were ever anxious to diffuse dominion nationalism, particularly threatening in South Africa, by an Irish settlement. Had the Anglo–Irish negotiations dragged on into late 1939 Ireland could have found itself unwillingly at war. Moreover, British departure was not conditional but was only made after Irish security guarantees had been given to Britain, and Irish apparent willingness to enter into detailed secret military discussions with the British further encouraged the latter to believe that Irish Government support could be counted on in a future war. It is greatly to the credit of Irish diplomacy that the British did not fully realise what they were giving away in the 1938 Agreement.[47]

The general picture which emerges from the historiography of Irish foreign policy is largely an heroic one, depicting the emergence of an intrepid corps of internationally-minded statesmen and accomplished, urbane envoys. These managed, in spite of residual civil war divisions, to transform Irish foreign policy from revolutionary and amateurish idealism into professional diplomatic pragmatism and succeeded in establishing, in a treacherous era in international relations, a viable and universally respected Department of External Affairs; all this in the face of parsimony, begrudgery and ridicule from Irish government and opposition parliamentarians, as well as external resentment, condescension and opposition from the still powerful British diplomatic establishment.[48] It is an appealing story: the virtuous and agile Irish David running diplomatic and constitutional rings around the disdainful, decadent Goliath of the British Empire; gaining popularity among nations great and small, and succeeding, in the face of British opposition, in projecting an independent national identity to the world. The survival and development of Irish diplomacy was indeed remarkable in the circumstances of the 1920s. It is understandable therefore that scholars, sometimes taking politicians and diplomats at their own estimation, with, perhaps, a somewhat excessive reverence for the institutions of the emerging state, there is a tendency to over-emphasise the effectiveness of Irish unilateral action, so that throughout Ireland's peculiar progress to republican status politicians and parliamentarians and envoys can appear to be always in the driving seat. A leading authority on Irish diplomatic relations, Ronan Fanning, wrote in 1983 that 'not one of the constitutional gains made by independent Irish governments between 1921 and 1949 was a product of Anglo–Irish negotiation. The abolition of the oath of allegiance, the External Relations Act of 1936, the 1937 constitution, the Republic of Ireland Act – all alike were the result of unilateral action taken by Irish governments which British governments chose to ignore rather than resist'.[49] He writes elsewhere that

> if the government were to prove their point that the treaty conferred what Collins had called the freedom to achieve freedom, it

was imperative that they show an ability to act independently of Britain. Such was the significance of their decision of 1 September 1922 to apply to join the League of Nations and, having been admitted on 10 September 1923, their registration of the treaty as an international agreement with the League on 11 July 1924, *both* in the face of British objections.[50]

Tim Pat Coogan makes an equally forceful argument for the autonomous strength of Irish diplomacy:

> While [de Valera] was busy portraying his opponents as lackeys of the British imperialism in both Ireland and America the Cosgrave administration had been quietly striking off the shackles in international relationships... They [The Irish] joined the League of Nations... (a significant gesture in itself) and in the teeth of British objections, succeeded in having the Treaty registered with the League... This gesture of independence was accompanied by another notable 'first' [when] Professor Smiddy was accepted by the Americans as the Irish 'Minister Plenipotentiary' to Washington. As Professor D. W. Harkness has noted, this acceptance meant that: The Irish Free State had penetrated the diplomatic unity of the Empire, successfully establishing in the American capital the first Dominion ambassador.[51]

These approaches to Irish foreign policy merit closer scrutiny, since the obstacles to Irish international assertiveness require no exaggeration. First of all, contrary to Fanning's contention, Britain did not object to Irish membership of the League of Nations, even if they were opposed to the Irish Free State, or any other dominion, asserting an independent foreign policy which would weaken imperial 'diplomatic unity'. Indeed, as Kennedy points out, League membership was an integral part of Irish acceptance of the Treaty. David Lloyd George assured Arthur Griffith that Britain would support Ireland's membership of the League of Nations as a 'co-equal with the other members of the Commonwealth'.[52] Certainly, the British Foreign Office viewed with suspicion Irish attempts at an independent foreign policy, but this was no different from its attitude to the other dominions. Lionel Curtis, imperialist adviser to the Cabinet, regarded Irish membership of the League as advantageous to Britain, since 'their immersion in this centre of world troubles has made them realise that there are other things which matter than the questions which have obsessed the Irish mind'.[53] Furthermore, as Ged Martin has argued, the changes initiated by Irish governments need to be closely examined with respect to their unilateral credentials.

The Irish succeeded in issuing passports in 1924 in the face of British opposition, but they were prevented from dropping the words 'Defender of the Faith' from the royal style on the passport in spite of Irish Catholic sensitivities on the issue. Similarly, although in 1926 O'Higgins managed, with dominion backing, to have a comma inserted to alter the King's title to 'King of Great Britain, Ireland, and the British Dominions...' (thus re-emphasising the ultimate unity of the country and perhaps paving the way for a dual monarchy), the Irish were unsuccessful four years later in their attempt to remove the word 'Britannic' from the King's title. They had sought admission to the jurisdiction of the International Court of Justice as early as 1924, but it took further five years to sort out British objections and enable Irish accession.[54] To Martin's reservations might be added the extraordinary position of the governor-generalship. The Irish, with the support of Thomas Jones, Assistant Cabinet Secretary, and Lionel Curtis, special Colonial Office adviser, succeeded in persuading the British to break with common dominion practice by appointing a native Catholic Irishman to the post in 1922. On the other hand this was on the unprecedented condition that the appointee, Tim Healy, sign a written pledge that he would withhold the Royal Assent to any Irish bill about which there existed the slightest constitutional doubt, unless he first consulted the Colonial Secretary.[55] In defence matters, the Free State and Newfoundland were alone among the dominions in being denied the normal privilege of access to the minutes of the Committee of Imperial Defence.[56] Irish constitutional assertiveness also seemed somewhat compromised in the 1926 Imperial Conference which conceded the principle of dominion equality, when the Free State joined with the other dominions in reaffirming the symbolic importance of the Crown in expressing the unity of the Empire and Commonwealth.[57]

The other 'constitutional gains' listed by Fanning – the abolition of the oath of allegiance, the External Relations Act of 1936, the 1937 Constitution and the Republic of Ireland Act – were only made after the passage of the Statute of Westminster of 1931, which conceded the principle of dominion sovereign competence to amend their constitutions and pass statutes which were repugnant to the statute law of the United Kingdom. More significant for Irish foreign policy was the acquisition of the Irish Great Seal in the same year, which enabled the Irish Free State to sign treaties with foreign states without going having to use the services of the British Foreign Office. This action, followed shortly afterwards by the South African procurement of a Great Seal, theoretically ended the diplomatic unity of the Commonwealth. The British continued to argue that the Treaty took precedence over the Statute and that it could only be amended with the consent of both governments, but this argument was rejected in 1934 by the Judicial Committee of the Privy Council which conceded that the Free State had inherited the dynamic status of Canada and the other dominions as it had developed since the Treaty, not Canadian status 'frozen' in 1921. De Valera, of course, rejected the authority of the Privy Council to pronounce on Irish sovereignty, even when, in this case, it upheld his legal – though not 'moral' – unilateral right to amend or abolish the Treaty and the Privy Council's jurisdiction within the Free State, and he proceeded with his constitutional changes without negotiation. Nevertheless, the Privy Council judgement was particularly significant, coming at a time when the Irish Supreme Court had been taking a much more rigid opinion of the Treaty and its Commonwealth provisions as being fundamental to Irish constitutional law. Even de Valera's successful embodiment of his idea of 'external association' in the External Relations Act of 1936 needs to be more critically evaluated. As Deirdre MacMahon has argued, de Valera was far more cautious in his dealings with Britain than the public rhetoric of the time suggested.[58]

After 1934, it was clear from the Privy Council judgement that there was no longer any external legal impediment to Irish republican secession from the Commonwealth. British attempts to retaliate against de Valera were hampered both by the Privy Council ruling and by pressure from Canada and South Africa, which advised against any attempt to push Ireland further out of the Commonwealth orbit, not least because of the effects that Irish secession might have on dominion nationalists. Thus, however much Irish governments wished to approximate a European Christian nation rather than a dominion, and in spite of de Valera's erosion of dominion status after 1932, the Commonwealth dimension was still inescapable for defence and economic reasons, and Irish policy was greatly aided by unsolicited dominion support. In 1965, de Valera remembered having had contact with Canadian and South African statesmen in the 1930s, but he recalled that he had not wished to be drawn further into the Commonwealth by using the clauses of the Statute of Westminster as weapons in Anglo–Irish relations. He did not know whether there were any favourable Commonwealth influences on British policy at the 1921 and 1937 Imperial Conferences, neither of which he attended. We know, however, from

British and dominion archives that the dominions exerted considerable influence on British policy in these years, and British officials were aware that their Irish policies might antagonise secessionist opinion in the dominions.

Canadian and South African refusals to alienate the Irish were crucial factors in the admission of the Irish to the Imperial Economic Conference in Ottawa in 1932, in the face of British opposition. Another example of the continuing importance of Irish–dominion relations was provided in South Africa shortly after de Valera's accession to power, when the Prime Minister, General Hertzog, appeared to support British-sponsored telegrams from the Australian and New Zealand governments to de Valera advising him to negotiate with the British. The ruling Nationalist Party was split from top to bottom on the issue, with Afrikaner republican hardliners sending a message of support to de Valera and prominent politicians advocating a policy of neutrality on the Irish model. Both pro-British elements in South Africa and British officials were particularly fearful of the effect of the Irish dispute in their most economically and strategically vital dominion, not least in the event of a European war.[59] 'If Ireland hives off', Smuts warned the Dominions Office, 'South Africa is sure to follow sooner or later.'[60] Sir William Clark, British High Commissioner to South Africa, reported ominously to the Dominions Office that Dr D.F. Malan, leader of the Purified National Party opposition, had demanded an assurance from Hertzog that he would ensure that no discussion of Ireland should take place at the 1937 Imperial Conference without the consent of the Irish Government. According to the South African delegation at the Imperial Conference, the 'extrusion of the Irish Free State from the Commonwealth [was] almost unthinkable', and Hertzog argued at the 1937 Imperial Conference that he would favour the continuance of Ireland as a member of the Commonwealth even if it declared a republic.[61] Malcolm MacDonald, Dominions Secretary, asked N.C. Havenga, one of the South African leaders, whether the new Irish Constitution might encourage Afrikaner republicanism, but was assured by him that with a moderate British response it would have the opposite effect by demonstrating that South Africa was 'perfectly free inside the British Commonwealth.'[62]

British fears of an Irish–South African linkage seemed to be fulfilled in September 1939, however, when in a crucial parliamentary debate on neutrality Hertzog cited the precedent of Irish neutrality while Afrikaner nationalist university students were inflamed by a pro-neutrality lecture on Ireland given by Eric Louw (friend and admirer of de Valera at the League of Nations and subsequently Minister of External Affairs) entitled *Ierland toon die weg aan* (Ireland shows the way).[63] Significantly, after the outbreak of war de Valera was careful to cultivate continuing Commonwealth connections by playing host in 1939 to Colonel Denys Reitz, South African Deputy-Prime Minister, and in 1941 to Sir Robert Menzies, Prime Minister of Australia, in an effort to circumvent British isolation.[64] The Commonwealth dimension became particularly apparent in early 1944, when the Americans demanded that de Valera expel the Axis legations in Dublin, and de Valera looked to the dominions for support. John Kearney, Canadian High Commissioner in Dublin, was privately annoyed by Anglo–American handling of the issue while maintaining public solidarity with the Allies; Australia was unsympathetic to de Valera, as was South Africa, now led by Smuts, although the latter was forced to engage in a bitter parliamentary battle with Malan, leader of the pro-neutralist Nationalist opposition, who had sent de Valera a telegram of support. Ironically, only New Zealand (which had once reminded Kevin O'Higgins of Northern Ireland, 'for it produces the same kind of jingo reactionary'), dissented from a hostile approach to de Valera, but it found itself pressed by a chagrined Dominions Office into a display of Allied and Commonwealth unity on the issue.[65] In this sense the Commonwealth continued to influence profoundly, if indirectly, both Irish and British foreign policies long after Ireland withdrew from active participation in the affairs of the organisation.

An appreciation of British legal impediments to Irish unilateral action, together with the context of great power relations, is also crucial to any understanding of Irish foreign policy and its achievements, particularly in the first decade of independence. The successful registration, in the face of British opposition, of the Treaty at the League of Nations in 1924, has often been hailed as a success for Irish diplomacy. Michael Kennedy, for example, has remarked:

> The League had firmly, if unofficially, supported the Irish Free State throughout its plan to register the Treaty. The Free State could now turn its attention to other matters.[66]

This registration amounted, however, to no more than a lodgement of the Treaty together with other constitutional documents. The Secretary-General had no power to reject Irish documentation, and the League published the Treaty in its *Treaty Series* together with the exchanges between the Irish and British governments on the issue, although, it should be stressed, without League comment on the extent of Irish international status.[67] Ged Martin has argued that 'by treating the [Treaty] as an international treaty, and so registering it at Geneva, the Irish had given Britain an additional hold over them – Cosgrave himself admitting that the Treaty could only be altered by consent'.[68] It might equally be argued that the unwillingness of the British as the other party to register the Treaty – even though such acknowledgement might later have bolstered British claims against Irish attempts to revise it – inevitably weakened Irish claims that the Treaty should be accorded international status.

Whatever subsequent Irish claims to the contrary, it should be stressed that was on the basis of Ireland's status as a dominion that the state was admitted to membership of the League. The limitations placed on Irish autochthony were again apparent over the issue of the Geneva Protocol of 1924–25. As Minister of External Affairs Desmond Fitzgerald and the Secretary of his department were aware, defence and economic dependency dictated that the Free State had no choice but to follow whichever way Britain decided to go, and while there was political acceptance within the League of Irish independence, the Free State was by the admission of Joseph Walshe, head of the diplomatic service, 'not an independent state as far as the purposes of the Protocol are concerned'.[69] While the successful 'registration' of the Treaty undoubtedly boosted Irish diplomatic morale, then, the objective significance of League membership for the recognition of Irish international sovereignty needs to be carefully weighed. Article 1.1 of the League Covenant allowed for the membership of 'any fully self-governing State, Dominion or Colony' with the backing of two-thirds of the Assembly, and it should be noted that the Indian Empire, still a Crown dependency and not fully self-governing, was exceptionally accorded League representation which was separate from that of the British Empire in 1919. Its delegates were effectively nominated by the British Government but it maintained a notional international profile, with a separate diplomatic service (and, after 1945, membership of the United Nations).

Moreover, the Free State weakened its own claim to sovereign treaty-making powers when in 1926 it, together with Britain and the dominions, subscribed to a resolution of the Imperial Conference. This resolution pointed out that the Legal Committee of the Arms Traffic Conference of 1925 had laid down that the terms of League conventions must not be regarded as regulating *inter se* the rights and obligations of territories which were subject to the same sovereign. Significantly, although the Free State continued to register agreements with the League while the Imperial Conference of 1926 was in session, this appears to have been the last occasion on which Irish agreements with other members of the Commonwealth were thus registered, even though South Africa continued to register such agreements with the League.[70] The *inter se* issue reappeared in 1929 during the negotiations surrounding the Optional Clause of the Statute of the Permanent Court of Justice which sought to make reference to the Permanent Court binding in certain circumstances. The British and dominion governments accepted the Clause, but reserved inter-imperial disputes. Although the Irish Free State made reciprocity the sole condition of acceptance, it was highly unlikely that the Permanent Court could override British reservations in the event of an Irish *inter se* dispute being brought before it.[71] Such questions remained academic, however, since the League was never required to adjudicate on these issues.

It might well be asked why other countries backed Irish membership of League bodies and, in some cases, established direct diplomatic relations. It is true that the Irish, backed particularly by the South Africans and Canadians, frustrated British attempts to speak on behalf of the dominions, and that Ireland's League policy was indeed – as Kennedy points out – based on more than anti-British reaction, but perhaps the very dominion status that the Irish sought to minimise was part of the Free State's international appeal. Take Ireland's membership of the League Council, for example. Michael Kennedy writes that

> Ireland's seat was a supposedly independent seat, but had from 1927 been occupied by Canada and in 1933 either Australia or Canada would stand for election. The seat was increasingly seen as the preserve of the Commonwealth, despite Ireland's independent Council position ... By replacing Canada, Ireland, despite her independence, had ironically ensured that the seat would become a Commonwealth seat.[72]

It might, however, be questioned whether there was anything ironic about the seat becoming regarded by other members as a Commonwealth preserve. Kennedy himself demonstrates the importance of Irish–dominion cooperation to Irish League policy.[73] After all, to other members of the League, Ireland was an English-speaking member of the Commonwealth, with British military bases on its territory, sharing common citizenship and enjoying a peculiar access to the Crown and the British government. In the early years of independence, Ireland's Commonwealth connections were clearly of major significance to those countries which established diplomatic relations with Ireland. Daniel Binchy, Irish Minister in Berlin (1929–31), found that the German Chancellor and his officials were chiefly interested in Ireland as one of the dominions, and, moreover, in whatever influence it might exert on the Commonwealth.[74] It also seems clear that German respect for wartime Irish neutrality was motivated more by a desire to divide the diplomatic unity of the Commonwealth than by any particular interest in, or respect for, Ireland's right to statehood, especially at a time when Germany was tearing up similar rights across the continent of Europe.[75] Even in their dealings with the Holy See, the Irish found that their connection with a great power, rather than their Catholicism, appeared to be of premier importance to the Papacy. The structures of the British Empire–Commonwealth were believed by the Papacy to offer unparalleled opportunities for the evangelisation of the English-speaking world, as well as for the process of England's reconversion to Catholicism, as Joseph Walshe wrote in 1929:

> One very striking impression received after a very few days contact is that the Holy See regards the peaceful maintenance of the British Commonwealth of Nations as the most important factor in the development and well-being of the Church. Great Britain's opinion becomes, therefore, of paramount interest … The quick decision [to appoint a Papal Nuncio to Dublin] was due, we believe, to the conviction that a foothold in some part of the British Commonwealth of Nations was useful, particularly in that part where positive service by the Church to the British Commonwealth of Nations and to its peaceful maintenance could most easily be rendered.[76]

Two years later Charles Bewley, Irish Minister to the Holy See, was made keenly aware of the Irish contribution, through emigration, to the Catholic Church in America and the dominions, and that the new Secretary of State, Eugenio Pacelli (the future Pope Pius XII), was not at all enthusiastic about Ireland's growing detachment from the Commonwealth:

> The Secretary of State has more than once pointed out to me the practical advantage to Ireland of remaining within the British Commonwealth of Nations, and amongst them has mentioned in particular the influence which she can exercise on England and the Dominions.[77]

Of course, Irish–Papal relations generally, together with such expressions of public religious devotion as the 1932 Eucharistic Congress, have tended to be regarded as a peculiar examples of Irish state religiosity and deference to clerical authority. It ought to be remembered, however, that in Great Britain, the ostensibly more secular country against which so much of Irish identity at this time was constructed, there remained until the Roman Catholic Relief Act of 1926 certain legal restrictions against Catholicism, including the forbidding of the ringing of church bells and the withholding of charitable status. The Protestant character of the British state was further emphasised by the official exclusion of Catholics from the Lord Chancellorship and, of course, the succession to the monarchy itself. In 1937, the Home Office refused to forward a loyal address to George VI presented by the English Catholic hierarchy on the grounds that their Catholic designation and territorial titles were unacceptable. The Home Office had adopted a similar attitude during George V's Silver Jubilee in 1935.[78] It is true, of course, that there were a number of prominent and influential Catholics in Britain, including Sir William Tyrell, Permanent Under-Secretary for Foreign Affairs in the late 1920s.[79] Nevertheless, Ramsay MacDonald, first Labour Prime Minister, was known for his contempt for Catholicism, as was Sir William Joynson-Hicks, sometime Conservative Home Secretary, who feared that Britain would be swamped by Irish Catholic immigration. Particularly revealing are the views concerning the assassination of Kevin O'Higgins to be found in the diary of Leo Amery, who, it should be remembered, as Colonial and Dominions Secretary between 1924 and 1929, had major responsibility for Britain's Irish policy at a crucial time:

> Poor fellow, he had many attractive personal qualities as well as real courage and patriotism. What a curse hangs over Ireland. To unravel it would be like the tale of Atreidae, but I fear the starting point is a fault in the blood, some element of ape-like savagery which has survived every successive flood of settlers... [I attended the] Memorial service to O'Higgins. These RC services strike me as curiously barbaric and in the direct line of descent from ancient Egypt.[80]

Such bigotry might seem to strengthen the portrayal of Ireland as a continuing victim of imperial racism and, by extension, as a protector of the colonised of the British Empire. In these circumstances, it might be questioned how real was Gavan Duffy's assertion of anti-imperialism as a defining feature of Irish foreign policy. It is true that the Irish Free

State along with Newfoundland, at its first Imperial Conference of 1923, had been unwilling to support South Africa's exclusionist Indian immigration policy, but, nevertheless, the Irish Free State – in common with other states – regarded South African 'Native Policy' as strictly an internal matter for the Union of South Africa, and the Irish continued to enjoy a more intimate relationship with South Africa than with any other dominion, not excluding Canada, until the late 1950s. Apart from the memory of the Irish pro-Boer movement in Irish nationalism in 1899–1902, this relationship was based on the realisation that South Africa was the only other dominion which was dominated by former republican guerrilla 'generals' who had experienced near-annihilation, whose state had originated in what many nationalists regarded as an ignominious treaty, and who appeared to share an Irish love of land, language, faith (even if somewhat different), and republican patriotism. Not surprisingly, the state visit to Dublin in 1930 of the South African Prime Minister, General Hertzog, was the largest such ceremony of the interwar years.[81]

Apart from the Afrikaners, who had proved to be a crucial dominion allies, and who were perceived to be traditional comrades in the struggle against British colonialism, successive Irish governments allowed earlier links with anti-colonial nationalist movements in Egypt and India to lapse, and, in spite of British fears to the contrary (which might have strengthened Irish leverage), even de Valera had no intention of allowing colonial issues to complicate Anglo–Irish relations. In 1948 he was happy to spend the last night of Lord Mountbatten's term as Governor-General of India in the company of Nehru and Mountbatten, but by this time de Valera was out of power.[82] Ironically, however, only New Zealand, that apparently most docile provided a lone voice in the League of Nations Assembly in the interwar years in support of the Indian National Congress's claim to a representative (as opposed to British-nominated) voice in League policy; on this and on the League's policies in the Mandated ex-German colonies and former Ottoman territories Ireland's opinion was not heard.[83] De Valera had, of course, provided League leadership in the early 1930s in the era of Japanese aggression, and he had supported the Ethiopian cause in spite of pro-Mussolini clericalist pressure at home. Nevertheless, Ireland was among the first states to recognise Italian sovereignty over Ethiopia by the accreditation in 1937 of a new Irish Minister to the 'King of Italy and Emperor of Ethiopia', in spite of protests in the Dáil from William Norton, the Labour Party leader, that Ireland had thus recognised *de jure* the legitimacy of the right of conquest, in defiance of the League

Covenant, the Kellogg Pact and international agreements banning the use of poison gas, as well as Ireland's own experience of colonial aggression.

It should be noted that under the 1937 Constitution de Valera could have chosen to accredit the Irish Minister without mentioning the Italian crown, but by advising George VI to recognise in the name of Ireland the Italian Emperor *de jure* (while Britain and the other dominions still recognised Haile Selassie), he sought to underline the subordination of the King in the government of Ireland. Equally, in the 1930s, Irish passive acquiescence in the proposed restitution of German colonies in the interests of appeasement would scarcely have convinced the native subjects of European empires of the essentially anti-colonialist character of the Irish Free State.[84] On the other hand, while Ireland's credibility as a model international good citizen might be further questioned because of its restrictive wartime policy on refugees, de Valera's personal support of Jewish refugees can be favourably set alongside recently emerging details of Swiss and Swedish active and profitable collaboration with Germany's racial policies during the Second World War.[85]

British obstructionism was not the only factor in hampering the Department of External Affairs campaign for Ireland to be recognised as a fully independent state. There was also the difficulty of conveying a sense of national identity in an era when nationality was widely regarded as being bound to language. The English-speaking world had little difficulty in recognising the political and cultural distinctiveness of Irish identity, and those European countries which had provided refuge to Irish Catholics in previous centuries were familiar with the uniqueness of Ireland as an English-speaking Catholic country in north-western Europe. Even this apparent familiarity, however, was no guarantee that a separate Irish nationality would be adequately recognised, and this extended beyond ensuring that the Irish rather than the British national anthem was played at official and sporting occasions. Official stationery with state offices and titles in Irish and French alone could not necessarily ensure recognition of Irish distinctiveness. When in 1931 William T. Cosgrave signed himself 'Liam MacCosgair' in a letter to Benito Mussolini, the Italian dictator and his cabinet colleagues were baffled as to who this man was, and asked the Italian Consul in Dublin for his assistance in identifying the writer of the letter. In 1934, the Holy See ineptly forwarded its reply to the credentials of the Irish Minister to the Cardinal Archbishop *of Westminster* for transmission to Dublin.[86] In spite of official attempts at language revival, independent

Ireland remained a predominantly English-speaking country, with a substantially 'Westminster' – or bicameral – system of parliamentary government, however much its institutions and officials were rechristened with Gaelic terminology in the interwar period. Even when popular sovereignty was made fully explicit in the 1937 constitution, it was circumscribed by the authority of the triune, Christian deity, in a unique effort to square the popular sovereignty of Rousseau with Joseph de Maistre's doctrine of divine authority. Even after 1937, British and dominion constitutional traditions remained significant. In 1944, at a time when Ireland was dramatically asserting its international sovereignty in the policy of neutrality, Frederick Boland of the Department of External Affairs advised de Valera on the Taoiseach's right to advise the President to dissolve parliament and call a general election in these terms:

> The parliamentary law of this State derives, like that of most democratically-ruled States, from the practice of the British 'Mother of Parliaments'. In our case, owing to our close association for so long with Great Britain and, latterly, with the British Dominions, we automatically turn to British and Dominion precedents in many of the constitutional problems with which we find ourselves from time to time faced.[87]

It was therefore not surprising that even pro-Irish elements in the Commonwealth should not always demonstrate sensitivity to Irish determination to avoid being considered part of the 'British' world. In 1946, Dr H.V. Evatt, Irish-descended Australian Attorney-General and Minister of External Affairs, who strongly supported Ireland's application for membership of the United Nations, described the decision to appoint a High Commissioner to 'Eire' as marking the completion of a process of establishing direct diplomatic relations with 'the two remaining *British countries* [Ireland and South Africa]'.[88]

The Irish judicial system inherited at independence was embedded in the tradition of English Common Law, and – notwithstanding a brief period of revolutionary sartorial austerity – its judges and barristers retained such English traditions as wigs and gowns. In Dublin, portraits of Crown-appointed Lord Chancellors continued to look down from the walls of the King's Inns on the 'benchers' as they 'kept commons'. In the early 1930s, moreover, the Irish Supreme Court took a more restrictive view than the British Privy Council of Irish rights to amend the Treaty, regarding it as the fundamental law of the State.[89] British recognition of a wholly separate Irish identity can also scarcely have been encouraged by Kevin O'Higgins's apparent willingness, as part of a proposed deal establishing Ireland as a reunited kingdom with a common crown, to accept the flying of the Union Jack alongside a revised Irish flag containing the harp and crown, and with 'someone like Lord Londonderry' as first viceroy of a reunified Ireland.[90] Although many imperial monuments had been removed and monarchical forms reduced to a minimum even under Cosgrave, there were still plenty of reminders of Ireland's recent imperial past in the capital, from learned institutions with royal prefixes, residual coats of arms on official buildings and Victoria's ample statue outside Dáil Eireann, to ubiquitous advertisements for British consumer 'household names', which gave Dublin the commercial feel of a British city, and viceregal street names (the German Legation, for example, was situated on Northumberland Road). Even the Irish police force, the Garda Siochana, resembled in function and ethos its unarmed British counterparts far more closely than any continental European force (or, indeed, the armed Royal Ulster Constabulary).

Ireland could thus seem to a non-Anglophone observer unfamiliar with Anglo-Irish trauma as less distinct, at least in terms of legal tradition, than Scotland, which remained within the United Kingdom.[91] Moreover, Ireland's currency enjoyed parity with Sterling, and – with the exception of the threepenny piece – the dimensions of its coinage exactly replicated those of their British counterparts, which circulated freely in the Irish economy. Thousands of its citizens regularly joined the British armed forces, or emigrated to Britain and the Empire as missionaries, settlers and administrators. Although great efforts were made to make the Irish National Army distinct from its British predecessor, British weaponry and British-style webbing were standard issue. Significantly, in 1940, at a time when Joseph Walshe, Secretary of the Department of External Affairs, in common with some members of the British Cabinet, believed Britain's cause to be lost, the Irish Army's 'German-style' helmet was replaced by the standard British infantry helmet, so that any potential invader would have found it extremely difficult to distinguish between Irish and British servicemen. This, together with Irish refusal to accept captured British armaments from Germany at a time of acute military shortages, spoke volumes for the benevolently pro-Allied character of Irish neutrality.[92]

The most conspicuous survival of the British connection was the title of the 'Department of External Affairs', which it shared with the foreign affairs departments of the other dominions until 1971, 22 years after the declaration of a republic outside the Commonwealth. This peculiar title, together with the fact that until 1947 Ireland's relations with other countries was at a ministerial and legation level rather than ambassadorial rank, reinforced the impression that Ireland belonged to that category of small emergent states which included the dominions, rather than to the grouping of great powers which possessed 'Foreign Offices' and large numbers of diplomats of full ambassadorial status. While Ireland chose to remain tied to the Crown in foreign relations, it could find itself restricted by political pressures as much as the conventions of diplomacy. These limitations became apparent in Irish relations with Germany at the beginning of the Second World War. When the eccentric pro-Nazi Charles Bewley retired as Irish Minister in Berlin in 1939, the legation was left in the hands of the First Secretary, William Warnock, who was given the rank of Chargé d'Affaires *ad interim*. Technically, de Valera could still advise the King to appoint a new Irish Minister, but he was tactful enough not to suggest this course after the outbreak of war, and, consequently, Cornelius Cremin was appointed to Berlin in 1943 as Chargé d'Affaires, a rank which did not require the presentation of credentials.[93]

Irish relative diplomatic weakness was further illustrated by the Australian insistence after 1946 on including the Irish envoy to Australia in the category of 'a representative of one of the Governments of His Majesty' in the Canberra Diplomatic List. It was also evident in Australia's hardline opposition after 1949 to the appointment of an Australian ambassador to Dublin while letters of credence incorporating the official title of 'Ireland' might be construed as tantamount to recognising the Irish constitutional claim – and therefore denying their Sovereign's claim – to Northern Ireland. On this point the Australians seemed even more pedantic than the British. The Canadians, moreover, who were generally more sympathetic to Irish feelings, anonymously continued after 1949 to acredit diplomats to Ireland in the name of the Sovereign 'of Great Britain and Ireland', since internal Canadian ethnic politics made difficulties for even a relatively minor territorial updating of the Canadian royal title as enshrined in the 1867 British North America Act. Most conspicuous of all, perhaps, was the unwillingness, if not the inability, of Irish governments in international organisations to challenge British legal authority over Northern Ireland. Irish diplomats understandably did not want to become regarded as anti-British cranks, and de Valera took the view that the national question transcended the jurisdiction of any other body.[94] Perhaps another explanation for Irish inertia lies in the fact that the Irish case would have been virtually impossible to argue in international law. Ireland could challenge Britain's 'moral right' to govern a part of Ireland, but British legal title to Northern Ireland had not only been enshrined in the Anglo–Irish Treaty, but it was continually reaffirmed in every international agreement and establishment of relations with other countries which recognised the Crown of the United Kingdom including Northern Ireland.

A common Irish–British culture could also, however, play to Ireland's advantage. A number of Irish diplomats posted in Britain and politicians responsible for Anglo–Irish relations scarcely fitted the description of revolutionary anti-imperialists. John MacNeill, Irish High Commissioner to London from 1923 to 1927 and Governor-General from 1927 to 1932, had become interested in Sinn Fein in the revolutionary period and had worked for the Dáil Ministry of Labour, but he was also an alumnus of Emmanuel College, Cambridge. He had had a distinguished career in the Indian Civil Service as a Commissioner of the Bombay Presidency and a member of the Imperial Legislative Council, before undertaking special duties for the Colonial Office in the West Indies and Fiji.[95] John Whelan Dulanty, veteran Irish High Commissioner to London from 1930 to 1950 and first Ambassador (July–September 1950), had an even less revolutionary background. He had been an Honorary Director, under John Redmond, of the United Irish League in 1910–17. Having worked for Winston Churchill during his 1906 Manchester election campaign. He also worked as Principal Assistant-Secretary of the Ministry of Munitions in 1917, when Churchill was Minister, and was an Assistant Secretary of the Treasury in Whitehall, before retiring from the civil service in 1920 with the accolades of Companion of the Bath and Commander of the Order of the British Empire, hardly the marks of an envoy of a post-revolutionary state.

Dulanty's diplomacy was crucial to what remained Ireland's nearest and most expensive diplomatic mission in the tense years between the advent of de Valera and the declaration of the republic. In 1939, Churchill, latterly so infuriated by Irish neutrality, remarked that 'Mr. Dulanty is thoroughly friendly to England…He acts as a general soother, representing everything Irish in the most favourable light'.[96] Like Walshe, with whom he enjoyed a sometimes combative relationship, Dulanty valued Ireland's Commonwealth connections, including its access to Foreign Office telegrams and, belatedly, confidential communications of the Committee of Imperial Defence. While de Valera's government continued to distance itself from connections with such imperial occasions as Armistice Day, Dulanty continued, with de Valera's tacit approval, to lay official wreaths at the Cenotaph in Whitehall until the outbreak of war. More crucially, throughout the period of the Economic War and until the outbreak of the Second World War, he continued to attend regular meetings of High Commissioners at the Dominions Office (even if these made him feel 'like a whore at a christening'), as well as the Imperial Conference of 1937 as an 'observer', thus maintaining intimate contacts with British and dominion representatives for the whole of his term in London.[97]

Anglophobia and anti-imperialism scarcely exuded from other leading personalities in Anglo–Irish and diplomatic relations. Tim Healey, former Parnellite MP and first Irish Governor-General (1922–28), was a regular guest of the well-connected Tory newspaper magnate and arch-imperialist Lord Beaverbrook. Beaverbrook even went as far as to throw a big party at the Hyde Park Hotel to celebrate Healey's elevation to the Governor-Generalship.[98] Patrick McGilligan, Irish Minister of External Affairs from 1927 to 1932, was so integrated into Commonwealth circles that his referees for the post of Professor of Law at University College Dublin in 1934 included Prime Ministers Bennett of Canada and Hertzog of South Africa, as well as O.D. Skelton, Canadian Under-Secretary of External Affairs, and N.C. Havenga, South African Finance Minister.[99] William MacCaulay, Irish Minister to the Holy See from 1934 to 1940, was a former officer in the Royal Navy and a close associate of the British Ambassador to Italy.[100] Charles Bewley, his predecessor, had been a Sinn Fein envoy in Berlin and later became pro-Nazi, but his anxiety not to give an impression of anti-Englishness seems excessive, in view of his own education at Winchester and Oxford University and his fondness for the British visiting élite in Rome.[101] The Irish diplomats who gathered at the Imperial Economic Conference in Ottawa in 1932 privately admitted to other dominion officials that they were pro-Commonwealth and more sympathetic to Cosgrave than to de Valera.[102] This common Irish-British culture also became advantageous in wartime and this was graphically illustrated by the close relationship which developed between the Irish Army Chief-of-Staff, Lieutenant-General Daniel McKenna, who was a native of Magherafelt, Co. Derry, and General Franklyn, commander of British forces in Northern Ireland, who hailed from Cork. Moreover, a complete Irish divorce from its Commonwealth connections was hardly illustrated by Brendan Bracken, wartime British Minister of Information and one of Churchill's closest confidants, who was the quixotic Jesuit-educated if deceitful son of a prominent Tipperary Fenian and Gaelic Athletic Association activist. There was still significant Irish emigration to the Empire, and – Establishment anti-Catholic condescension notwithstanding – southern

Irish Catholics continued to occupy positions of senior administrative authority across the Empire from the Punjab to Kenya; again these were hardly the hallmarks of a hostile and irreconcilable subject people.[103]

An enduring feature of Irish foreign relations has been the claim that Ireland has enjoyed a special relationship with the United States, based on the presence of a large Irish and Irish-descended community in the USA, and a common revolutionary-republican tradition of resistance to Britain, notwithstanding the 'White Anglo-Saxon Protestant' – indeed anti-Catholic – character of the founding generation of American revolutionaries. Ireland was not alone, of course, in claiming such a singular relationship and peculiar leverage in American policy; all European countries with substantial emigrant populations in America recreated to some extent the 'Great Republic' in their own image. There were indeed millions of Americans of Irish descent who were particularly vocal and well-organised in American eastern and mid-western cities. The great bulk of Irish-descended Americans, however, a large proportion of whom were Protestant, were not ethnically politicised in the least, and had long been assimilated into the mainstream of American culture. The British also had, of course, their own developing myth of a 'special relationship', based on legal and linguistic affinity, aristocratic connections with wealthy Anglo-Americans, and the common kinship with at least one third of Americans who could claim British descent, still a larger proportion of Americans than the Irish could claim. Yet, while the British recognised their relative inability to mobilise British-descended Americans to their support, they had an exaggerated fear of the Irish-American 'millions'. The British largely took the claims of Irish-American activists at face value, thus underestimating their own influence in Washington and unintentionally strengthening Irish diplomatic influence.[104]

The reality of Irish issues in Anglo–American relations was very different. While Irish affairs were a continuing irritant, and – during the Great War – a matter of concern even to the avowedly anglophile President Woodrow Wilson, there was never very much likelihood that the State Department, still dominated by the 'White Anglo-Saxon Protestant' élite, would allow the Irish question to threaten co-operation between the two great powers.[105] During the revolutionary period Congressional resolutions on Ireland were amended to avoid explicit support for Irish republican status. Indeed, Wilson, himself of Ulster Protestant descent, thought that American diplomatic intervention in Ireland in the face of British opposition would be 'inexcusable' and might cause 'serious international embarrassment'.[106] Besides, Sinn Féin was unlikely to gain a sympathetic hearing from Wilson, then reliant on the British to support his idea for collective security based on a League of Nations. De Valera's position was further weakened by associating himself with Irish–American opposition to the League, which they regarded as a WASP conspiracy.[107] There was thus a gulf between the nationalist image of America as a 'Greater Ireland', and the hard realities of postwar Anglo–American diplomacy. Donal O'Callaghan, TD and leading anti-Treatyite, admitted that it 'was all a myth talking about 20 millions of [the Irish] people in America. There was never more than half-a-million in the Irish movement in America'; a view with which de Valera and leading Irish–American opinion privately concurred.[108]

The limitations of Irish leverage in America continued to be apparent in the post-1922 period. The significance of the appointment of the first Irish minister to Washington can be exaggerated, as Ged Martin points out, since the Canadians had already in 1920 gained – though not yet exercised – the right to representation in Washington. Moreover, the Irish appointment took place at the formal request of the British Ambassador to the USA, Sir Esmé Howard, while the initial American moves to reciprocate were channelled though Leo Amery at the Dominions Office.[109] This formal process hardly conveys the impression of a headlong rush to establish diplomatic relations over the heads of the British, and, ironically, for all British fears of Irish-American strength, American administrations consistently came down on the British side whenever Anglo–Irish issues intruded into US foreign policy. Joseph Walshe privately had few illusions about American policy, warning de Valera shortly after coming to power that in the event of an Anglo–Irish confrontation 'even the Americans' would choose the British side.[110] In 1933, Walshe's caution was vindicated when, in reply to a question about whether he would enter into a trade agreement with the Irish Free State, President Franklin D. Roosevelt told a press conference: 'No. Tell me, can we enter into a trade agreement with Ireland without the consent of Great Britain?' When a reporter replied, 'I think so; Ireland claims they can', Roosevelt responded with a laugh.[111] It should be noted that this exchange had followed the Imperial Economic Conference held in Ottawa in the previous year. In spite of latent Anglo–Irish tension and apparent Irish–American friendship, Ireland had sent a delegation to Ottawa, where Britain, the dominions, India and Southern Rhodesia attempted to work out a scheme of imperial tariffs in defiance of the wishes of the USA.[112]

Not surprisingly, the Americans tended to see Ireland as part of the British 'camp'. The secret US 'War Red Plan', evolved in the 1920s to deal with the unlikely event of war with the British Empire, bizarrely envisaged the Irish Free State contributing a division to the defence of Canada against an American invasion.[113] In 1933, when Sean T. O'Kelly, Vice-President, used the occasion of the accreditation of the new American Minister to Dublin to de Valera, rather than, as customary, to the Governor-General, as evidence of growing recognition of Irish independence in defiance of British wishes. In fact George V had already formally approved the new procedure of accreditation and the American State Department had no wish to become further involved in Anglo–Irish affairs. This incident further illustrates that in the emergence of Ireland into sovereignty even the Americans chose to move at the pace of a British-defined legalism, rather than adhere to Irish definitions of independence.[114] Even when, in this period, Ireland could claim a wider significance, through its presidency of the League Council, de Valera's American birth and Irish nationality counted for nothing in his efforts to promote South American peacekeeping in the face of American opposition. The truth about American foreign policy was that it was primarily motivated neither by Irish, nor British, nor any other ethnic considerations, but by American national self-interest, which, in the 1930s, demanded cooperation with the other anglophone great power, with which the USA, for all its historical rivalry, shared a common interest in the obstruction of German, Italian and, particularly, Japanese militarism.[115] The appointment in 1938 of Joseph Kennedy as American Ambassador to the Court of St James was far less significant than de Valera had hoped. In the same year Roosevelt wrote to inform de Valera that he had instructed Kennedy to discuss Anglo–Irish relations privately with the British, but he warned that he could not 'officially or through diplomatic channels accomplish anything or even discuss the matter'.[116] This was substantially the case. There was very little the USA, already locked in isolationism but keen on the business opportunities offered by British rearmament, could do, if it had the will, to influence Anglo–Irish relations. Generally, however, it lacked the conviction, and such leverage as it possessed was weakened by Kennedy's increasingly obvious faith in an Axis triumph in Europe.[117] Ireland was again forced to learn the lesson not to place too much trust in Irish-American influence.

It is instructive to contrast the apparent powerlessness of the Irish-American Kennedy in London with the growing influence in American policy of the decidedly patrician US Minister to Dublin, David Gray. He was the very antithesis of Kennedy: a WASP authority on fox-hunting and social etiquette who was Roosevelt's uncle by marriage. Although the Irish Government generally despised Gray as anti-Irish, they liked to believe that his views were unrepresentative of American opinion, when in fact he echoed prejudices of the American administrative elite all too well.[118] The war and its immediate aftermath further proved how marginal Irish influence had become, when the Americans and the British formed what was to become the closest military alliance in modern times. In 1940–41, the Americans, even while still neutral, brought pressure to bear on the Irish Government to enter the war, and Roosevelt personally blocked Irish attempts to secure American arms, while Britain was being provided with enormous quantities of Lend-Lease material. In 1941, when Frank Aiken travelled to America in search of food and arms for neutral Ireland, he encountered a deep hostility from both Roosevelt and the State Department, which was so hostile that it almost asked him to leave the country; it should be noted that this came at a time when Winston Churchill was being lionised in the USA as 'the greatest Anglo-American'.[119] Significantly, the first wartime posting of American troops in Europe was in Northern Ireland (where the warm welcome afforded by the Unionists was noted by the US State Department), in defiance of de Valera's protest that this constituted a violation of Irish national territory.

In the postwar decade, British persuasion again prevented the sale of American arms to Ireland, while, ironically, Britain continued herself to provide a trickle of arms.[120] After the end of the Second World War, Ireland found itself temporarily blackballed by the Americans, manifested in their refusal to send the customary message of congratulations to Sean T. O'Kelly on his election as President. This was due not only to disapproval of Ireland's wartime neutrality, but also because the State Department feared that such a message might amount to American acknowledgement that 'Ireland is completely dissociated from the British Commonwealth'.[121] In American politics, then, although the relationship with Ireland was powerfully sentimental and certainly important in key local areas at election time, in foreign policy terms Ireland was, at most, of episodic interest. In contrast, the American alliance with Britain was, for all its jealous intimacy, strategic and coherent, and for these reasons the Anglo–American and Irish–American relationships would remain entirely different in character. Whatever the public rhetoric of Irish–American friendship, the wartime experience reminded Irish politicians and diplomats that they could not command the support of American governments on the issue of partition, and this provided an added incentive to the Irish Government to pursue after the war a policy of military detachment, even without ideological neutrality in the developing Cold War confrontation with the communist East.[122]

What, then, is the significance of dominion status in Ireland's progress to republican status outside the Commonwealth? In 1966 Nicholas Mansergh observed that 'succeeding generations find it increasingly hard to comprehend' the importance of dominion status in Irish history, in spite of its central importance in the differences between the pro- and anti-Treaty sides in the Civil War and the emotional intensity it aroused.[123] More recently, Paul Kennedy has observed:

> The theory of dominion status which could be redefined as circumstances changed, and the concept of a metamorphosis from Empire into Commonwealth, stayed the hand of nationalists who otherwise might have pressed for outright independence – Hertzog, for example; for a while it even bemused de Valera and the more extreme Irish nationalists.[124]

The controversies surrounding the nature and extent of dominion status provided the dominant influences on Irish foreign policy for over a generation, and it could equally be argued that these dominion issues 'stayed the hand' of the British as much as it did de Valera. True, Ireland was not a dominion in spirit, but that status nevertheless defined its relations with both the Commonwealth and the world at large, and Britain was hampered in any pressure in might bring to bear on Ireland because of the wider need to maintain good relations with the dominions and India. The recently published histories of Irish involvement in international bodies other than the Commonwealth, facilitated by the opening of Irish diplomatic archives, have provided valuable understandings of the genuine internationalism which motivated the first generation of Irish diplomats. Nevertheless, this new scholarship does not successfully challenge the view that the British and Commonwealth context of Irish diplomacy remained of overwhelming importance in the first three decades of independence. For most of this period, de Valera was dominant, and in a telling remark in 1952 Frederick Boland told Nicholas Mansergh that de Valera was fundamentally a 'Commonwealth man':

> [De Valera's] feeling was that once external association had been more formally established, the Irish mission in the Commonwealth would be much strengthened, particularly in respect of partition. Throughout, he believed strongly in Irish cooperation with the

Commonwealth overseas. The great difference of emphasis between him and MacBride [External Affairs Minister] was that the latter believed in Western European cooperation, de Valera in Commonwealth cooperation.[125]

This impression seems entirely consistent with de Valera's policies in government. Ironically, dominion status as it developed in the 1930s proved to be his greatest constitutional ally. In 1936, he told the Dominions Secretary Malcolm MacDonald that the responsibility for an Irish secession from the Commonwealth would lie with Britain; in other words, he would not leave formally and only a British-inspired expulsion would be responsible for an Irish secession.[126] De Valera shared with MacDonald and Neville Chamberlain a liberal democratic culture. His relationship with MacDonald was increasingly marked by personal warmth and a realisation, that the cruelties of Irish history paled in comparison with the fascist and communist excesses of contemporary Europe and Asia. Whether he realised it or not, the dominions, particularly Canada and South Africa, proved to be particularly valuable in deterring a British reaction. In 1947, de Valera encouraged a visiting delegation of Indian nationalists to devise a form of external association with the Commonwealth, and in October 1951 he told the visiting South African High Commissioner, Dr A.L. Geyer, that he would have been satisfied with the status of a republic within the Commonwealth recently accorded to India.[127] When he lost power in 1948 his anti-partition world tour took him to the dominions of Australia and New Zealand, and he confided to Niall MacDermott, a member of the Central Committee of the European Union of Federalists, that while he generally supported a European federation:

It would depend necessarily to some extent on Britain's position. If Britain found it necessary owing to her Commonwealth to remain outside a European Federation, then it would be better for Ireland in the first place to join some other regional grouping, based perhaps on the British Commonwealth of Nations.[128]

We can only speculate, but it seems unlikely that de Valera, had he remained in power, would have taken Ireland completely out of the Commonwealth. We know that he had informed the British that, in the absence of an initiative from them on partition, he would be forced to bring in legislation removing the vestiges of the Crown from Irish diplomacy. Here, again, the timing was crucial. After the war, the

British to a great extent proved willing put the neutrality issue behind them and were prepared, for example, to support Irish efforts to join the United Nations, and there is evidence to suggest that de Valera was considering transferring diplomatic formalities from the King to the Irish President without openly breaking with the Commonwealth, a move which almost certainly would have worked with Indian and South African support.[129] Such a course was precluded however by the accession of the inter-party government committed to ending all constitutional ambiguity by taking Ireland out of the Commonwealth altogether.[130] Even here, however, Commonwealth opinion remained important in hampering British attempts at diplomatic pressure. In 1948 the Irish High Commissioner in London accepted an invitation to a South African official dinner in honour of Field Marshal Smuts, along with the High Commissioners of Canada, Australia, New Zealand, India, Pakistan and Southern Rhodesia, as well as such leading Imperial figures as L.S. Amery, Lord Tweedsmuir, General Ismay and Marshal of the Royal Air Force Lord Tedder, thus signalling Ireland's rehabilitation in the highest Commonwealth circles.[131] It was difficult for the British to be hostile in such circumstances. When the British held meetings with the dominions at Chequers to discuss the implications of Irish secession, they were careful to exclude from these discussions the newly-elected Afrikaner Nationalist government in South Africa, which had indicated its strong support for the Irish position and enjoyed close personal relationships with both Taoiseach Costello and External Affairs Minister MacBride.[132]

The other dominions, however, proved to be equally unwilling to pressurise the Irish on the issue of the republic and they encouraged the British to do likewise. The result was in many ways an unofficial continuation of 'external association'. The British, until the mid-1960s, continued to deal with Ireland through the Commonwealth Relations (formerly the Dominions) Office, rather than the Foreign Office, so that Ireland could continue to seem like a Commonwealth absentee rather than as an imperial escapee. The British were encouraged in this approach by an apparent willingness on de Valera's part to consider rejoining the Commonwealth in the 1950s if the issue of partition was addressed.[133] Each of the Dominions passed legislation recognising Irish secession, but continued to treat the Irish as though they had not left the Commonwealth. Ireland had not been an active participant in Commonwealth proceedings for almost twenty years, so its departure did not seem so drastic.[134] This relative complacency seems to be in keeping with Irish confusion about whether Ireland might continue to be a member of various Commonwealth organisations such as the Agricultural Bureau, and British suggestions that Ireland might be readmitted to Commonwealth committees on an *ad hoc* observer basis.[135] Irish diplomacy may have been aided by another factor that was largely outside its direct control: the British Foreign Secretary Ernest Bevin's belief that it was essential to include Catholicism in a unified Christian response to communism as part of Britain's Cold War strategy.[136]

However skilled Irish diplomats were, then, in common with other representatives they did not always control the pace of events or necessarily recognise key influences which lay outside the confines of Anglo–Irish relations. Nevertheless, Irish foreign policy, in terms of Commonwealth relations, seemed to end in the best of all worlds, retaining most of the benefits of Commonwealth membership, but with neither obligations nor any apparent need to confront Ireland's extensive, practical rather than principled, participation in British imperialism which continued into the post-Second World War era. In this sense, both Collins and de Valera's seemingly opposing positions on Commonwealth membership seemed to be vindicated by events. Collins had predicted that dominion status would provide the 'freedom to achieve freedom' and that the other dominions would provide safeguards for Irish freedoms, but that Britain would or could not in 1922 accept an overt Irish break with the Crown.[137] In 1922 it was the British rather than the Irish who proved to be unimaginative, doctrinaire and obsessed with dominion status. De Valera, on the other hand, was prophetic in his conviction that Commonwealth elasticity could be stretched to encompass a virtual republic. In his belief that it was wiser to leave some relationships undefined he was closer to the organic, Burkean traditions of British constitutionalism than the British themselves seemed. He was also proved correct, but only in the very different circumstances of the 1930s, when Britain, confronted by economic and military danger, but by no means abdicating imperial aspirations, sought to readjust its treaty relationships with Ireland, Egypt and Iraq, in order to make these less provocative to local nationalists.[138] The Commonwealth factor was significantly, if belatedly, recognised in Taoiseach John A. Costello's speech introducing the Republic of Ireland Act in November 1948, when he sought to reassert a 'special' relationship with Britain and the Commonwealth:

> [I]t would be unthinkable for us, by the action which this Bill proposes to take, to go further away from those nations with which we have had such a long and, I think, fruitful association in the

past 25 or 26 years ... Our people pass freely from here to England. We have trade and commerce of mutual benefit to each other. We have somewhat the same pattern of life, somewhat the same respect for democratic principles and institutions. The English language in our Constitution is recognized as the second official language of this nation ... Our missionary priests, nuns and brothers have gone to England and brought the faith there, and are giving no inadequate contribution to the spiritual uplift which is so necessary in the atheistic atmosphere of the world today ... Ireland does not now ... intend to regard [Commonwealth] citizens as 'foreigners' or their countries as 'foreign' countries.[139]

This might seem a strange admission for a government to make on the eve of republican status and final secession from the Commonwealth. A number of phrases have been used to describe Ireland's peculiar constitutional position from 1922 to 1949, from 'Restless Dominion' to 'Dictionary Republic'. In the light of these continuing and uniquely intimate connections to Britain and the Commonwealth, it could be argued that 1949 ushered in the age of the 'Aberrant Republic'.

Notes

1 Quoted in N. Mansergh, *The Unresolved Question: The Anglo–Irish Settlement and its Undoing, 1910–1972* (London, 1971), p. 321. Only slightly less bizarre, perhaps, was the constitutional progress of Canada, which exercised its sovereign right, gained through the Statute of Westminster (1931), to declare war a week after Britain in 1939, so that the 'King of Canada' was not at war until so advised by his Canadian cabinet. Canada abolished the right of appeal to the United Kingdom Privy Council in 1947, yet only achieved the right to amend the Canadian constitution in 1982, when the British Parliament 'patriated' the British North America Act of 1867. In South Africa, where de Valera's precedent of neutrality was unsuccessfully cited by General Hertzog, the declaration of war was delayed until 6 December, when Smuts formed a pro-war government, so that the 'King of South Africa' was not officially at war until three days after his British constitutional persona. See F. Madden and J. Darwin (eds), *The Dominions and India Since 1900: Select Documents on the Constitutional History of the British Empire and Commonwealth*, vol. 6 (Westport, 1993). ch. 31.

2 N. Mansergh, *Unresolved Question*, p. 321. The irony that the papal title, *Fidei Defensor*, had originally been awarded by Pope Leo X to Henry VIII for his defence of Catholic doctrine against Luther, was commonly regarded as irrelevant by Irish Catholics and British Protestants, since the title had become 'Protestantised' in the course of the Reformation and had long since lost its original Catholic significance.

3   N. Mansergh, *Documents and Speeches on British Commonwealth Affairs, 1931–1952* (London, 1953), pp. 794–6.

4   N. Mansergh, *The Commonwealth Experience*, vol. 2, *From British to Multi-Racial Commonwealth* (rev. edn, London, 1982), p. 143.

5   The Statute of Westminster of 1931, which guaranteed the sovereignty of the dominions in international affairs, was adopted by the Irish Free State, Canada and South Africa between 1931 and 1934, and by Australia and New Zealand in 1942 and 1947 respectively. However, the right to amend the Canadian Constitution (the British North America Act of 1867) was retained by the United Kingdom parliament until 1982, while the British Government also possessed reserve powers relating to the Australian states until 1986. India's advance to independence was even more unusual, gaining while still under British control membership of the League of Nations in 1919, followed by the appointment of diplomats overseas, and it became a founder member of the United Nations in 1945, two years before independence. India, Pakistan, Ghana and Nigeria all passed through dominion status before becoming republics within the Commonwealth, while most other states gaining independence in the 1960s opted for immediate republican status. Of those territories gaining independence in the post-war decades only Burma chose to leave the Commonwealth outright. At the time of writing several Commonwealth states, including New Zealand and Jamaica, retain the right of appeal to the Judicial Committee of the Privy Council at Westminster, even though fully sovereign in international affairs. See H.J. Harvey, *Consultation and Co-operation in the Commonwealth* (London, 1952), ch. 8; K.C. Wheare, *The Constitutional Structure of the Commonwealth* (Oxford, 1960), chs. 4–5.

6   See B. McKercher, 'Wealth, Power and the New International Order: Britain and the American Challenge in the 1920s', *Diplomatic History*, vol. 12 (1988), pp. 411–41; J. Major, 'War Plan Red: The American Plan for War with Britain', *The Historian*, no. 58 (1998), pp. 12–15.

7   D. Keogh, *Ireland and Europe, 1919–1948* (Dublin, 1988), p. 5. For a useful summary of traditional Irish nationalist awareness of the importance of world opinion see H.V. Brasted, 'Irish Nationalism and the British Empire', in O. MacDonagh (ed.), *Irish Culture and Nationalism* (Canberra, 1983).

8   Patrick Keatinge, 'The Formative Years of the Irish Diplomatic Service', *Eire–Ireland*, vol. 6 (1971), pp. 57–71; Dermot Keogh, 'The Origins of the Irish Foreign Service in Europe (1919–1922)', *Etudes Irlandaises*, no. 7 (1982), pp. 145–63; Keogh, *Ireland and Europe*, ch. 1; Arthur Mitchell, *Revolutionary Government in Ireland: Dail Eireann 1919–22* (Dublin, 1995), pp. 25–8, 38–43, 99–119, 254–64.

9   Arthur Mitchell, *Revolutionary Government in Ireland: Dail Eireann 1919–22* (1995), pp. 106–10; Eamon de Valera, *India and Ireland* (New York, 1920); Sean T. O'Kelly, *India and Ireland* (New York, 1924); T.G. Fraser, 'Ireland and India', in K. Jeffery, *'An Irish Empire'?: Aspects of Ireland and the British Empire* (Manchester, 1996), p. 77.

10 P. Keatinge, 'The Formative Years of the Irish Diplomatic Service', *Eire–Ireland*, vol. 6 (1971), pp. 57–71; D. Keogh, 'The Origins of the Irish Foreign Service in Europe (1919–1922)', *Etudes Irlandaises*, no. 7 (1982), pp. 145–63; Keogh, *Ireland and Europe*, ch. 1; Mitchell, *Revolutionary Government*, pp. 25–8, 38–43, 99–119, 254–64.

11 De Valera Papers, UCDA MS 1462: Report of Colonel Moore's Mission to South Africa, April 1921, and Note to the Envoys in London or Irish Republican Government, about October 1921; Maurice Moore Papers, NLI, MS 10,581: Copy of letter, Moore to Smuts, 'about 20 August 1921'. I am grateful to Seamus Helferty of the Archives Department, University College Dublin, for his assistance with the de Valera papers.

12 A.B. Keith, *Letters on Imperial Relations, Indian Reform, Constitutional and International Law, 1916–1935* (London, 1935); M. Collins, *The Path to Freedom* (Dublin, 1922), pp. 87–92.

13 N. Mansergh, 'Ireland and the British Commonwealth', in D. Mansergh (ed.), *Nationalism and Independence: Selected Irish Papers by Nicholas Mansergh* (Cork, 1997), p. 98.

14 N. Mansergh, 'Commonwealth Membership', in N. Mansergh *et al.*, *Commonwealth Perspectives* (Durham, 1958), p. 1.

15 PRO:CAB 43/2. SFB 13, Curtis Memorandum.

16 See, for example, T.D. Williams, 'Ireland and the War', in T.D. Williams and K.B. Nowlan (eds), *Ireland in the War Years and After* (Dublin, 1969); T.D. Williams, 'Irish Foreign Policy', in J.J. Lee, *Ireland 1945–70* (Dublin, 1979).

17 See, for example, D.G. Boyce, *The Irish Question in British Politics, 1868–1996* (London, 2nd. edn. 1996); G. Boyce, 'From War to Neutrality: Anglo-Irish Relations, 1921–1950', *British Journal of International Relations*, vol. 5 (1978), pp. 15–36; J. Bowman, *De Valera and the Ulster Question* (Oxford, 1982); P. Keatinge, 'Unequal Sovereigns: The Diplomatic Dimension of Anglo–Irish Relations', in P. Drudy (ed.), *Ireland and Britain Since 1922* (Cambridge, 1985); C.C. O'Brien, 'Ireland in International Affairs', in O.D. Edwards (Ed.), *C. C. O'Brien introduces Ireland* (London, 1969). The relevant works of Nicholas Mansergh include: 'Ireland: External Relations, 1926–39', in F. MacManus (ed.), *The Years of the Great Test* (Cork, 1967); *The Irish Free State: Its Government and Politics* (London, 1934), ch. 15; *Prelude to Partition: Concepts and Aims in Ireland and India* (Cambridge, 1978); and *The Unresolved Question: The Anglo–Irish Settlement and its Undoing* (New Haven and London, 1991). Mansergh's essays, articles and diary entries, ranging over four decades, are usefully collected in D. Mansergh (ed.), *Nationalism and Independence: Selected Irish Papers by Nicholas Mansergh* (Cork, 1997).

18 See A.B. Keith, *The Dominions as Sovereign States* (London, 1938); R.M. Dawson (ed.), *The Development of Dominion Status, 1900–1936* (London, 1937); K.C. Wheare, *The Constitutional Structure of the Commonwealth* (Oxford, 1960), *passim*; W.K. Hancock, *Problems of British Commonwealth Affairs 1918–1939*, vol. 1: *Problems of Nationality* (London, 1937), ch. 3. See also R.F. Holland, *Britain and the Commonwealth Alliance 1918–39* (London, 1981), ch. 9; N. Mansergh, *The Commonwealth Experience*, vol. 1: *The Durham Report to the Anglo–Irish Treaty* (Revised edn. Toronto, 1983), ch. 7, and vol. 2: *From British to Multi-Racial Commonwealth* (Revised edn. Toronto, 1983), ch. 5; D.B. Swinfen, *Imperial Appeal: The Debate on the Appeal to the Privy Council, 1833–1986* (Manchester, 1987), pp. 88–13, *passim*. For a particularly scathing and avowedly Anglocentred view of Irish assertiveness, as well as dominion nationalism generally in this period, see C. Barnett, *The Collapse of British Power* (London, 1972), pp. 121–234.

19   The Irish Free State possessed an 'essentially republican constitution on most advanced continental lines', according to L. Kohn's authoritative *The Constitution of the Irish Free State* (London, 1932), p. 80. Relevant works by David Harkness include: *The Restless Dominion: The Irish Free State and the British Commonwealth of Nations, 1921–31* (London and Dublin, 1969); 'Mr de Valera's Dominion: Irish Relations with Britain and the Commonwealth', *Journal of Commonwealth Political Studies*, vol. 8 (1970), pp. 206–28; 'Britain and the Independence of the Dominions: The 1921 Cross-Roads', in T.W. Moody (ed.), *Historical Studies XI: Nationality and the Pursuit of National Independence* (Belfast, 1978); 'Patrick McGilligan: Man of Commonwealth', in N. Hillmer and P. Wigley (eds), *The First British Commonwealth* (London, 1980); 'The Constitutions of Ireland and the Development of National Identity, 1919–1984', *Journal of Commonwealth and Comparative Politics*, vol. 26 (1988), pp. 135–46. Harkness's work has also underpinned J.M. Curran, 'The Issue of External Relations in the Anglo–Irish Negotiations of May–June, 1922', *Eire-Ireland*, vol. 13 (1970), pp. 15–25.
20   G. Martin, 'The Irish Free State and the Evolution of the Commonwealth, 1921–49', in R. Hyam and G. Martin (eds), *Reappraisals in British Imperial History* (London, 1975), p. 206. Martin's view is echoed in G.M. MacMillan, *State, Society and Authority in Ireland: The Foundations of the Modern Irish State* (Dublin, 1993), pp. 233–35.
21   D. MacMahon, 'Ireland, the Dominions and the Munich Crisis', *Irish Studies in International Affairs*, vol. 1 (1979), pp. 30–37; and *Republicans and Imperialists: Anglo–Irish Relations in the 1930s* (New Haven and London, 1984), ch. 10; P. Canning, *British Policy Towards Ireland 1921–1941* (Oxford, 1985), pp. 110–114, 126, 130.
22   Swinfen, *Imperial Appeal*, p. 139; Harkness, *Restless Dominion*, pp. 251–2. See also G.M. MacMillan, 'Legislative Authority, Sovereignty, Legitimacy and Political Development: The Constitutional Basis of the Irish Free State', (Unpublished Ph.D. dissertation, National University of Ireland, 1987).
23   J. Darwin, 'Imperialism in Decline?: Tendencies in British Imperial Policy Between the Wars', *Historical Journal*, vol. 23 (1980), pp. 661–64; J. Darwin, 'Dominions or Nations?', paper delivered at 'The British World: Diaspora, Culture and Identity since c. 1880', Institute of Commonwealth Studies, University of London, 26–27 June 1998. D. Lowry, 'Ulster Resistance and Loyalist Rebellion in the Empire', in Jeffery (ed.), *'An Irish Empire'?*, pp. 191–215.
24   L. Lloyd and A. James, 'The External Representation of the Dominions, 1919–1948', *The British Yearbook of International Law 1996* (Oxford, 1997).
25   See F. McEvoy, 'Canada, Ireland and the Commonwealth: The Declaration of a Republic', *Irish Historical Studies*, vol. 24 (1983), pp. 506–27; P. O'Farrell, 'Irish-Australian Diplomatic Relations', *Quadrant*, vol. 34 (1980), pp. 11–19; A. Martin, 'An Australian Prime Minister in Ireland: R.G. Menzies, 1941', in F.B. Smith (ed.), *Ireland, England and Australia* (Canberra, 1990); N. Quirke, 'Australia's Role in Ireland's Declaration of a Republic and Withdrawal from the Commonwealth', in *Irish-Australian Historical Studies* (Canberra, 1989); J. O'Brien, 'Australia, Britain, Ireland and the Ottawa Conference', in O. MacDonagh and W.F. Mandle (eds), *Ireland and Australia* (Canberra, 1989); J. O'Brien, 'Ireland's Departure From the British Commonwealth',

Round Table, No. 306 (1988), pp. 179–194; D. W. Dean, 'Final Exit? Britain, Eire, the Commonwealth and the Repeal of the External Relations Act, 1945–1949', *Journal of Imperial and Commonwealth History*, Vol. 20 (1992), pp. 391–418; D. Lowry, ' "Ireland Shows the Way": Irish-South African Relations and the British Empire-Commonwealth, c. 1902–1961', in D. McCracken (ed.), *Ireland and South Africa in Modern Times* (Durban, 1996); I. McCabe, *A Diplomatic History of Ireland 1948–1949: The Republic, the Commonwealth and NATO* (Dublin, 1991).

26 D. Akenson, *The United States and Ireland* (Cambridge, 1973); C.J. Carter, 'Ireland: America's Neutral Ally, 1939–1945', *Eire-Ireland*, vol. 12 (1977), pp. 5–13; T. Ryle Dwyer, *Irish Neutrality and the USA 1939–1947* (Dublin, 1977); T. Ryle Dwyer, *Strained Relations: Ireland at Peace and the USA at War 1941–45* (Dublin, 1988); R.J. Raymond, 'American Public Opinion and Irish Neutrality, 1939–1945', *Eire-Ireland*, vol. 18 (1983), pp. 20–45; R.J. Raymond, 'David Gray, the Aiken Mission and Irish Neutrality, 1940–41', *Diplomatic History*, vol. 9 (1985), pp. 55–71; R. Fanning, 'The Anglo–American Alliance and the Irish Application for Membership of the United Nations', *Irish Studies in International Affairs*, vol. 2 (1986); F. Carroll, *American Opinion and the Irish Question 1910–1923* (Dublin, 1978); F. Carroll, 'Protocol and International Politics: The Secretary of State goes to Ireland, 1928', *Eire-Ireland*, vol. 26 (1991); J.L. Rosenberg, 'The 1941 Mission of Frank Aiken to the United States: An American Perspective', *Irish Historical Studies*, vol. 22 (1980), pp. 162–77; S. Cronin, 'The Making of NATO and the Partition of Ireland', *Eire–Ireland*, vol. 20 (1985); S. Cronin, *Washington's Irish Policy, 1916–1986* (Dublin, 1987); J. Carroll, 'U.S.–Irish Relations', *The Irish Sword*, vol. 9 (1993–5), pp. 99–105.

27 See Keogh, *Ireland and Europe*; P. Keatinge, 'The Europeanization of Irish Foreign Policy', in P.J. Drudy and D. McAleese (eds), *Ireland and the European Community* (Cambridge, 1983); P. Sharp, *Irish Foreign Policy and the European Community: A Study of the Impact of Interdependence on the Foreign Policy of a Small State* (Aldershot, 1990); M. Hederman, *The Road to Europe: Irish Attitudes, 1948–67* (Dublin, 1983); P. Keatinge, 'Irish Neutrality and the European Community', in B. McSweeney (ed.), *Ireland the European Community* (Dublin, 1985).

28 D. Keogh, 'De Valera, the Bishops and the Red Scare', in John A. Murphy and P.J. Carroll (eds), *De Valera* (Cork, 1983); *The Vatican, the Bishops and Irish Politics 1919–1939* (Cambridge, 1986); 'Ireland, the Vatican and the Cold War: The Case of Italy', *Historical Journal*, vol. 34 (1991), pp. 931–52; *Ireland and the Vatican: The Politics and Diplomacy of Church–State Relations, 1922–1960* (Cork, 1995).

29 See B. Sexton, *Ireland and the Crown, 1922–1936: The Governor-Generalship of the Irish Free State* (Dublin, 1989); R. Sherry, 'The Story of the National Anthem', *History Ireland*, vol. 4 (1996), pp. 39–43. It should be noted that the adoption of a distinctively Irish national flag had a significant effect on nationalist politics in South Africa, where the flag issue seemed to bring Afrikaner nationalists and British South African Empire loyalists to the brink of civil war. See H. Saker, *The South African Flag Controversy, 1925–1928* (Cape Town, 1980), p. 9.

30 R. Fanning, 'Irish Neutrality – A Historical Review', *Irish Studies in International Affairs*, vol. 1 (1982), pp. 27–36; R. Fanning, 'Anglo–Irish Relations: Partition and the British Dimension in Historical Perspective', *ibid.*, vol. 4

(1985), esp. pp. 15–16; R. Fanning, *Independent Ireland* (Dublin, 1983), pp. 82–6; R. Fanning, 'Irish Neutrality', in B. Huldt and A. Lejins (eds), *Neutrals in Europe: Ireland* (Stockholm, 1990); J.P. Duggan, *Neutral Ireland and the Third Reich* (Dublin, 1985); T. Ryle Dwyer, *De Valera's Finest Hour: In Search of National Independence, 1932–1939* (Cork, 1982); J.T. Carroll, *Ireland in the War Years 1939–1945* (Newton Abbot, 1975); R. Fisk, *In Time of War: Ireland, Ulster and the Price of Neutrality, 1939–45* (London, 1983); T. Salmon, 'The Changing Nature of Irish Defence Policy', *The World Today*, vol. 35 (1979); T. Salmon, 'Ireland: A Neutral in the Community?', *Journal of Common Market Studies*, vol. 20 (1982); T. Salmon, *Unneutral Ireland: An Ambivalent and Unique Security Policy* (Oxford, 1989); D. O'Drisceoil, *Censorship in Ireland 1939–1945: Neutrality, Politics and Society* (Cork, 1996).

31   National Archives of Ireland, Cabinet Memorandum by de Valera, Cabinet File S8083, cited in Salmon, *Unneutral Ireland*, p. 95.

32   C.C. O'Brien, 'Ireland in International Affairs', in O.D. Edwards (ed.), *Conor Cruise O'Brien Introduces Ireland* (London, 1969); P. Keatinge, 'Ireland and the League of Nations', *Studies*, vol. 59 (1970), pp. 133–147; P. Keatinge, 'Ireland and the World', in F. Litton (ed.), *Unequal Achievement* (Dublin, 1982); P. Keatinge, *A Singular Stance: Irish Neutrality in the 1980s* (Dublin, 1984); S. Barcroft, 'Irish Foreign Policy at the League of Nations, 1929–1936', *Irish Studies in International Affairs*, vol. 1 (1979), pp. 19–29; D. Driscoll, 'Is Ireland Really "Neutral"?', *Irish Studies in International Affairs*, vol. 1 (1982), pp. 55–61; N. MacQueen, 'Eamon de Valera, the Irish Free State and the League of Nations', *Eire-Ireland*, vol. 17 (1982), pp. 110–27; T. Mulkeen, 'Ireland at the UN', *Eire-Ireland*, vol. 8 (1973); N. MacQueen, 'Ireland's Entry in the United Nations, 1946–56', in T. Gallagher and J. O'Connell (eds), *Irish Contemporary Studies* (Manchester, 1983); N. MacQueen, 'Frank Aiken and Irish Activism at the United Nations', *International History Review*, vol. 6 (1984). Michael Kennedy's works include: 'The Irish Free State and the League of Nations', *ibid.*, vol. 3 (1994), pp. 9–24; 'Candour and Chicanery: The Irish Free State and the Geneva Protocol', *Irish Historical Studies*, vol. 29 (1995); 'Prologue to Peacekeeping: Ireland and the Saar, 1934–5', *ibid.*, pp. 420–428; *Ireland and the League of Nations 1919–1946: International Relations, Diplomacy and Politics* (Dublin, 1996); J.M. Skelly, 'Ireland, the Department of External Relations, and the United Nations', *Irish Studies in International Affairs*, vol. 7 (1996); J.M. Skelly, *Irish Diplomacy at the United Nations 1945–1965: National Interest and the International Order* (Dublin, 1996).

33   M. Holmes, N. Rees and B. Whelan, *The Poor Relation: Irish Foreign Policy and the Third World* (Dublin, 1993), p. 180. See also B. Laffan, *Ireland and South Africa* (Dublin, 1988); B. Whelan, M. Holmes and N. Rees, 'Ireland and the Third World – A Historical Perspective', *Irish Studies in International Affairs*, vol. 5 (1994), pp. 107–119.

34   Keogh, *Ireland and Europe*, p. 10.

35   D. Keogh, 'Ireland. Department of Foreign Affairs', in Zara Steiner (ed.), *The Times Survey of Foreign Offices of the World* (London, 1982), p. 279.

36   The enduring totemic power of Irish 'anti-imperialism' is evident in a speech given by President Mary Robinson to the South African Houses of

Parliament on 26 March 1996, in which she stated:

> Let us remember our own past suffering and link with the suffering of the poorest countries who need support in their self development... Although Ireland is a small country and a member of the European Union, its history and sense of identity are closer in many ways to the African, than to European experience. Ireland has a genuine interest in the future of Africa as its history has been one of struggle for freedom and justice. When European countries were engaged in the scramble for Africa, the Irish were struggling to achieve their own independence... [Our] story of colonization, famine and dispersal of people is one mirrored in the story of many African peoples. [*Cape Times*, 26 March 1996.]

Such a view of Irish history, however, completely ignores the nature of the Irish home rule movement, which included staunch Irish supporters of colonialism (including Charles Stewart Parnell, who had accepted £10 000 from Cecil Rhodes), the prominent involvement of Irishmen and women of all religious and ethnic traditions in the 'Scramble for Africa', and the intimate relationship which developed between Irish and the Afrikaner nationalists. Moreover, as Liam Kennedy has argued, in socio-economic terms Ireland has resembled a European metropolis rather than a colonial periphery, and more importantly, has behaved in its economic policies towards the developing world as pragmatically as its fellow members of the European Union. See Liam Kennedy's essay on 'Modern Ireland: Post-Colonial Society or Post-Colonial Pretensions', in *Colonialism, Religion and Nationalism in Ireland* (Belfast, 1996), p. 180; D. Lowry, 'The alliance that dare not speak its name: Afrikaner and Irish Nationalists and the British Empire-Commonwealth, c. 1902–1961', *Institute of Commonwealth Studies Collected Seminar Series*, 14 November 1996.

37 Skelly, *Irish Diplomacy*, pp. 25–6.

38 *Ibid.*, p. 74. Lowry, 'Ireland Shows the Way', *passim*.

39 See W.K. Hancock, *Survey of British Commonwealth Affairs 1918–1939*, vol. 2: *Problems of Economic Policy* (London, 1942), ch. 3; Darwin, 'Imperialism in Decline?', pp. 661–64; J. Darwin, *Britain and Decolonisation: The Retreat from Empire in the Post-War World* (London, 1988), p. 150; P.J. Henshaw, 'Britain, South Africa and the Sterling Area: Gold Production, Capital Investment and Agricultural Markets, 1931–1961', *Historical Journal*, vol. 39 (1996), pp. 197–223.

40 J. Lee, *Ireland 1912–1985: Politics and Society* (Cambridge, 1989), p. 156.

41 Keogh, *Ireland and the Vatican*, pp. 133–34.

42 P.J. Cain and A.G. Hopkins, *British Imperialism: Crisis and Deconstruction 1914–1990* (London, 1993), ch. 6; I. Drummond, *British Economic Policy and the Empire* (London, 1972); O'Brien, 'Australia, Britain, Ireland and the Ottawa Conference', is a notable exception to the general neglect of Irish-Commonwealth economic relations. For Marxist interpretations see T.A. Jackson, *Ireland Her Own: An Outline History of the Irish Struggle* (London, 1947); D.R. O'Connor Lysaght, 'British Imperialism in Ireland', in A. Morgan and B. Purdie (eds), *Ireland: Divided Nation, Divided Class* (London, 1980).

43 See D.C. Watt, *What About The People? International History and the Social Sciences* (London, 1985); E.R. May, 'The Decline of Diplomatic History', in G.A. Bilias and G.N. Grob (eds), *American History: Retrospect and Prospect* (New York, 1971).

44 J. Lee, *Ireland 1912–1985*, p. 91, n. 144.

45 Kevin O'Higgins (Vice-President and sometime Minister of External Affairs 1922–1927); Eamon de Valera (Minister of External Affairs 1932–1948); Joseph Walshe (Secretary to the Department of External Affairs, 1922–1946, and first Irish diplomat to serve with the rank of Ambassador – to the Holy See – 1946–1954); Patrick McGilligan (Minister of External Affairs 1927–1932). See T. de Vere White, *Kevin O'Higgins* (London, 1948); D. Harkness, 'Mr. de Valera's Dominion: Irish Relations with Britain and the Common-wealth, 1932–1938', *Journal of Commonwealth Political Studies*, vol. 8 (1970), pp. 206–208; D. Harkness, 'Patrick McGilligan: Man of Commonwealth', in N. Hillmer and P. Wigley (eds), *The First British Commonwealth* (London, 1980); D. Keogh, 'Profile of Joseph Walshe, Secretary, Department of Foreign Affairs, 1922–46', *Irish Studies in International Affairs*, vol. 3 (1990), pp. 59–80; D.H. Akenson, *Conor: A Biography of Conor Cruise O'Brien* (2 vols., Montreal, 1994). For Charles Bewley (1888–1969, eccentric and pro-Fascist Minister-Plenipotentiary to Rome from 1929 to 1933, and Berlin from 1933 to 1939, when his retirement was forced by de Valera), see his autobiographical *Memoirs of a Wild Goose* (J. Duggan ed., Dublin, 1989). The papers of Frederick Boland (Secretary of the Department of External Affairs, 1946–50; Ambassador to the UK, 1950–56; Irish Permanent Representative at the UN, 1956; President of the General Assembly, 1960) are held at Trinity College Dublin, but – unfortunately for scholars – few papers survive from the office of John Whelan Dulanty, Irish High Commissioner and later first Irish Ambassador to London, who characteris-tically conducted much of his business by telephone or in person. His unparalleled knowledge of British, imperial and Anglo–American affairs was based on two decades of service at the heart of the Empire.

46 MacMahon, *Republicans*, ch. 10.

47 See Fisk, *In Time of War*, chs. 1–2; Canning, *British Policy*, chs. 9–10; Harkness, 'Mr. de Valera's Dominion', *passim*.

48 See M. Maguire, *A Bibliography of Published Works on Irish Foreign Relations* (Dublin, 1984); D. Keogh, 'Ireland: Department of Foreign Affairs', in Z. Steiner (ed.), *The Times Survey of Foreign Offices of the World* (London, 1982), p. 279. The revolutionary origins of the Irish foreign service are examined in Mitchell, *Revolutionary Government*, pp. 25–42, 99–119, 254–64.

49 Fanning, 'Anglo–Irish Relations', p. 15.

50 Fanning, *Independent Ireland*, p. 83. (My italics.)

51 T.P. Coogan, *De Valera: Long Fellow, Long Shadow* (London, 1995), p. 422.

52 Kennedy, *Ireland and the League*, p. 21.

53 Canning, *British Policy*, p. 113.

54 See Martin, 'The Irish Free State', p. 217.

55 Canning, *British Policy*, p. 75.

56 S. Roskill, *Hankey: Man of Secrets: vol. 2, 1919–1931* (London, 1972), p. 480.

57 See R.B. Stewart, *Treaty Relations of the British Commonwealth of Nations* (New York, 1939), pp. 338–42.

58 MacMahon, *Republicans*, pp. 237–86.

59 State Archives Pretoria, Department of External Affairs, BTS 1/31/1, Charles te Water to Hertzog, 18 May 1932; National Archives of Ireland, Department of Foreign Affairs, DFA 5/211, de Valera to Hertzog, 31 May 1935; State Archives Pretoria, Charles te Water Papers, Hertzog to de Valera, 4 June 1935. See also 'Mr. de Valera and Gen. Hertzog – Reply to Appeal on the Oath', *Manchester Guardian*, 9 April 1932; 'South Africa and Free State – General Hertzog's Message', *The Times*, 9 April 1932; 'Interest in Capetown – General Hertzog and the Republicans', *The Times*, 9 April 1932; 'Die Kabelgramme aan de Valera', *Die Burger* [Cape Town], 11 April 1932; 'General Smuts and the Irish "Family Trouble"', *Cape Argus*, 18 April 1932; 'Anglo–Irish Dispute – General Hertzog as Arbitrator', *Pretoria News*, 2 July 1932.

60 MacMahon, *Republicans*, p. 74.

61 State Archives, Pretoria, Department of External Affairs, BTS 1/31/1, vol. 2: Imperial Conference Minutes, 14 June 1937; N. Mansergh, *Survey of British Commonwealth Affairs: Problems of External Policy 1931–1939* (Oxford, 1952), pp. 270–333; McMahon, *Republicans*, pp. 47–9, 142, and ch. 10; Fisk, *In Time of War*, pp. 30–33; Lowry, 'Ireland Shows the Way', pp. 104–116; Bowman, *De Valera*, p. 111; Holland, *Commonwealth Alliance*, ch. 9; R. Tamchina, 'In Search of Common Causes: The Imperial Conference of 1937', *Journal of Imperial and Commonwealth History*, vol. 1 (1972–3), pp. 81–2.

62 MacMahon, *Republicans*, p. 213.

63 A. van Wyk, *Vyf dae: Oorlogskrisis van 1939* (Cape Town, 1985); Eric H. Louw, L.V., *Ierland toon die weg aan: konstitusionale ontwikkeling sedert 1921. Lesing gehou voor die Afrikaanse Nasionale Studentbond van die Universiteit van Stellenbosch op 31 Julie 1939* [*Ireland shows the way: constitutional development since 1921. Lecture delivered before the Afrikaans Student League of the University of Stellenbosch on 31 July 1939*] (Beaufort West, 1939). I am grateful to Dr. Dirk Kotze of the University of South Africa, Pretoria, and Professor J.C. Moll of the University of the Orange Free State, Bloemfontein, for these references.

64 National Archives of Ireland, Department of Foreign Affairs DFA235/108: J.P. Walshe to Assistant Secretary, 28 November 1939: Visit of Colonel Reitz; D. Reitz, *No Outspan* (London, 1943), pp. 256–60; A. Martin, 'An Australian Prime Minister in Ireland: R.G. Menzies 1941', in F.B. Smith (ed.), *Ireland, England and Australia* (Canberra, 1990), pp. 195–200; R. Menzies, *Afternoon Light: Some Memories of Men and Events* (London, 1967), pp. 36–43.

65 Carroll, *Ireland in the War Years*, pp. 145–6, 153–4.

66 Kennedy, *Ireland and the League*, p. 74.

67 N. Mansergh, *The Irish Free State: Its Government and Politics* (London, 1934), p. 271.

68 Martin, 'Irish Free State', p. 217.

69 Kennedy, *Ireland and the League*, p. 50.

70 See Stewart, *Treaty Relations*, pp. 338–42; Kennedy, *Ireland and the League*, ch. 1 and p. 258; H.J. Harvey, *Consultation and Co-Operation in the Commonwealth* (London, 1952), pp. 282–3; A.B. Keith, *The Governments of the British Empire* (London, 1936), pp. 95–6.

71 A.B. Keith, *The Constitutional Law of the Dominions* (London, 1933), p. 80.

72 Kennedy, *Ireland and the League*, pp. 184–5.

73 M. Kennedy, 'The Irish Free State and the League of Nations: The Wider Implications', *Irish Studies in International Affairs*, vol. 3 (1992), pp. 18–19.

74 Keogh, *Ireland and Europe*, p. 30.

75 Carroll, *Ireland in the War Years*, p. 37.

76 Keogh, *Ireland and the Vatican*, p. 40.

77 *Ibid.*, pp. 79–80. For Irish ecclesiastical anger with the dominance of English Catholic interests at the Vatican see Keogh, *The Vatican, the Bishops and Irish Politics*, p. 261, n. 39.

78 *The Times*, 21 May 1937.

79 Lady Drummond, wife of Sir Eric Drummond, British ambassador to Italy in the early 1930s and former Secretary-General of the League of Nations, was the aunt of the Duke of Norfolk, the 'Premier Catholic Peer' and Earl Marshal of England, a connection which, William Macaulay noted, appeared to impress the Vatican 'not a little'; see Keogh, *Ireland and the Vatican*, p. 118.

80 Canning, *British Policy*, pp. 87, 113, 115–17; Keogh, *Ireland and the Vatican*, p. 118; J. Barnes and D. Nicholson (eds), *The Leo Amery Diaries*, vol. 1: *1896–1925* (London, 1980), pp. 515–16 (entries for 10 and 13 July 1927).

81 See Lowry, 'Ireland Shows the Way', *passim*.

82 This was not, as is often inaccurately reported, the last night of British rule, since India had gained its independence a year earlier, so that this was a far less significant occasion. Coogan, *De Valera*, p. 639, incorrectly describes the de Valera visit as 'the last night of British rule in India'.

83 Mansergh, *Survey*, p. 359. The one exception to Ireland's voice not being heard related to Palestine. In late 1937 the British were aware of, and expressed regret, that de Valera did not agree with their policy, see PRO, CP 237 (37) 14 October 1937, Cabinet printed note, Mr de Valera and Palestine. In 1937 de Valera did briefly intervene in League discussions of British proposals to partition the Palestine Mandate, but he later explained to Malcom MacDonald, Dominions Secretary, that he would have consulted the British beforehand and he knew that the Palestinian issue would come up for discussion, since, in his view, this was a British rather than a Commonwealth responsibility. See University of Durham, *Malcolm MacDonald Papers* 10/4/22–4 Cabinet Printed Note, C.P 237 (37) 14 October 1937.

84 A.B. Keith, *The Dominions as Sovereign States: Their Constitutions and Governments* (London, 1938), pp. xiii–xiv.

85 Keogh, *Ireland and Europe*, pp. 107–11; D. Keogh, *Jews in Twentieth-Century Ireland: Refugees, Anti-Semitism, and the Holocaust* (Cork, 1998).

86 Keogh, *Ireland and the Vatican*, p. 118.

87 Trinity College Dublin, Frederick H. Boland Papers, MS 10470/9: Memorandum on the Taoiseach's right to advise a Dissolution, 11 May 1944.

88 O'Farrell, 'Irish-Australian Diplomatic Relations', p. 12. (emphasis added)

89 See C. Kenny, *The King's Inns and the Kingdom of Ireland* (Dublin, 1992); J.F. McEldowney and P. O'Higgins (eds), *The Common Law Tradition in Irish Legal History* (Dublin, 1990); W.N. Osborough (ed.), *Explorations in Law and History: Irish Legal History Society Discourses, 1988–1994* (Dublin, 1995); D. Hogan and W.N. Osborough (eds), *Brehons, Serjeants and Attorneys: Studies in the Irish Legal Profession* (Dublin, 1990).

90 *Leo Amery Diaries*, p. 483.

91 Notwithstanding the differing role of the Supreme Court in the interpretation of the Constitution, the Irish system of government remained substantially British in origin. See B. Chubb, *The Government and Politics of Ireland* (3rd. edn, Dublin, 1992).

92 E. O'Halpin, 'The Army in Independent Ireland', in K. Jeffery and T. Bartlett (eds), *A Military History of Ireland* (Cambridge, 1996), p. 417. The 'German-pattern helmet' was in fact manufactured in Birmingham by Vickers to a Belgian pattern.

93 Fisk, *In Time of War*, p. 372; Keogh, *Ireland and Europe*, p. 105. For the conventions of diplomatic appointments in this period see E. Satow, *A Guide to Diplomatic Practice* (London, 1922), chs. 16, 25. It is clear from an inventory of constitutional law and political science texts held by the Department of External Affairs Legal Adviser after the Second World War that British and dominion predominated. See Trinity College Dublin, Frederick H. Boland Papers, MS 10470/18–19: Inventory, 4 January 1946.

94 Skelly, *Irish Diplomacy*, p. 36.

95 Sexton, *Ireland and the Crown*, p. 112.

96 MacMahon, *Republicans*, p. 24; Carroll, *Ireland in the War Years*, p. 15. It may be relevant to quote from the diary of Charles te Water, South African High Commissioner in London in the 1930s and a close associate of Dulanty, who recalled the atmosphere of an Irish-South African dinner at the World Economic Conference, attended by Dulanty and Smuts: 'The Irish are I think Europe's most charming and cultured conversationalists. Indeed they are all poets and quotations from the major poets are part of every Irishman's conversational armoury. Dulanty in his cups was a master at this. After dinner they arranged a circle of chairs for that they said was the only way for friends to converse with one another – circle! See what it brought forth!': State Archives, Pretoria, te Water papers, AE2/37, diary, entry for 11 July 1933.

97 *What's Past is Prologue: The Memoirs of the Right Honourable Vincent Massey, C.H.* (London, 1963), p. 298.

98 A. Chisolm and M. Davie, *Beaverbrook: A Life* (London, 1992), p. 181.

99 Harkness, 'Patrick McGilligan', p. 118.

100 Keogh, *Ireland and the Vatican*, p. 118.

101 *Ibid.*, p. 81.

102 State Archives, Pretoria, Department of External Affairs, BTS1/31/1: Memorandum to Dr Bodenstein, Ottawa, 23 July 1932.

103 O'Drisceoil, *Censorship*, pp. 111, 208; K. Fedorowich, 'Recruitment and resettlement: the politicisation of Irish migration to Australia and Canada, 1919–39', *English Historical Review*, vol. 114 (1999).

104 See H.C. Allen, *The Anglo–American Relationship Since 1783* (London, 1959), ch. 4; R.H. Heindel, *The American Impact on Great Britain, 1898–1914* (New York, 1968); P. Kennedy, *The Realities Behind Diplomacy: Background Influences on British External Policy* (London, 1981); M. Hunt, *Ideology and United States Foreign Policy* (London, 1987); W.R. Louis and H. Bull (eds), *The Special Relationship: Anglo–American Relations Since 1945* (Oxford, 1987).

105 K.M. Burk, *Britain, America and the Sinews of War, 1914–1918* (Boston, 1985); F. Cosigliola, 'Anglo–American Financial Rivalry in the 1920s',

Journal of Economic History, vol. 37 (1977), pp. 911–34; M.J. Hogan, *Informal Entente: The Private Structure of Cooperation in Anglo–American Economic Diplomacy, 1918–1928* (Columbia, 1977); D.C. Watt, 'America and the British Foreign Policy Making Elite: From Joseph Chamberlain to Anthony Eden', in D.C. Watt (ed.), *Personalities and Policies: Studies in the Formulation of British Foreign Policy in the Twentieth Century* (London, 1965).

106 S. Hartley, *The Irish Question as a Problem in British Foreign Policy, 1914–18* (London, 1987), p. 198; E.D. Batzell, *The Protestant Establishment* (New York, 1964), *passim*. For Irish issues in Anglo–American relations see F.M. Carroll, *American Opinion and the Irish Question, 1910–23* (Dublin, 1978), esp. chs. 5–6. American fear about offending British diplomatic protocol persisted long after the establishment of the Irish state. In 1934, when the US Minister presented his credentials to de Valera rather than, as was customary, to the Governor-General, and this appeared to lend support to a triumphantly republican speech made by Sean T. O'Kelly on the same day. At the request of de Valera the American Secretary of State Cordell Hull was asked to explain the affair in full, but Hull, having ascertained that George V had approved the accreditation procedure was unwilling to pursue the matter. See T. Ryle Dwyer, *De Valera: The Man and the Myths* (Dublin, 1994) p. 194.

107 Coogan, *De Valera*, pp. 141–5.

108 M. Hopkinson, *Green Against Green: The Irish Civil War* (Dublin. 1988), p. 47.

109 Harkness, *Restless Dominion*, pp. 63–4.

110 Keogh, 'Profile of Joseph Walshe', p. 71.

111 Dwyer, *De Valera*, p. 180.

112 O'Brien, 'Ottawa', *passim*; MacMahon, *Republicans*, pp. 48–55, 68–87, 251–3.

113 Major, 'War Plan Red, p. 13.

114 MacMahon, *Republicans*, p. 194.

115 C.A. MacDonald, *The United States, Britain and Appeasement 1937–1939* (London, 1981).

116 Dwyer, *De Valera*, p. 215.

117 Canning, *British Policy*, p. 286.

118 J. Carroll, 'US–Irish Relations', *Irish Sword*, vol. 19 (1993–5), pp. 99–100.

119 J.L. Rosenberg, 'The 1941 Mission of Frank Aiken to the United States: An American Perspective', *Irish Historical Studies*, vol. 22 (1980), pp. 163–74; D. Keogh, *Twentieth Century Ireland: Nation and State* (New York, 1995), p. 119.

120 O'Halpin, 'The Army in Independent Ireland', pp. 429–23.

121 R. Fanning, 'The Anglo–American Alliance and the Irish Application for Membership of the United Nations', *Irish Studies in International Affairs*, vol. 2 (1986), p. 45.

122 See Skelly, *Irish Diplomacy*, p. 93. The myth of an Irish–American special relationship remains strong, however, fuelled by the latent influence of Irish politics during the Clinton presidency, as descibed by Conor O' Clery in *The Greening of the White House: The Inside Story of How America Tried to Bring Peace to Ireland* (Dublin, 1996), esp. ch. 14. While changes in American policy cannot be minimised, the notion of the 'greening' of American policy, may, however, be somewhat premature, if not misleading.

American intervention has not been on the basis of support for Irish reunification sought by Irish–American activists for generations.

123 N. Mansergh, 'Ireland and the British Commonwealth of Nations: The Dominion Settlement' [1966], in Mansergh, *Nationalism and Independence*, p. 93.

124 P. Kennedy, 'Why Did the British Empire Last So Long?', in *Strategy and Diplomacy* (London, 1989), p. 209.

125 Mansergh, *Nationalism and Independence*, p. 189.

126 PRO ISC(32)108, Memorandum by Malcolm MacDonald, July 1936, quoted in MacMahon, *Republicans*, p. 182.

127 *Ibid.*; A.L. Geyer, *Vier Jaar in 'Highveld': Diplomatieke Ervarings – Soms Sonder Dorings – As Hoë Kommissaris in Londen 1950–1954* (Cape Town, 1969), pp. 50, 70–1; National Archives of Ireland, Dublin, Department of the Taoiseach, S15153: Secretary of External Affairs to Secretary of An Rialtas, 4 October 1951; M. Broodryk and J. van der Westhuizen, *Die Nasionale Party, 1940–1948* (Bloemfontein, 1994), p. 701.

128 Keogh, *Ireland and Europe*, p. 207.

129 Mansergh, *Commonwealth Experience*, p. 140; Mansergh, *Unresolved Question*, p. 315.

130 I. McCabe, 'John Costello 'Announces' the Repeal of the External Relations Act', *Irish Studies in International Affairs*, vol. 3 (1992), pp. 67–77.

131 A. Worrall and W. Lorimer, *'Highveld': The Story of a House. The Residence of the South African Ambassador to the United Kingdom* (Johannesburg, 1986), pp. 37–8.

132 State Archives, Pretoria, Havenga Papers, A38/19/8/2: John A. Costello to N.C. Havenga, 23 December 1949; Institute of Contemporary History, Bloemfontein, Eric Louw Papers, File 85: Louw to Malan, 4 October 1948. This was especially ironic in the case of Sean MacBride, son of the executed 1916 leader and commander of the Irish Transvaal Brigade, Major John MacBride. Sean MacBride was especially close to the South Africans, but later became a prominent leader of the anti-apartheid movement and United Nations High Commissioner for Namibia.

133 J. Horgan, *Sean Lemass: The Enigmatic Patriot* (Dublin, 1997), p. 252.

134 See R. Fanning, 'The Response of the London and Belfast Governments to the Declaration of the Republic of Ireland, 1948–49', *International Affairs*, vol. 58 (1981–2), pp. 95–114; McEvoy, 'Canada, Ireland and the Commonwealth: The Declaration of a Republic', pp. 506–27; O'Farrell, 'Irish-Australian Diplomatic Relations', pp. 11–19; Martin, 'An Australian Prime Minister in Ireland'; Quirke, 'Australia's Role in Ireland's Declaration'; O'Brien, 'Australia, Britain, Ireland and the Ottawa Conference'; O'Brien, 'Ireland's Departure From the British Commonwealth', pp. 179–194; Dean, 'Final Exit?', pp. 391–418; Lowry, 'Ireland Shows the Way'; McCabe, *Diplomatic History of Ireland*.

135 Trinity College Dublin, Frederick H. Boland Papers, 10470/21: Memorandum of 6 December 1948.

136 R. Ovendale, *The English-Speaking Alliance: Britain, the United States, the Dominions and the Cold War 1945–51* (London, 1985), p. 75.

137 Collins, *The Path to Freedom*, pp. 88–9. See also F. Costello, *Michael Collins: In His Own Words* (Dublin, 1997), pp. 72–5; N. Mansergh, 'Ireland and

the British Commonwealth of Nations: The Dominion Settlement', in Mansergh (ed.), *Nationalism and Independence*, p. 98.

138   Darwin, 'Imperialism in Decline?', *passim.*

139   John A. Costello, Dáil Eireann speech, 24 November 1948, in N. Mansergh (ed.), *Documents and Speeches on British Commonwealth Affairs, 1931–1952*, vol. 2 (London, 1953), pp. 805–806.

10
Trinity College Dublin and the New Political Order

Pauric Dempsey

The history of the ex-unionist community in the Irish Free State has been written of largely as the history of a benign silence.[1] FSL Lyons wrote that in the 1920s and 1930s, the unionist minority had 'fallen back on the defensive' in society, politics and the arts. He found the persistence of the ghetto mentality 'the most striking characteristic of the minority'.[2] To Professor W.B. Stanford, a fellow of Trinity College Dublin (TCD) writing in the 1940s, 'there was a wait and see policy, a lie low and say nothing policy, a policy dictated by a leadership that was old, conservative and cautious.[3] Dr E.C. Hodges, the Church of Ireland Bishop of Limerick and one-time principal of the Church of Ireland Teacher Training College in Dublin, writing at the same time as Stanford believed that 'In relation to a majority whose objectives and standards are inscrutable for the outsider in religion. Criticism and co-operation alike, must remain unprofitable, misleading and open to misrepresentation'.[4] Such avowed stocism belies the volubility of the *Irish Times*, Trinity College, and the Church of Ireland at a time when their collective attitude toward the new state was nothing less than querulous. This chapter will look anew at one of these three institutions, TCD, and assess its alleged and much vaunted stoicism and support for the new order.

Where Oxford and Cambridge undergraduates vehemently ranged themselves on one side or another of a political question, the Earl of Midleton found in the early 1920s that 'the men at Trinity have made hardly any appearance with regard to this crisis [Irish question] although it has been going on at their gates all these years'.[5] As a ruling class, Standish O' Grady saw unionist Ireland as being guilty for its 'neglect of duties and responsibilities, love of pleasure, sport and ease, lack of union and public spirit, selfishness, stupidity, and poltroonery'.[6]

Unionist Ireland which had 'gibed at Ireland and everything Irish'[7] failed to give leadership to the people, preferring instead to foster disdain and exclusivity. The Board of Trinity College made the appropriate public noises of support after the Treaty had been signed, but it was, as Andrée Sheehy Skeffington wrote, 'still dominated by men whose eyes were turned towards England and who continued to feel besieged'.[8] To Terence de Vere White 'the board of TCD was still unashamedly unionist in sentiment, and while it obeyed the law and sent representatives to the Dáil, these usually spoke in the voices of reprieved prisoners'.[9] Trinity actively discouraged members of the College from expressing in public, political or religious views, and forbade the use of the College address for such correspondence. To R.B. McDowell and D.A. Webb this was part of the 'policy of inconspicuousness' that was the guiding principle of College up to 1946. Despite this avowed policy, the Union Jack flew from on high over TCD until 1935,[10] *God Save the King* resounded until 1939, and the King's health was toasted at the Fellow's High Table until 1945. To further exasperate matters, the Trinity Week Committee wantonly insulted the Governor General by refusing to play *The Soldiers Song* at the College races in 1929[11] and Provost Edward J. Gwynn refused the government's invitation to attend the official reception to welcome Ireland's first Papal Nuncio in 1933.[12] Away from symbols, emblems and anthems, TCD did manage to be more tactful in its election of provosts. In 1927 Gwynn, a scholar in old Irish succeeded J.H. Bernard as Provost. Gwynn, despite his dislike for Irish nationalism in general and language revival movement in particular, 'served to some extent as a lightning conductor against attacks on the College as un-Irish'.[13] Privately Gwynn confided to J.H. Bernard that he was 'essentially English and not Irish in spite of certain sympathies and antipathies':

> A man is what he inherits and what he draws from his surroundings, and for me and most of us Protestants these things are 90% English or Scotch [sic] – traditions, beliefs and customs, mental furniture, all that and why I mainly fear and draw back from the new order which I now suppose will flood in upon us … is not so much the material loss and annoyance as the tendency to cut us away from our roots, our civilisation which is the bone of our bone, flesh of our flesh … I don't want myself and I don't want them [his children] to feel alien in their own country.[14]

Andrée Sheehy Skeffington wrote that the appointment of Gwynn could not have but assisted 'in the development of the new spirit of

Trinity'.[15] Sure enough in 1928 a year after Bernard's death TCD conferred honorary degrees on Eoin MacNeill, historian, revolutionary, and former Minister of Education (1922–25), and W.T. Cosgrave, President of the Executive Council. Twelve years earlier J.H. Bernard, Gwynn's predecessor as Provost, used his influence as president of the Royal Irish Academy (RIA) to have MacNeill expelled from the academy because of his connections with the Volunteers and his part in the Easter rising.[16] Likewise in July 1933 Douglas Hyde was awarded a D.Litt by his *alma mater*. Hyde wrote to W.M. Crooks, a friend from student days in Dublin, that 'Trinity has certainly changed its tone very much since our time. It looks on me quite tolerantly or even favourably now!'[17] In 1896 TCD had turned down Hyde for the Chair in Irish. At the time Hyde wrote 'They would not have me at any price and I fancy the worse the man was the better pleased they were, so that no attention could be drawn to Gaelic studies by him'.[18]

Ill-health forced Gwynn's retirement in 1937 and he was replaced by W.E. Thrift who in turn was succeeded by Ernest Henry Alton in 1942, both of whom had represented TCD in Dail Eireann. To Cosgrave, the four Trinity parliamentary representatives 'had taken a most helpful part in the discussions [on the Constitution of the Free State in 1922] and were amongst the most trusted, popular and influential members of the legislature'.[19] The four TDs were Gerald Fitzgibbon K.C., William Henry Thrift (Provost 1937–42), Sir James Craig and Ernest Henry Alton (Provost 1942–52). On the death of Sir James Craig in 1933, Dr Robert James Rowlette was elected and retained his seat unopposed until the abolition of university representation in 1937. So obliging were the University of Dublin TDs in 1922 that they temporarily forgot that they had ever been unionists. Gerald Fitzgibbon,[20] a senior freemason and leading layman of the Church of Ireland, declared that he did not 'represent anybody calling themselves southern unionists, or anybody of that such. ... The people who purported to represent southern unionists [in the London negotiations with Griffith] ... I do not consider them as representing me ... I represent the constituency that sent me here'.[21] Prior to Fitzgibbon's reincarnation as an Independent TD, he was returned for Trinity as a unionist MP in the 1921 general election. He served in the Dáil until 1924, when he was appointed a Supreme Court judge.

Fellow mason W.E. Thrift represented Trinity in the Dáil between 1922 and 1937[22] declared that he represented University of Dublin (TCD) and that it had no connection with the southern unionists.[23] Later Thrift was to change his mind. In 1932 in the debate on the

Removal of the Oath of Allegiance, Thrift defended the oath 'for those whom I have the honour to represent, and I refer to those who used to be called the Southern Unionists'.[24] Moreover, in 1934 Thrift told the Dáil that 'university representation was a reasonable attempt to give that minority some representation, which, I hold, might correspond with its weight in numbers and value'.[25] Such denials were obviously the nonsense of political expediency as the Dublin University constituency was overwhelmingly unionist and continued to be so for several decades after the Treaty, be it as a constituency of the Dáil or the Seanad. The sheer nonsense is brought into focus by the agreement in June 1922 between the representative southern unionists and the provisional government. One of the terms of that agreement arrived at for securing unionist representation in the legislative Assembly was university representation.[26] The *Church of Ireland Gazette* had no doubt of Trinity's political pallor. In August 1923 it declared that the only representative of the 'ex-unionist' or Protestant community in the Dáil were the four members for Trinity College.[27] The provisional government considered three of the four Trinity TDs to be representative southern unionists including both Fitzgibbon and Thrift.[28]

In the Dáil, Trinity's public men were other than timorous. Gerald Fitzgibbon was instrumental in the framing of the constitution during 1922, and in the Dáil he spoke frequently and did not restrict himself to any single portfolio. In addition to his work on the Constitution Bill, Fitzgibbon exerted considerable energy on the Electoral Bills (1922, 1923), Public Safety (Emergency Powers) Bill (1923), the Land Bill (1923), Criminal and Malicious Injuries (Amendment) Bill (1924), and the Enforcement of Law (Occasional Powers) Bill (1924). He was instrumental in agitating for the transfer of university representation from the Seanad to the Dáil. Ernest Blythe told the Seanad in 1934 that the reason university representation was transferred to the Dáil was because 'the members of the Dáil were impressed with the help they got from those … representatives of the universities … particularly one of the Trinity representatives, who is now Mr Justice Fitzgibbon'.[29] Fitzgibbon's achievement was indeed considerable as only months earlier Provost J.H. Bernard had failed to achieve this end. At that time Eamonn Duggan, Minister of Home Affairs, feared that such a proposition would not have been well received, but by October 1922 he could write to Winston Churchill that:

This position has been altered by subsequent events. The four members representing Trinity College in the Dáil have been constant in their attendance at the debates, and have taken considerable part in them. When they proposed that the Universities should be given special representation in the Dáil/Chamber of Deputies, in lieu of the representation given in the Senate, the proposition was well received by the House so that the government felt justified in all the circumstances in leaving the matter to an open vote of the House.[30]

Outside the House Fitzgibbon was also consulted by W.T. Cosgrave on legal matters before being appointed a Judge of the Supreme Court. Despite his close relationship with the Cumann na nGaedheal Government he was not slow to express his disapproval of some of its actions. In September 1922, he expressed his misgivings about giving special, powers to the army and in December he criticised, albeit in palid terms, the illegality of the government's reprisal executions of four anti-Treaty prisoners.

William Edward Thrift was also a very active parliamentarian. Deputy speaker of the Dáil, and chairman of Joint Committees of both Houses of the Oireachtas, he was a member of the Second House of Oireachtas Commission (1936). He clung doggedly to the Treaty and resisted any alteration of its character. Speaking on the abolition of the right of appeal to the Privy Council he told the Dáil that he attached no value to it but, as it was part of the bargain with the representative southern unionists, it should not be tampered with.[31] A member of the National Commission on National Education and the Censorship of Publications Board (1930–36) he was lauded 'as one of the most useful and one of the most valuable members of the House'. Ernest Blythe deemed his interventions as always most helpful,[32] but Deputy Martin Corry of Fianna Fáil held that Thrift and those associated with him used their power to dragoon the unfortunate individuals outside the Dáil, for 'in respect of every type of coercion bill introduced here during the last ten years, they were in the forefront of the voting line'.[33] Fianna Fáil considered him too close to Cumann na nGaedheal to be independent whilst James McGuire, of Fine Gael, told the Dáil that although they might call themselves Independent it was obvious to everybody that if they continually voted with Fine Gael and were opposed to the policy of the Fianna Fáil government, they were not Independent in spite of their chosen nomenclature.[34] In a Fianna Fáil pamphlet entitled *The Economic History of the land of Erin*, Thrift, 'the mason', was associated with the economic ills of the country:

> And there was one among them who came over deep waters, the Grand Sword bearer and Squarer, the mighty maker of rings, the

powerful puller of strings, the soft tongued smooth-spoken son of
Thrift, who arose and passed around the hat [for the waiting
Cosgrave] saying 'Brethren; if you would thrive, give heed to Thrift!
Hail ye the prophet! For it has been revealed to me that he will give
light unto the many to see that nought is good that is not damn
good for the brethren of Good [John Good T.D.] and Thrift.³⁵

In the Dáil Thrift was at times the spokesman of the Independent
Group in the Senate which echoed his own political views. In a letter
to Midleton, Provost J.H. Bernard wrote in 1924 that:

... the heads of the Irish government are sensible of the contribution
of loyalists like Andrew Jameson and our Professor Thrift could render if they were ministers, but they are afraid to take them into the
Executive Council or to give them high office for fear of Republican
criticism.³⁶

In 1925 Thrift was nominated by the other Independent members of
the Dáil³⁷ to speak on their behalf on the issue of the prohibition of
divorce:

I regard this motion as one which will have the effect of imposing
on the whole population the religious views, in respect of divorce,
of the majority of the population ... It is imposing on a section, in a
way which I contend is not permissible, the views of the majority of
the population ... the passing of this motion will raise up one more
barrier against a possible union between the north of Ireland and
the south of Ireland ... it is not really a question of divorce or not.
It is a question as to whether the passing of this motion will, or
will not, leave the individual the liberty of conscience which our
constitution gives.³⁸

In April 1932 Thrift spoke in favour of the Oath of Allegiance. 'It was
because of the Oath and because of what it contained that I, for one,
was able to accept the Treaty ... in so doing I swept away all my previous views. I understood that I was wiping the slate.'³⁹ Thrift believed
that the retention of the oath was important for two reasons. Firstly, he
believed it to be of great importance to the unionist community, and
secondly that its abolition would violate the Treaty:

Do not let happen what will happen if you pass this Bill. What will
Great Britain say? They will not proceed to argue it. It will be said

that you have broken the Treaty. We know that is going to be said. What will the whole world say? The Irish Free state took a step that they were told by the other signatories to the bargain was breaking the Treaty, and nevertheless they took it, careless as to how it would affect other treaties and possible international obligations.[40]

In 1934 Thrift stood up in the Dáil as the representative of the unionist minority to protest against the abolition of the senate. In an impassioned speech he argued that the abolition of the upper house would be 'a definitely fatal step for the future spirit of goodwill, for future harmony in the country and its future prosperity':

> I feel that in this last attempt to whittle away any academic provision which was in our Constitution before, and on the strength of which many people gladly gave their whole hearted co-operation to the building up of this state, you are taking a grave step which will put backward, rather than forward our development...I claim no privilege...but I do say that by removing these paper academic provisions, if you like things which, in themselves, mean little and which do not practically affect, to the extent of the weight of a feather, our actual being, we are cutting ourselves off definitely for many years to come from those with whom we would all wish to be united, and making thousands of people in the country say: Why did I ever lend my support to a separate Irish Free State Government?[41]

When the government abolished university representation Thrift reiterated this point. University representation was the means by which a minority section in the country could express its views in the House. The effects of the Bill, Thrift believed, would be 'a definite curtailment in its powers of expression in the Dáil, and, far from wanting its co-operation, it [the government] is seeking a curtailment of its powers of expression'.[42] Thrift felt strongly for the Treaty. To him at least it was the final settlement of the Irish problem.

Professor Ernest Henry Alton, as a Fellow of Trinity, commanded a company of the University of Dublin Officer Training Corps in 1914. During the 1916 rising he had the presence of mind to bar the gates before the rebels could seize the College and was later awarded the Military Cross. In June 1921, the day before de Valera invited unionists representatives to the Mansion house, Alton invited de Valera into Trinity to meet him and his three parliamentary colleagues. Alton explained to David Robinson, a former British Army Officer and Sinn

Féin neophyte who was acting as an intermediary 'It is only intended for friendliness and has no political element'.[43] In 1922 Alton wrote to Bernard advising him against pressing the British government to compel the Irish government to grant Trinity a guarantee of either financial support or absolute freedom from constitutional interference.[44] In 1925 Alton also spoke in the Dáil against the prohibition on divorce. He would, he argued, make divorce difficult if not almost impossible and went on to say that he believed that there was 'one chance in a million, one chance in ten millions...that a divorce should be given'.[45] At the same time he felt that for a very small minority there was the possibility of a dissolution of marriage *a vinculo*, and this minority should not be deprived of the possiblity of redress. McDowell and Webb wrote that Alton was anxious to have Trinity's merits and status appreciated by all Irishmen, and 'by ignoring the great difficulties which lay in the path of this ideal he had some success in promoting it'.[46]

Sir James Craig, who was King's Professor of Medicine at Trinity, sponsored and piloted through the Dáil the first Charitable Hospital's Bill (which with amending legislation saw the scope of the Irish Hospitals' Trust Sweepstakes scheme extend to nearly all the hospitals in the Irish Free State within two years).[47] Craig protested successfully against ministerial interference in the internal management of hospitals and outside of public health concentrated his efforts in the areas of education and finance. A resident and a commissioner of Merrion Square, he favoured the handing over of the Square for use as the Irish National War Memorial in 1927.[48] He argued that its use as a public open space in the city centre would be of enormous benefit to those who lived in the slums of the area.

Robert James Rowlette was elected to Dáil Eireann on the death of Sir James Craig in 1933. He was the first deputy returned to the Dáil after the abolition of the Oath of Allegiance and, like Craig, largely avoided the sectional politics which Thrift and Alton indulged in concentrating mainly on matters to do with health and medicine. In 1934 he opposed the outright prohibition of the sale of contraceptives arguing that their use in certain circumstances were necessary as a woman's life or health could be endangered should she have to undergo the trials of pregnancy and childbirth.[49] He objected to legislation prohibiting prostitution because he felt that the legislation whilst giving protection to male members of the community from being accosted or solicited in the streets, it did not give protection to women who may be accosted for improper purposes by males while going about their legitimate business.[50] In 1937 he was the one Protestant deputy to question the recognition of the special position of the Catholic Church embodied in article 44 of the 1937 Constitution.[51] He felt that such recognition had no place in the Constitution for such a clause might be interpreted as giving special privilege to one Church.[52] He also expressed his reservations concerning article 41 of the Constitution, relating to the place of women in the home, which he argued 'might be misread so as to put some bar in the way of the freedom of action of women in their work'.[53]

On the question of divorce Rowlette expressed the opinion that in certain cases the dissolution of a marriage 'would conceivably give an opportunity for establishing a happy home which would be useful to society'. He also argued that the outlawing of all forms of divorce might well render certain marriages illegal even though recognised in canon law.[54] Rowlette studiously avoided marginalising himself as a representative of the minority community in contrast to Alton and Thrift who while preaching about integration took every opportunity to plead a special case. The 1934 Constitutional amendment to abolish university representation was an exception. He told the Dáil that no institution in the country nor any group of voters had been more loyal to the state than the voters of Trinity. He also told the House that two of the three Trinity TDs had been nationalists for as long as many of the members on the government side of the House. Rowlette recognised that university representation granted the right of representation to 'certain classes, which would otherwise find it difficult to obtain representation in a popular assembly'. Rowlette asked the Dáil not for 'minority protection or for any favour except the favour to be allowed to work for our country in the best way we believe we can'.[55] In 1942 the efforts of Rowlette and others to set up a nationwide anti-tuberculosis campaign were thwarted by Dr John Charles McQuaid, the Roman Catholic Archbishop of Dublin. McQuaid expressed in a letter read out at the public meeting called to establish the campaign the opinion that the groups proposed programme could only be carried out by the Red Cross Society. In the light of the Archbishop's letter of disapproval, Rowlette who chaired of the meeting, felt that he could not put forward a motion to establish any such organisation.[56]

The student body at large was more gauche in expressing their political allegiance than the College's representatives in the Dáil. In November 1922 at one of the most important junctures in Ireland's history, editor of *TCD: A College Miscellany*, wrote that

One is conscious that about Irish affairs there definitely remains nothing more to be said; or at least nothing helpful. Ireland is not where she is for want of discussion and, for our part, we are going to talk about something else.[57]

J. Marshall Dudley of the Historical Society believed that Trinity's natural allegiance should be to the country that founded her and that provided scope for her sons in the empire. 'She was not founded nor did she ever pretend to be the university of an Irish Ireland' he wrote 'She was founded as an Anglo-Irish University... when the Anglo-Irish race shall die out, then let Trinity die... her work in life will be consummated'. Dudley feared that the 'spirit of nationalism would reduce Trinity from being the third university of the British empire to being the first university in an obscure island on the western seaboard of the continent of Europe'. Richard G.H. Carter shared Dudley's opinions. Writing in 1929 he reflected:

> We of the Anglo-Irish have sacrificed much. Our most hallowed traditions and beliefs have been flouted. No opportunity has been lost to 'rub it in'. Trinity has lost more than any individual. She had an Army School. [established 1904] Where is it now? She had one of the finest contingents of the O.T.C. – Where is it now?

Robert Wyse Jackson editor of the *College Pen* believed that Trinity should adopt a similar position to that adopted by Harvard, Princeton and Yale after the American Revolution. These universities calmly accepted the change which revolution brought, without, fawning upon the new order. Such a position earned respect, and in time they assimilated the best of what the new order had to offer.[59] Peter O'Flaherty, a lonely Republican within Trinity, wrote in 1929 that the college was segregated from all outside influences.[60] O'Flaherty believed that the mental attitude of Dublin's suburbia had to be suppressed and he saw that mental attitude as 'a certain narrow-minded intolerance and suspicion of all opinions which happen to differ from their own'. 'Trinity' wrote O'Flaherty 'must accept the fact that she cannot be English, therefore let her recognise that she is Irish'.[61] Owen Sheehy Skeffington concurred in a subsequent edition of the *College Pen*:

> It is true that the jingo national anthem of a nation which has ever been hostile to ours is played without interference on almost all important occasions. Yet, when the Gaelic society hold their annual opening meeting, are they allowed to do so without interference?... surely the reactionary majority in this college, if indeed it is a

majority might choose a better emblem than the stink bomb, a better method of voicing their opinions than the slap bang and the smashing of windows.[62]

On Armistice Day the more raucous element of Trinity declared their unionist sentiments to the crowds in College Green. Lionel Fleming remembered linking arms with his fellow students right across College Green, and stopping all the traffic in the centre of Dublin for the duration of the two minutes silence 'for although this city might not wish to honour Armistice day, Trinity could still see that it was honoured'.[63] After the disorder and violence which accompanied the 1926 commemorations A.A. Luce writing in the *College Mecelany* warned that the involvement of civilian students in the Armistice Day parade was unwise:

TCD as an institution has no special claim to be represented on that parade...If civilians march in formation wearing the poppy, the complexion of the act is altered. It becomes provocative, may cause opposition, and is likely to sour the sentiment of the day...eo ipso the parade appears a political demonstration, and the poppy snatchers find the pretext they seek.[64]

In 1929 a small group of students marching back from the Phoenix Park after the official armistace ceremonies, halted outside the front gates of Trinity, whilst the rest of the parade marched into Front Square. Brandishing a dirty cotton royal standard on a bamboo curtain pole, they commenced bawling *God Save the King*, waving their hats and cheering. 'Gratified grins wreathed their faces as old shawlies from Townsend street surged in amongst them patting them on the back and making much of "the grand old Trinity fellas"...and for thousands of outsiders in College Green this pitiable exhibition represented the mind and policy of Trinity College.'[65] In 1932, the 'over zealous young loyalists attempted the 'supreme act of defiance' by removing a field gun from the OTC parade ground, in order to push it out into College Green. This artillery push had been a recurring theme of Armistice day throughout the 1920s, and, in 1932 *TCD* recognised that 'It was only due to the reasonable and tactful interference of the Civic Guards that a most unpleasant situation was averted'.[66] The two minutes silence for those who had fallen during the Great War was marred by this 'band of puny fools squabbling with the police and proclaiming a raucous homage to their king'.[67]

Between November 1932 and November 1933 the field guns were removed, and on Armistice day 1933 a College Fellow took up a position near the Front Gates to ensure there would be no repeat of what happened the year before. In successive years a lower profile was maintained but this was not as W.J. White, a TCD graduate, argued, proof of Trinity's political maturity but merely a more astute rein on political passions. To White, writing in the *avante guard* journal *the Bell* in April 1945, the blame for such excess lay with the Catholic church and the Irish State who were 'striving to keep Trinity in the bottle and to prove that her traditions are inimical to the religious and political faiths of the Irish people':

> They are doing their utmost, in fact, to turn her towards her old allegiance, and to prevent her from playing a part in the building of Ireland. Nothing could be more foolish. Trinity's tradition is not political or sectarian, but scholastic.[68]

To mark the allied victory in Europe one month later, Trinity's students took to the College roof and hoisted the Union Jack on the west front. Amidst the flags of the Soviet Union, France and the USA, the tricolour appeared 'in one of the numerous permutations of bunting, below the Union Jack'.[69] This incensed the crowd in College Green, and in particular several members of Ailtirí na hAiséirighe (Architects of the Revolution) who staged an impromptu anti-Trinity demonstration during which a Union Jack was burnt. To the continued refrain of *God Save the King, Tipperary, Land of Hope and Glory* and *La Marseillaise*, Trinity's scholars, wearing red, white and blue rosettes, burned the tricolour in response and by so doing brought down upon the university near siege conditions for the next two days.

In 1930 a voice of reason was heard in TCD:

> We are forever being told to leave politics alone. 'Keep Quiet' is the motto of the average [Trinity] man. You are only likely to stir up ill-feeling, he says, if you mention political relations. Yet we entirely disagree with the attitude of the average man. A controversial matter, like that of politics, cannot and should not be left alone. If it is, it becomes like a sore and breaks out as a disease, when it is least expected. You will have opinions and patriotic feelings suppressed to such an extent that in the end they will break out as bitter hatreds and narrow, absurdly narrow bigotry… in Trinity we are always meeting these political sores, breaking out because our

suppressed opinions have become tinged with party hatreds and party narrowness...Why cannot we be open, and express our opinions candidly and not lie dormant until a crisis actually arises? Far be it however, that we should advocate the 'die-hard' spirit, which is also unfortunately prevalent in college at the present time.[70]

In conclusion the history of post-1922 Trinity belies the notion of a minority too timid to stand up for its rights. Trinity was at times arrogant and jingoistic, at times demanding and occasionally conciliatory but it was seldom abashed, fearful or retiring. Both fellows' and the student body's lives within the College walls went on after the Treaty very much as they had before. Lyons's ghetto was not a construct of independence. It predated 1922, and for that matter 1800, and would persist late into the century. Wolfe Tone wrote of the Anglo-Irish in 1791 that 'They distained to occupy the station they might have held among the people, and, which the people would have been glad to see them fill'. Echoing Tone, Hubert Butler has written, of the Anglo-Irish of the 1920s and 1930s, that they could have dodged their fate, if, 'their interest in Ireland, let alone their love, had been more than marginal'.[71]

Notes

1 A notable exception is K. Bowen, *Protestants in a Catholic State: Ireland's Privileged Minority* (Dublin, 1983).
2 F.S.L. Lyons, 'The Minority Problem in the 26 Counties', in F. MacManus (ed.), *The Years of the Great Test* (Cork, 1978), p. 95.
3 W.B. Stanford, *A Recognised Church. The Church of Ireland in Eire* (Dublin, 1944), pp. 16–23.
4 Dr Hodges, 'Protestantism since the Treaty' in *The Bell*, vol. 8, no. 3. June 1944.
5 Midleton Papers PRO London 30/67/43 – Memo by Midleton: Notes as to the leading men in Southern Ireland.
6 S. O'Grady, *Selected Essays and Passages* (Dublin, n.d.), p. 202.
7 Herbert Butler, 'Anglo–Irish Twilight', in *Escape from the Anthill* (Dublin, 1986), p. 77.
8 A. Sheehy Skeffington, *Skeff* (Dublin, 1991), p. 36.
9 T. de Vere White, *A Fretful Midge* (London, 1957), p. 66.
10 J.A. Birmingham, *The Red Hand of Ulster* (London, 1912), pp. 176–7, also R.B. MacDowell and D.A. Webb, *Trinity College Dublin 1592–1952: An Academic History* (Cambridge, 1982), p. 553n.
11 B. Sexton, *Ireland and the Crown 1922–36: The Governor-Generalship of the Irish Free State* (Dublin, 1989), p. 119.
12 Rev. J. Dignam, *Catholics and T.C.D.* (Dublin, 1934), p. 6.

13 R.B. McDowell and D.A. Webb, *Trinity College Dublin*, p. 441.
14 E.J. Gwynn to J.H. Bernard, 6 December 1921. Bernard papers British Library MS 52783.
15 Sheehy Skeffington, *Skeff*, p. 38.
16 Terence Brown, *Ireland; A Social and Cultural History, 1922 to the Present* (New York, 1990), p. 90. R.B. McDowell and D.A. Webb, *Trinity College Dublin*, p. 424.
17 Douglas Hyde to W.M. Crook, 13 July 1933. W.M. Crook papers, Bodleain Library, Oxford. Crook and Hyde were students together at TCD and remained lifelong friends.
18 Quoted in J.E. Dunleavy and G.W. Dunleavy, *Douglas Hyde: A Maker of Modern Ireland* (Los Angeles, 1991), p. 201.
19 Memo of a meeting between Mr Bonar Law and the Irish ministers at the Board of Trade, 24 October 1922. P.R.O. London CO 739/7.
20 *Irish Times*, 7 December 1942.
21 *Dáil Debates*, 4 October 1922, col. 1153. Fitzgibbon overlooks the fact that Provost J.H. Bernard was one of the representative unionists in London.
22 *Irish Times*, 24 April, 1942.
23 *Dáil Debates*, 4 October 1922, col. 1153.
24 *Dáil Debates*, Constitution (Removal of Oath) Bill, 29 April 1932, col. 922. See also *Dáil Debates*, Constitution (Amendment no. 24) Bill, 12 December 1934, col. 2652. 'Whatever you may think of me I stand as a representative of the minority'.
25 *Dáil Debates*, Constitution (Amendment no. 23) Bill, 5 July 1934, col. 1496.
26 Duggan to Churchill, 16 October 1922. P.R.O. London CO 739/2. See also *Seanad Debates*, 18 July 1934, col. 1977–1979, speech by Andrew Jameson.
27 *Church of Ireland Gazette*, 3 August, 1923. See also 15 December 1922.
28 Duggan to Churchill, 16 October 1922. P.R.O. London CO 739/2.
29 *Seanad Debates*, 12 July 1934, col. 1959.
30 Duggan to Churchill, 16 October 1922. P.R.O. London CO 739/2.
31 *Dáil Debates*, Constitution (Amendment no. 22), 12 October 1933, cols. 2389–2390.
32 *Seanad Debates*, 12 July 1934, cols. 1960–1961.
33 *Dáil Debates* (Constitution No. 23) Bill, 5 July 1934, col. 1506.
34 *Dáil Debates* (Constitution No. 23) Bill, 5 May 1934, col. 584.
35 Fianna Fáil pamphlet, *The Economic History of the land of Erin* (Dublin, n.d.).
36 Bernard to Midleton 24 October 1924. BL Bernard papers MS 52781.
37 Deputy Davin told the Dáil that Thrift was speaking 'for the first time I think, on behalf of the United Independent Party'. *Dáil Debates*, Private Bills for Divorce, 11 February, 1925, col. 175.
38 *Dáil Debates*, Private Bills for Divorce, 11 February, 1925, cols. 162–163.
39 *Dáil Debates*, Constitution (Removal of Oath) Bill, 29 April 1932, col. 923.
40 *Dáil Debates*, Constitution (Removal of Oath) Bill, 29 April 1932, col. 932.
41 *Dáil Debates*, 12 Dec. 1935, col. 2652.
42 *Dáil Debates*, Constitution (Amendment No. 23) Bill, 8 May 1934, cols. 491–492.
43 Letter from D.L. Robinson to ? 29 June 1921. NAI DE2/2.
44 Bernard Papers 2922 quoted in McDowell and Webb, *Trinity College Dublin*, p. 464.

45 *Dáil Debates,* 11 Feb. 1925, col. 179.
46 R.B. McDowell and D.A. Webb, *Trinity College Dublin,* p. 433.
47 *Dáil Debates,* vol. 48, col. 2375, 1933.
48 *Dáil Debates,* Merrion Square (Dublin) Bill 1927, vol. 19, cols. 416, 418.
49 *Dáil Debates,* col. 2017–2020, 1 August 1934.
50 *Dáil Debates,* col. 2014, 1 August 1934.
51 J.H. Whyte, *Church and State in Modern Ireland 1923–1979* (Dublin, 1980), p. 58. See *Dáil Debates,* 1891–1892, 4 June 1937.
52 *Dáil Debates,* col. 1891, 4 June 1937.
53 *Dáil Debates,* 4 June 1937, col. 1895–1898.
54 *Dáil Debates,* col. 1886 (4 June 1937). See also: D. Fitzpatrick, 'Divorce and Separation in Modern Irish History' in *Past and Present,* no. 114, Feb. 1987.
55 *Dáil Debates,* Constitution (Amendment no. 23) Bill, 5 July 1934, cols. 1507–1518.
56 Sheehy Skeffington, *Skeff,* p. 119.
57 *T.C.D., A College Miscellany,* 30 November 1922.
58 *The College Pen,* 5 November 1929, 19 November 1929.
59 *The College Pen,* 19 November 1929.
60 *The College Pen,* 29 October 1929.
61 *The College Pen,* 29 October 1929. Peter or Peadar O'Flaherty was later to join the I.R.A. See Sheehy Skeffington, *Skeff,* pp. 44–5.
62 *The College Pen,* 12 November 1929.
63 Lionel Fleming, *Head or Harp* (London, 1965), p. 96.
64 *T.C.D: A College Miscellany,* 18 November 1926.
65 *T.C.D: A College Miscellany,* 14 November 1929.
66 *T.C.D: A College Miscellany,* 9 November 1933.
67 *T.C.D: A College Miscellany,* 9 November 1933.
68 W.J. White, 'Inside Trinity College' in *The Bell,* vol. 10, no. 1, April 1945. White was an *Irish Times* journalist, born in Cork and educated at Midleton College and T.C.D. At Trinity he was President of the College Philosophical Society and editor of *T.C.D.* (1940). After the War he went to the *Irish Times* London office from where he wrote the daily 'London Letter' which proved to be one of the most popular features of the newspaper. In 1952 he was made Features Editor of the newspaper despite the best efforts of the newspaper's management to install him as Editor. He remained on as Features editor until he was appointed Controller of Television Programmes with R.T.E. He died in 1980. See Tony Gray, *Mr Smyllie, Sir* (Dublin, 1991).
69 R.B. McDowell and D.A. Webb, *Trinity College Dublin,* p. 464.
70 *T.C.D: A College Miscellany,* 13 November 1930.
71 Wolfe Tone, *Argument on behalf of the Catholics of Ireland* (1791), p. 69 quoted in Butler, *Escape from the Anthill,* p. 101.

Index